Taekwondo

Taekwondo

THE STATE OF THE ART

MASTER
SUNG CHUL WHANG
and
MASTER
JUN CHUL WHANG
with
BRANDON SALTZ

and Special
Contribution from
MASTER
DAE SUNG LEE

BROADWAY BOOKS New York

BROADWAY

Broadway Books titles may be purchased for business or promotional use or for special sales. For information, please write to: Special Markets Department, Bantam Doubleday Dell Publishing Group, Inc., 1540 Broadway, New York, NY 10036.

BROADWAY BOOKS and its logo, a letter B bisected on the diagonal, are trademarks of Broadway Books, a division of Bantam Doubleday Dell Publishing Group, Inc.

Library of Congress Cataloging-in-Publication Data
Whang, Sung Chul.
        Taekwondo : the state of the art / Sung Chul Whang and Jun Chul
    Whang with Brandon Saltz ; and special contribution from Dae Sung Lee.
            p.   cm.
        Includes bibliographical references (p.   ) and index.
        ISBN 0–7679-0214-9 (pbk.)
        1. Tae kwon do.   I. Whang, Jun Chul.   II. Saltz, Brandon.   III. Title.
    GV1114.9.W53   1993   98-44960
    796.815'3—dc21

FIRST EDITION

Designed by Tina Thompson

Illustrated by Rich Miller

99   00   01   02   03   10   9   8   7   6   5   4   3   2   1

This work is dedicated to our students,
past, present, and future.

To my Father and Mother, and my family.
JUN CHUL WHANG

To Sue, Derek and Dylan.
SUNG CHUL WHANG

To my wife, Heon Mi Lee, my daughter, Nikita Da Hee Lee,
my son, Daven Tae Hyung Lee; and to my father and mother,
Won Kil Lee and Kyong Ok Lee.
DAE SUNG LEE

To my wife, Sallie, and to my grandmother,
Florence Zunser Saltz.
BRANDON SALTZ

CONTENTS

ACKNOWLEDGMENTS

No matter how extensive a master's experience, no matter how many students a master has trained, and no matter how many black belts carry forth a master's message to the larger world of Taekwondo, that master always owes a debt of gratitude to the family of Taekwondoists who have made all these accomplishments possible. This book could never have been written were it not for Master Young Man Park, who was our first instructor in the Philippines and to our knowledge was the first Korean master to bring Taekwondo to the Philippines. We remain ever grateful to the late Grandmaster Pong Ki Kim, from whom we received our black belts and learned to be gentlemen in Taekwondo; to Grandmaster Dong Keun Park, a legend in his own time; to USTU president Grandmaster Sang Chul Lee; to Master Javier Arizmendi, who taught us the meaning of passion; to Master Han Don Cho, with whom we shared a vision and made it reality; and Master Dae Sung Lee, an inspiration whose direct contribution to this book has, we feel, elevated it to the foremost ranks of instructional martial arts books.

To Master Han Won Lee, Sammy Pejo, and Mayumi Pejo, we are indebted for insights into the evolution of modern Taekwondo sparring and training at the Olympic Training Center, a beacon for Taekwondoists all over the country.

In addition, we would like to thank Youn Sang Lim, our little brother who makes it possible for us to live out our dreams of owning a dojang; Alfredo Torruella, a good friend and training partner; and Todd Holzman, faithful student and partner in a grand adventure.

These acknowledgments would not be complete without mentioning Dr. Un Young Kim, president of the World Taekwondo Federation, for his herculean efforts and ultimate success at promoting Taekwondo internationally and elevating this very special discipline to the level of true art and Olympic sport. Every practitioner of Taekwondo around the world, from the rawest white belt to the most seasoned Grandmaster, owes him special appreciation.

We would also like to thank Master Malick Coulibaly Dit Fall, Andrew Cohen, Alex Chung, Joseph Incognoli, Jr., Chris Abramson, Miki Foged, Sallie Sills, Steffee Sloane, Kenneth Kaplan, Isabelle Charbonneau, Debbie Squires-Lee, James Ziglar, Richard Gilman, Barbara Riccardi, Cynthia Crowley, Mirta Citrone, Morgen Bowers, Daniel Lee, David Mandelbaum, Moda Thiam, Bill Knauer, Teresa Throckmorton, Nanice Lund, Pedro Espino, Eddie Garcia, Martine Colmant, Shiraz Tangri, and Chi Chi Tse; our Three Musketeers, David Birdoff, Pascal Dadoun, and Andy Krieger; and the rest of the faithful staff and our students at West Side Taekwondo.

Brandon Saltz and Jennifer Huang deserve special mention and appreciation for the grueling photo sessions that ultimately resulted in the drawings appearing in this book.

Brandon Saltz would like to thank Dr. Ken Min, the visionary Taekwondo leader who was his first Taekwondo instructor at the University of California at Berkeley, who helped him learn the meaning of Taekwondo, and from whom he received his black belt.

This book would not have been possible without the savvy of our editor, Charlie Conrad, or the talents of the design team at Broadway Books; without the guidance of our agent, Arielle Eckstut; or without the brilliant work of Suzy Jurist, Matt Birdoff, and the rest of the staff at SJI, Inc.

Last, but certainly not least, we would like to thank artist Rich Miller, whose talents truly set this book apart.

Finally, Brandon Saltz cannot escape another special mention. This book was Brandon's idea, and throughout the long and arduous course of this project, he remained its moving force. With Brandon, we experienced the fun of mapping out a course for this project and the elation of securing a publisher for the book. Often we faced sheer terror at the amount of work that would have to go into creating a manuscript that would live up to everyone's expectations. Brandon quickly dispelled that sense of panic with his unbelievable hard work and unflagging enthusiasm. Without Brandon, this book would not be.

FOREWORD
BY MASTER DAE SUNG LEE

I've seen many Taekwondo books by many different instructors. Those books have great value, but this Taekwondo book is the most modern in its coverage of not only sparring but also training and conditioning. I am very honored to have had a part in contributing to it and to have had a chance to share some of my knowledge and experience. I hope readers of all kinds will find it and use it, not only Taekwondo students but also the general public. To people who already practice Taekwondo, I hope this book will give some new ideas about sports and martial arts. To people who do not practice Taekwondo, I hope this book can provide some inspiration in their own training, and maybe persuade them to try Taekwondo.

As a teacher of Taekwondo, my personal goal is to teach Taekwondo to everybody, all kinds of people: children and adults, people just interested in martial arts, and people who want to be international competitors. Everybody can enjoy Taekwondo as a martial art and as a sport. I want Taekwondo to be a part of the lives of people who practice it. I know that Taekwondo can change the lives of students. The next Olympics will make more people than ever before aware of Taekwondo. Sometimes I worry, though, that if Taekwondo turns into a pure sport, there will be a limitation on the number of practitioners. Not every practitioner is there for the sake of competition. One day I would like to build a huge dojang and be able to give scholarships to the most deserving students, to foster their enjoyment and encourage everyone.

I would like to share some of my own background with you. I started my Taekwondo training in 1968, when I was ten. I lived in Korea at the time. Soon afterward, in 1971, I moved to Hawaii. Because there were so few Koreans in Hawaii in 1971, I couldn't find a Taekwondo dojang, so for a short time I studied Hapkido. Then I found a great instructor, Master Randy Chun, and I trained under him for eight years. He retired in 1979. After that, I trained under

Master Song. Unfortunately, he moved to Florida that same year. Then I found Master Sang Chul Lee. To this day, I consider Master Lee my master and coach. I began training under him in 1979, and that year I became a national team member. Master Lee gave me great knowledge about technique, and I also learned a great deal from him about coaching. He supported me during my entire competitive career. I was national champion from 1979 to 1987 and competed at the World Championships five times. While I never won at the World Championships, I was able to become a gifted coach, and I have produced Olympic champions. Master Lee helped me get where I am now.

In 1989, I was unofficially invited to teach Taekwondo in China. I was the first person to go to China to teach Taekwondo. For two and a half weeks, I taught Taekwondo to sixteen of China's best wu shu players at the University of Beijing in the Department of Physical Education. Those two and a half weeks of Taekwondo must have had a huge impact on the Chinese. China established the Chinese Taekwondo Association in 1995, and four of the original athletes became coaches. The summer of 1998, I was invited back (this time officially) for three weeks to help train their national team. Former United States national team member Tim Connolly went with me. Master Connolly now has the honor of being the first white man to teach Taekwondo in China.

The level of their Taekwondo is incredible. Their women's team is amazing. The authorities there recruit men and women from members of the basketball, volleyball, and track teams. They train for six hours a day, and have been doing this for three years. But they treat Taekwondo purely as sport. Seventy percent of the team did not actually enjoy Taekwondo. All they trained to do was kick and punch for competition. They did not know any poomse or any self-defense principles. Master Connolly and I helped to introduce the art of Taekwondo, as opposed to the sport. We taught them poomse and self-defense. When we left, the entire team loved Taekwondo. Now the United States has one more country to worry about at the World Championships and at the Olympics.

There are some differences in the way Taekwondo competition is approached in the United States and in other countries. In many countries, the high-level competitors are very young—from seventeen to about twenty-three. Here, in the United States, competitors peak between twenty-three and twenty-eight. I peaked at twenty-nine. Some countries, such as South Korea, start training competitors when they are in elementary school and high school. Spain and Chinese Taipei also do this, and some European countries are starting to do this, too. In many of these countries, Taekwondo is a sport first. As Taekwondo becomes more popular, this trend will increase.

Although I had great success as a Taekwondo competitor, my emphasis is on Taekwondo as a martial art, not as sport. Sport Taekwondo can be very exciting and very valuable. But my experience with students and with the Chinese team tells me that the martial art of Taekwondo cannot be neglected. That is where its permanent value lies. In the end, sport Taekwondo is only for competitors. Taekwondo as a martial art is for everybody. The 2000 Olympics will absolutely enhance Taekwondo's popularity, but the future shape of Taekwondo in the United States will depend on the instructors. I hope this book will help everyone to practice both kinds of Taekwondo and, with our help, become better martial artists, athletes, and more complete human beings.

INTRODUCTION

Every one of today's Taekwondoists, students and masters alike, will witness one of the most exciting events in the ancient history of their martial art: the arrival of Taekwondo at the 2000 Olympics. This is the first time a martial art has been officially introduced to the Olympics in nearly forty years, and its appearance represents a great achievement for Taekwondo grandmasters, masters, practitioners, and officials everywhere, not to mention the legions of athletes themselves. This pivotal moment in the evolution of our martial art calls for a fresh look at our history, our philosophy, and, of course, our techniques, all the stuff that makes Taekwondo the fastest-growing martial art in the world. With this book, we present what we believe to be the clearest and most modern text available anywhere on Taekwondo techniques, training, sparring, and philosophy.

In the spirit of modernity, we chose to use a collaborative approach to the presentation of our information. Through interviews, meetings, and reflection on our own experiences, we have tried to include the accumulated wisdom of many teachers and leaders of the Taekwondo community.

Even with so much input, it is difficult to imagine a single book on Taekwondo that could discuss every aspect of this martial art. Our intention is to provide an authoritative sourcebook for basic Taekwondo, including the changes modern Taekwondo has experienced. Here you will find every hand technique and every stance in the Taegeuk poomse, plus a carefully selected variety of others. Similarly, we have included all the kicks most common to modern Taekwondo, with special emphasis on those that have helped establish Taekwondo's reputation as the world's preeminent kicking art. To our knowledge, this is the first book to devote a complete chapter to steps and footwork, those essential elements of Taekwondo training. In our chapter on sparring, we have made every effort to provide an essential guide to strategy, technique, and training. We believe that the material presented here will help all students, from beginners through black belts, to enhance their sparring and think about it in more sophisticated ways.

The poomse chapter includes all eight of the Taegeuk forms, which are among the most commonly practiced poomse in World Taekwondo Federation dojangs. We have included several features that we hope will make it easier for you to learn new forms. Each poomse comes with an abbreviated chart for quick reference, lots of advice about proper chambering and how to generate power in tricky techniques, and clear, intelligently laid-out illustrations that make the pattern of each form easier to follow.

One of the least traditional aspects of this book is our use of illustrations rather than photographs. As an alternative to the usual martial arts photography, we sought out the cleanest, sharpest illustrative style we could find. Every drawing in this book is based on photographs of national champions demonstrating the best possible technique.

The figures we use are shown wearing their belts and dobok pants, but not the tunics. This conveys a more precise image of their body positions. While it differs from the standard depiction of World Taekwondo Federation martial artists, we believe that you will find the illustrations here more instructive than traditional photographs.

We very much hope that this book will enhance your practice of Taekwondo, and that within these pages you will find the inspiration to try something new, to think about your training in a new way, and to reach a new level of performance.

Finally, we have capitalized "Taekwondo" throughout this work, but have left the names of other martial arts in lowercase. We have done this to contrast our familiarity with our subject, Taekwondo, to our comparative lack of familiarity with other styles. That is, in referring to "Taekwondo" we refer to a style that we take pains to define. In referring to "karate," however, we are aware that the very term describes a number of different styles. By drawing this distinction, we hope to avoid giving offense to any of our fellow martial artists.

Taekwondo

CHAPTER 1

History of Taekwondo

Early Korea and Wiman Choson • Three Kingdoms •
The Middle Period: Koryo and the Yi Dynasty • Occupation and Liberation

Taekwondo's history stretches back to the annals of ancient Korea, long before anything resembling the two nations we now know had come to exist. It is thought that Taekwondo originated as a martial art first called tae kyon and later called soo bak, and that it was practiced by soldiers of the Koguryo kingdom before being passed on to the famed hwarang of Silla. To understand the nature of Taekwondo as we practice it today, and to gain a better appreciation of the philosophical code that governs our training (which is discussed in the next chapter), it is helpful first to look into the origin of the Three Kingdoms and their martial culture.

Early Korea and Wiman Choson

Before actual kingdoms emerged in Korea, walled town-states and village communities dominated the political landscape, such as it was. Some of these, such as Old Choson, Chin, Imdun, and Chinbon, had been able to spread their influence through trade or conquest, and developed into what can be called confederated kingdoms, each loosely ruled by a central figure. By the fourth century B.C.E., Old Choson and the other confederated kingdoms had become large enough to attract the attention of China, and hostilities between Old Choson and the Chinese state of Yen were common as they confronted each other across the Liao River. Records indicate that Old Choson had actually acquired a reputation among the Yen Chinese for being arrogant and cruel.

Nonetheless, Old Choson suffered from long exposure to conflict and ceaseless pressure, and entered into a period of gradual decline. Under the leadership of Ch'in K'ai, Yen invaded the Liaotung Peninsula (to the northwest of Old Choson) at the end of the fourth century B.C.E. For the next hundred or so years, tension between the Korean states and China seemed to have diminished. But around 206 B.C.E., the Ch'in establishment fell to Liu Pang, the founder of the Chinese Han dynasty. Turmoil in the Yen territory ensued, and refugees streamed out of the area, heading east.

One of these refugees was a man named Wiman, who is said to have taken with him a band of a thousand followers. Wiman and his supporters appealed to King Chun of Old Choson, who appointed him protector of the northwest border. Wiman accepted, but had different ideas for himself, and soon overthrew King Chun. Shortly, Wiman was able to subjugate the neighboring states of Chinbon and Imdun, giving him a territory extending hundreds of miles in every direction. Wiman Choson thus became the first real Korean power, and, realizing the advantage of his geographic position between China and the rest of the Korean peninsula, his kingdom profited from control of the trade routes.

Han China did not appreciate losing direct control of its trade with southern Korean states. It also feared the likely alliance of Wiman Choson with the Hsiung-nu of Mongolia and Manchuria. In 109 B.C.E., Emperor Wu of Han was able to launch an all-out campaign against Wiman Choson, ruled at this time by Wiman's grandson, King Ugo. Wiman resisted fiercely for a year, but was weakened by defections and Ugo's assassination by dissenters. The struggle continued for a time following King Ugo's death, but Wiman Choson fell in 108 B.C.E., and the kingdom perished.

By 107 B.C.E., Han had divided Wiman Choson into four commanderies—militarily governed districts—claiming Korean territory as far south as the Han River. Resistance from the local populations seems to have been stiff, however, because within twenty-five years, by 82 B.C.E., the commanderies governing Chinbon and Imdun had to be withdrawn. Within another ten years yet another withdrawal occurred, removing the Hsüan-tu commandery from the middle reaches of the Yalu river basin and abandoning effective control of its Korean territory.

The Three Kingdoms

Han withdrawal signaled the germination of the Three Kingdoms period of Korean history, a time of great cultural and political advance marked equally by constant warfare and the growth of the military as an institution. It is to this we look as the primary source of the martial heritage behind modern Taekwondo.

Koguryo

Legend has it that Koguryo was founded in 37 B.C.E. by Chumong and a band of his followers from Puyo, north of the Korean peninsula, in a region thought to be centered around the middle of the Yalu and T'ung-chia river basin. Modern scholars disagree, however. They point to the failure of the Han to keep its commanderies functional, and indicate that this failure must have been due to determined, organized resistance from the local people. It seems this organized resistance must have been offered by the nascent state of Koguryo.

Because Koguryo came into being in a context of continual conflict with the Chinese, it is perhaps no surprise that its culture seems to have been predominantly martial. Its ruling aristocracy was a warrior class, and even in times of peace, combat training was in evidence everywhere. Tomb murals from the period depict figures apparently engaged in unarmed combat, using techniques similar to those practiced by modern Taekwondoists. It is likely that this is the birthplace of tae kyon, an indigenous form of foot fighting, and, most likely, the birthplace of Korean wrestling. It is also safe to conclude that the martial arts developed in Koguryo must have been influenced by Chinese styles as well; it is probably to this exposure that Taekwondo owes certain stances and its emphasis on circular defensive movements. Koguryo's additional preoccupations were land, populations, and domestic animals, hallmarks of a militant society. Perhaps not surprisingly, the Chinese gained the vivid impression that the Koguryo people were vigorous and warlike—tendencies that the people of Koguryo may well have developed out of determination to expel their Chinese occupiers.

Koguryo began to reach the height of its power during the reign of King Kwanggaet'o, who ruled from 391 to 413 C.E. During this time, he expanded Koguryo's territory to encompass Manchuria to the north and reach as far south as the Han River. His remarkable victories included the conquest of sixty-four fortress domains and some 1,400 villages. Under his rule occurred an episode pivotal to the history of the kingdom of Silla and, therefore, to the history of Taekwondo.

Silla and Paekche

At the southern end of the Korean peninsula, a number of city-states were struggling to acquire power and territory, and as they fought and maneuvered against each other, three fledgling kingdoms began to emerge: Paekche, Kaya, and Silla. Paekche occupied the southwestern portion of the peninsula and Silla the southeast, with Kaya filling in a wedge between them, dominating the Naktung river basin.

In the year 400 C.E., Paekche sought to conquer Silla and dominate the southern portion of the peninsula by enlisting the aid of both Kaya and the Wa of Japan. Kaya agreed to allow the Wa safe passage through its territory to Silla, and this Japanese invasion might have succeeded in overwhelming Silla had King Naemul not successfully called on Koguryo for assistance. By some accounts, King Kwanggaet'o sent as many as 50,000 troops to Silla's aid. Whatever the number, it is from this infusion of Koguryo military power that knowledge of tae kyon most likely came to Silla.

A price accompanied Koguryo's assistance. For a number of years following the defeat of the Japanese, Koguryo insinuated itself into Silla's internal affairs. This was a situation that Silla could not tolerate, and in 433 C.E., Silla and Paekche forged an alliance, in spite of their antagonistic past. Their mutual strength eventually allowed Silla to shake off the influence of Koguryo, although this took another twenty-five years, probably accomplished during the reign of King Chabi (458–479 C.E.).

Within the next forty years, Silla became a fully centralized autocratic state. Under King Pophung (514–540 C.E.), the "true-bone" system had been formalized. This was a ranking system that essentially delineated the potential any noble had to serve in government, and at what level, with the highest levels reserved for those of pure true-bone status. There is evidence that Paekche and Koguryo had similar institutions, although the intricacy of Silla's rivaled both.

The Three Kingdoms also nationalized their military structures. Kings were warriors and frequently led their troops into battle personally—a feature of monarchy that would be repeated throughout the history of medieval Europe, among many others. More striking was the integration of the military into all levels of government throughout each of the Three Kingdoms. Virtually every official charged with some kind of executive authority, from the local village headman up to regional governors and royal officials, also held military responsibilities. The size and importance of their commands varied with their rank, as might be expected. There was no separation of political duty and military command until some centuries later, after Silla managed to unify the Korean peninsula for the first time. No doubt the frequency of armed conflict contributed to this style of government. Given the circumstances, it is no surprise that this part of the world succeeded so notably at conceiving of and promoting martial arts.

The Hwarang

Little, if anything, is known about the precise structure of military command throughout the Three Kingdoms at this time. However, it is known that Silla established six primary garrisons, the *chong,* one in each of the six provincial administrations. These garrisons were commanded by generals of true-bone rank. The garrisons themselves were composed of men who lived in each respective capital, so the garrisons bore an elite status. Serving in the military was considered to be an honor and a privilege.

Attached to each of these corps were the famous hwarang bands, the "flower of manhood," companies of young men, probably in their teens. Bands like the hwarang were common to each of the kingdoms, but it appears that those of Silla fulfilled a unique role. Based on similar bands that had appeared in the much earlier clan-centered society, the hwarang were conceived of as a means to provide a literal body to the state that would both serve the state and exemplify its highest virtues. This is most clearly exemplified by the hwarang's adherence to the five secular injunctions laid down by the Buddhist monk Won'gwang in the early 600s. The five injunctions were:

1. Loyalty to the king
2. Fidelity, respect, and obedience to one's parents
3. Fidelity in friendship

4. Never to retreat in battle
5. Never to make an unjust kill

These are still the guiding tenets of Taekwondo, and in the next chapter we discuss their relevance to us as modern martial artists.

The hwarang were also expected to pursue education in music, dancing, poetry, Buddhism, and Confucianism. They made pilgrimages to sacred sites to pray, through song and dance, for their nation's prosperity and tranquility. But their primary function was military, and they constantly practiced their skills, acquiring new knowledge when possible, as when the troops from Koguryo arrived to help them drive back the dual invasion of Paekche and the Japanese. In time of war, they fought in the front lines, and some of their greatest fighters, such as Sadaham, Kim Yu-sin, and Kwanch'ang, became the stuff of Korea's greatest legends. It is a great pity that the writings of the eighth-century Buddhist monk Kim Tae-mun, among them *Chronicles of the Hwarang,* do not survive.

The Valor of Koguryo and Silla's Rise

As the sixth century progressed, the military and political situation for all three of these kingdoms became even more complex. The 120-year alliance between Silla and Paekche had come to a shocking end in 554, when Silla turned on Paekche after they had driven Koguryo from the Han river basin. The Sui dynasty had managed to reunite China after a lengthy division into the Northern and Southern dynasties, and it had now turned its attention west to the emerging power of the Turks. Koguryo, meanwhile, still held vast territories extending throughout Manchuria, and now hoped to confront the Sui by allying itself with the Turks. At the same time, Paekche was seeking to reopen its relationship with the Japanese. The Sui dynasty and Silla were each confronted with the specter of a formidable series of alliances, and so they joined forces to counteract the bloc formed by Koguryo, the Turks, Paekche, and Japan. The resulting network of military relationships set the stage for a pivotal showdown in the history of Northeast Asia.

Hostilities opened with Koguryo's attack against the Sui across the Liao River in 598. The Sui emperor, Wen Ti, retaliated, but was turned back. Then, in 612, Yang Ti, the next Sui emperor, mounted an enormous invasion, marshaling a force said to consist of more than a million men. That earthshaking army reached Koguryo's Liao-tung fortress but failed to take it. Yang Ti then sent a third of his forces—some 300,000 men—to attack the capital at Pyong-yang directly, but they were trapped by Koguryo's forces in an ingenious maneuver and suffered near-total devastation; it is said that of the original force, only 2,700 men found their way back. Yang Ti was forced to retreat, and although he continued to mount attacks against Koguryo, his army was too weakened to be effective. His dynasty fell and was replaced by the Tang dynasty.

Yon Kaesomun emerged as absolute leader of Koguryo in 642, and he took a forceful position with respect to Silla. Paekche hastened to invade Silla that same year. Silla bravely requested assistance from Koguryo against Paekche's attacks, which Yon Kaesomun not only denied but replied to by demanding the cession of the Han river basin. He also ignored Tang entreaties to halt operations against Silla.

The Chinese Tang responded to Koguryo's hard line by invasion, and destroyed a number of Koguryo fortresses, including Liao-tung, which had so valiantly withstood the Sui siege. They besieged the fortress at An-shih, but here Koguryo made its stand. Over the course of the sixty-day siege, defenders repelled as many as seven attacks per day, and the Chinese eventually withdrew. Further attacks were equally repelled, and the Chinese withdrew from the entire Korean peninsula, at least for a time.

Having failed to find support from its neighbor to the north, Silla then turned to the Tang for support, and they agreed to take Paekche first, then Koguryo. Accordingly, in the year 660 the Tang attacked Paekche's west coast by sea, while Silla closed in from the east. Paekche mounted an impressive resistance in spite of treachery at the highest levels of state, including a series of assassinations, but after three years Paekche came to an end.

Silla and the Tang now directed themselves toward their ultimate objective, the conquest of Koguryo. Their task was made somewhat easier by the disaffection surrounding Koguryo's strongman leader, Yon Kaesomun. After his death, conflict broke out between his two sons and his younger brother. The elder son was driven out and surrendered himself to the Tang, while the younger brother fled to Silla. Tang and Silla lost no time in taking advantage of this misfortune, and in 667 they coordinated an attack that overpowered Koguryo within a year.

Silla Unification

Silla discovered that the Tang had ulterior motives for their assistance with the dismantling of Paekche and Koguryo, for once those territories had fallen, the Tang set up a series of commanderies in Koguryo and Paekche, naming natives of those areas as its commanders. Silla perceived the nature of these puppet governments, however, and soon found itself at war once again. Silla's first step was to mount a fresh campaign and render assistance to the restoration forces in Koguryo. Silla then turned to the Paekche commanderies, and in 671, eventually prevailed after a series of bloody battles. In 676, Silla confronted the Tang forces in the Han river basin directly and expelled China, once again, from Korea.

Through the defeat of Paekche and Koguryo, followed by the successful rout of the Tang's imperialist incursion into formerly allied territory, Silla accomplished what had not been done before: the unification of the Korean peninsula under one banner. It is true that the large portion of Manchuria ruled by Koguryo remained under the control of remnants of Koguryo, which eventually fashioned itself into the kingdom of Parhae, but the vast majority of the peninsula now answered to one king, and the Korean people now had an environment in which a mainstream culture could develop.

The Middle Period: Koryo and the Yi Dynasty

For all its significance, Unified Silla was not to last. Over time, the growing gap between the ruling class and the general populace resulted in a series of uprisings, and, some two hundred years after its formation, Unified Silla splintered back into the three kingdoms from which it had emerged. However, they did not retain their sovereignty either. By the end of the tenth century, Korea had once again been unified, this time nearly permanently (until the current division of Korea following World War II). The new kingdom was known as Koryo.

Like many of its predecessors, Koryo came to life in the midst of armed conflict, essentially as a rebirth of Koguryo. Its society, therefore, took on trappings similar to those of the earlier kingdoms in the extensive influence of its military. Garrisons were common sights, and Koryo maintained a large and well-organized standing army. For some time, study of the martial arts had declined and become primarily a means of attaining physical fitness. But as Koryo's power increased and its military forces grew, there seems to have been a resurgence in combat practice. This may well have been reinforced after the reorganization of Koryo's military forces, which were modified to include a division of armed Buddhist monks called the Subdue Demons Corps. Their purpose was to increase the odds of victory through active prayer, but they were also trained as soldiers, and they bore arms and battled alongside their more secular compatriots.

Buddhism flourished under the Koryo government, and monks came to be granted a great number of privileges, including free grants of land, exclusion from certain taxes, and other economic benefits. Their growing wealth led increasing numbers of princes and other royalty to seek admission to their ranks. And as they became wealthier, monks found it necessary to be able to defend their wealth—armed monks became common enough themselves, and it was from this pool that the Subdue Demons Corps was formed. There is every reason to believe that tae kyon, or soo bak, flourished during this period. If it is true that unarmed combat techniques were passed secretly from master to student, as some sources indicate, then it is likely that this occurred within Koryo's Buddhist monasteries.

Koryo's aristocracy indulged itself and its servants, at the expense of the military, even those military commanders of true-bone status. As a result, the military rose and overthrew the regime in 1170. This marked the establishment of military rule in Korea, which continued through a series of popular uprisings, and invasions by both the Mongols and the Japanese, until the late fourteenth century.

At that time, a Koryo general by the name of Yi Songye seized political power in a perfectly timed, near-bloodless coup, and established the Yi dynasty. In one form or another, this dynasty ruled Korea until the twentieth century. Practice of the martial arts began to wane during this time, however, partly owing to the increasing use of gunpowder and other technological advances that made traditional arts obsolete, except as forms of exercise.

Occupation and Liberation

If there can be said to be a dark period in Korean history, it would probably have begun at the end of the nineteenth century. By then, international politics had, of course, changed considerably, and the relative isolation of Asia that had predominated for centuries had evaporated. Throughout its history, Korea had maintained relations—peaceful, trade oriented, or conflicted, at different times—with Japan, China, Manchuria, and Russia. Now, however, the Western powers were on the rise, and had come to dominate international trade. The Asian nations had in various ways insisted on isolationist policies to defend themselves against the dangers of Western economic imperialism, but Korea's resistance eventually succumbed to the irresistible pressures of the Russian and Japanese military.

By the 1890s, Russia and Japan had become involved in a lethal struggle, and as Korea stood between them geographically, the peninsula became hotly contested. Russia had claimed Manchuria, and it was Japan that watched this growth with the greatest concern as Russia prepared to drive into Korea as well. The two nations came to a noninterference agreement regarding Korea in 1898, but that in fact did not halt Russia's efforts to expand in that direction.

Negotiations regarding Korea's fate continued between Russia and Japan, but the two could not agree on mutually beneficial terms, and in 1904, war broke out between them. Korea proclaimed its neutrality immediately, but the Japanese response was first to occupy Seoul and then to sign a protocol agreement with Korea that allowed the Japanese to set up what became known as a "government by advisers" in Korea, with Japanese advisers active in many branches of the Korean government. Japan surprised the world with a series of victories against Russia, and in 1905, the United States stepped in to help the two work out a peace.

The Russo-Japanese war was concluded on catastrophic terms for Korea, for in signing the Treaty of Portsmouth, Russia recognized Japan's paramount interest in Korea's economic, military, and political affairs, and promised not to interfere in whatever actions Japan deemed necessary for the guidance, protection, and control of the Korean government. Japan's first step was to draft a protectorate treaty with Korea, which was signed under controversial circumstances, to say the least. The result of this step was the complete divestiture of Korea's right to govern itself or to carry out foreign policy in any manner. Japan's grand plan was apparently to transform Korea into a Japanese colony, which it formally achieved in 1910.

This was nearly a death knell for Korean martial arts, as well as for all other forms of Korean expression, whether cultural or political, for Japan instituted a policy of complete repression, making the maintenance of law and order its top priority. Soo bak survived, was taught secretly, and was handed down from masters to students at the risk of imprisonment. It is virtually certain, however, that during this period elements of Japanese martial arts were introduced to the traditional Korean style, and it is to this time that we must look for the influence of karate in modern Taekwondo.

Korea was finally liberated after the Japanese defeat in World War II, although not without the tragic division of the nation by the United States and Soviet Union into today's North Korea and South Korea, formalized in 1948. Following the expulsion of the Japanese, Korean martial arts reemerged under a handful of names: Soo Bak Do, Kwon Bop, Tang Soo Do, Hwarang Do, and others, all somewhat different from each other, depending on how much Chinese or Japanese influence the various masters had absorbed. Reputedly, the first dojang to teach a native Korean martial art opened in Seoul in 1945 and was called Chung Do Kwan. During the next ten years, a number of other schools opened as well.

For a number of years, dissension among the masters prevented the centralization of any kind of regulation authority for the martial arts. However, tae kyon had caught on with the military, and it became a regular part of military training in 1945. During the Korean War in 1952, South Korean president Syngman Rhee witnessed a demonstration by a number of masters and was sufficiently impressed by the experience to make martial arts instruction an integral aspect of military life. In 1955, a meeting was convened to decide upon a single name for the Korean martial arts, but no decision could be reached. Two years later, however, the name Taekwondo was suggested, and, for the most part, Taekwondo became the commonly recognized name.

The Korean Tae Kwon Do Association was formed in 1961, and under its early leadership, masters traveled all over the world to spread the art. Taekwondo became highly popular in Korea, and dojangs opened everywhere. By the end of the decade, Taekwondo was established worldwide, and in 1973, the World Taekwondo Federation was formed to serve as the central governing body for the dynamic growth of Korea's martial art. Since then, Taekwondo events around the world have been overseen and coordinated by this organization. The WTF's crowning achievement was the introduction of Taekwondo to the 1988 Olympics as a demonstration sport. In the year 2000, Taekwondo will make its appearance as a fully official Olympic sport, the first martial art to appear in the Olympics since judo in 1964.

All Taekwondoists can look forward with excitement to the continuing spread and popularity of this martial art—one whose techniques and traditions have survived for as long as two thousand years, and one that has continued to evolve, improve, and grow with the passage of time. In studying Taekwondo, you participate in an ancient and ongoing ritual. Treasure the experience.

CHAPTER 2

Philosophy of Taekwondo

The Hwarang Code • Indomitable Spirit • Three-Way Unification • The Dojang •
The Dobok • Rank • The Black Belt • Combat and Competition: Martial Arts and Sports

Written on the shingles of Taekwondo dojangs all over the United States appear words like "Confidence," "Self-Respect," "Discipline," "Fitness," "Focus," and, of course, "Self-Defense," like some magic formula or mantra. What exactly is meant by these vague if wondrous promises? The meanings of some, like "Self-Defense," seem apparent, but how do the others relate to Taekwondo training? And why are they touted in the first place? Could a master not do just as well by promising "Washboard Abs!" and "Killer Kicks!"? Why does it even matter how all these promises are phrased? What are we to make of the word "Taekwondo" itself, and its translation "the way of hand and foot"? What is really meant by *do,* the "way"?

Sometimes students who are drawn to the study of martial arts by those very phrases are puzzled to discover that some dojangs place relatively little emphasis on the instruction of such qualities as self-respect and discipline. Some students find themselves wondering why, if Taekwondo is about focus, clarity, or inner peace, so little formal practice is devoted to meditation or other techniques specifically designed to clear and relax the mind. And, they wonder, if Taekwondo is about inner strength and clarity of mind, then what's the story with all the ranks and the fuss of promotional tests? In the end, aren't those just distractions from the true goal of "enlightenment"? And isn't Taekwondo really pretty violent? In this day and age, should students really be practicing a martial art that publicly declares itself to be devastatingly powerful? Who exactly are we planning to devastate?

In the time that we have been teaching Taekwondo, all of these questions have arisen at one time or another. And they are on the minds of most beginners as they first enter the strange and foreign world of the dojang, with its uniforms, its bows, its foreign phrases and rituals. In this chapter, we will try to sweep some of the mystery from the trappings of Taekwondo.

The Hwarang Code

As you will recall, in the Three Kingdoms period of early Korean history, the establishment of the hwarang played an important role in the unification and dissemination of hand-to-hand combat methods. To remain a powerful fighting force, the hwarang had to have the best training available, and they practiced constantly, in times of peace as well as war. The influence of the Koguryo military on the practices of the fighting forces of Silla cannot be overestimated, and the infusion of Koguryo strength and fighting prowess into the Sillan military had a lasting effect, notably in the promulgation of the early Korean martial art of tae kyon.

Equally important to Taekwondo's evolution as a martial art, however, is the Buddhist code by which hwarang soldiers were encouraged to live. The very fact that there was such a code in the first place is significant. The hwarang were not conscripts; they were the sons of nobles and nobles in their own right, and were expected to embody the virtues of Korean, and specifically Sillan, society. Their training consisted of the expected military skills, including swordsmanship, archery, horsemanship, and tae kyon (Taekwondo's historical predecessor), but becoming good fighters was not sufficient. They were also expected to become knowledgeable in Buddhism, Confucianism, music, dance, and literature. Their destiny was to develop themselves into complete and enlightened individuals, exemplary citizens. The code that governed their lives, their training, and their development is known as *hwarangdo,* or "the way of flowering manhood."

Five principal values governed the hwarang, and those values and their rules of conduct still apply to Taekwondo students today. Taken together, the hwarang code is known as *Hwarang Ae O Gae,* the "five principles of the Hwarang." Its tenets are *Sa Koon Yi Choong, Sa Chin Yi Hyo, Kyo Woo Yi Shin, Im Jeon Moo Tae,* and *Sal Saeng Yoo Taek.* These are commonly translated as loyalty, fidelity, honor, courage, and the practice of justice.● The principles themselves derive from concepts found in both Buddhism and Confucianism, and obviously come from an era and world different from ours. However, the lessons to be learned are of universal application.

Sa Koon Yi Choong

LOYALTY TO THE KING. To a member of a democratic society, this tenet has a particularly anachronistic ring. It also rings of patriotic fervor; it could be read as nationalistic, even jingoistic. Insofar as the hwarang were concerned, it may well have been strongly both. They were, after all, an elite warrior class charged with the mortal protection of their society. In some circles today, patriotism itself has lost some appeal—while some feel stirred by the national anthem, others invariably smirk, or yawn with boredom when the time comes to stand and face the flag. Some are offended by insults to the flag, while others feel it their Constitutional right to deface it in order to make a point about their views of government in general, about the current administration in particular, or about political speech itself. The diminishment of patriotism as a core value of American society does not necessarily mean that Americans have no respect for authority. Americans generally show respect to certain classes of people; judges and senators are referred to as "The Honorable . . . ," the President of the United States is addressed as "Mr. President," and most folks feel it is wise to address a police officer as "Officer" or "Sir."

But the principle of *Sa Koon Yi Choong* has less to do with reverence for the trappings of authority and the state than it does with the order of society. In many dojangs, for example, it is customary at the beginning and end of class to bow first to the flag—American, Korean, or both—and then to the instructor or master. Bowing to the flag is not the same as reciting the pledge of allegiance in school. In pledging one's allegiance to the United States of America, one is specifically swearing to uphold the laws of the state and body of the state itself. However, when we bow to the flag in the dojang we are not

---

● The precepts of *Hwarangdo,* as well as the place the hwarang occupied at the pinnacle of Sillan society, call to mind the familiar Japanese samurai, with their emphasis on honor, bravery, respect, obedience, and fearsome prowess. But it may be instructive to note that the hwarang preceded the samurai by a margin of centuries, which has led to some ironic speculation that the philosophical roots of the samurai may lie in Korean history.

necessarily allying ourselves with the entity of the United States or with the Republic of South Korea. Instead, we are acknowledging our obligation to the society in which we live, and our connection to it and to our fellow citizens— our community. This is one of the levels on which Taekwondoists demonstrate respect, for if it weren't for the benefits we have gained as members of society, no matter how shortchanged some may occasionally feel or how much we may occasionally envy others, how could we have found our way to our particular station in life and society, or even to our dojang?

Because we, as Taekwondoists, have gained so much from our practice of Taekwondo, and because we continue to benefit from Taekwondo throughout our lives, we also owe a debt of loyalty to the place that has contributed so substantially to our physical, mental, and spiritual well-being: the dojang itself. Your dojang can be a home away from home, a second family, a source of inspiration, of challenges, of encouragement and support. In return, it deserves your support. Even if you find it necessary to seek out a new place to continue your training, you should honor your roots—in a sense, your birthplace as a martial artist, as one who seeks personal improvement.

When you bow to the flag, then, whether it be to the American flag, the Korean flag, the WTF flag, or some other symbol, remember that you are not swearing to lay your life down in the defense of a political entity. You are acknowledging your respect and appreciation for that which has nurtured you and provided you certain opportunities—the opportunity to practice Taekwondo, among others.

Sa Chin Yi Hyo

FIDELITY, RESPECT, AND OBEDIENCE TO PARENTS AND ELDERS. This is the precept most familiar to Taekwondo students, even if the phrase itself is not. As described above, by bowing to the flag we show our appreciation for the benefits of membership in society itself. On a more immediate scale, and a more intimate one, we owe respect to our parents, our elders, and our siblings. Our parents or other caregivers have given us love and nurture. Most of what many of us have been able to achieve has, in large measure, come from what our parents have given us. They have fed and clothed us, given us love and advice, and, throughout our childhoods, helped us to survive. We have relied on their love and trustworthiness.

Siblings occupy a unique position outside of our relationships to our parents or our relationships with elders and teachers. Elder siblings often instinctively understand that they bear some responsibility for the well-being of their younger brothers and sisters (granted, they are not always known to act on their understanding!). In Korean society, elder siblings really are responsible for looking after their youngers, and younger brothers and sisters need to respect their elders for the responsibilities expected of them. By demonstrating respect for his or her youngers, an elder sibling acknowledges that responsibility.

Likewise, those who are older than we understand more about living, because they have done it. Just because they are older doesn't mean that they are always right, of course, but it does mean that it would be foolish not to listen to them, and it means that they deserve our respect for weathering storms we have yet to face. One day, we will be like them. They already know that; many of us, however, are so distracted by the noise in our lives and the commotion in our thoughts that something so simple is easily forgotten. As keepers of memory and tradition, the elders of society deserve all the respect we can muster, and we should be mindful that however much we feel deserving of respect ourselves, it is deserved even more by those who bear the weight of years.

The relationship between instructor and student is best understood in the context of the network of family relationships and the burdens of responsibility shared by all family members. It is easy to understand the respect students owe to their sabomnim. The master leads classes, teaches techniques, coaches, gives advice, and, generally, supplies us with Taekwondo itself. It is unimaginable not to show respect for the sabomnim or kyobunim's role. But the respect that students owe to their instructors and masters extends to another level as well. A sabomnim does not only teach Taekwondo techniques. In teaching Taekwondo, sabomnim also teaches a way to live, a way to behave, and a way to approach the world. Sabomnim, in short, is like the eldest sibling, and treats each student like a younger sibling who needs to be helped along through the world. The sabomnim's obligation reaches beyond the level of basic hand and foot techniques to every student's well-being. It is for this reason, ultimately, that students owe respect to their masters.

Masters and instructors, on the other hand, owe respect to their students first in acknowledgment of their own burden as dispensers of knowledge and as worldly guides who use Taekwondo as a lantern. In reciprocating their students' respect, they also demonstrate an appreciation for their students' interest in learning from them and for the trials students experience at their hands. Taekwondo training should not be easy, after all, and no student is required to undergo it. Training is not compulsory. Masters, therefore, respect their students' decision to stick with it, to sweat and ache and practice in their own pursuit of proficiency and excellence.

Finally, Taekwondo students demonstrate the same respect for each other as siblings ought to show. Students are all in it together, and it is their responsibility to be good training partners, to look out for one another, and to give aid when needed and advice when asked. Senior students, like elder siblings, have to help their juniors learn new forms and new techniques. Just as sabomnim seeks to nurture the health and well-being of all students in the dojang, so the students need to help each other in whatever way they can. This is the reason we show respect to each other in the dojang, and adhering to this principle is the best way to engender that respect.

Kyo Woo Yi Shin

TRUSTWORTHINESS AMONG FRIENDS. The very notion of trustworthiness among friends calls to mind a number of related qualities: integrity, dependability, and reliability are some examples. But perhaps "honor" best sums up the whole of these values. Your ability to demonstrate genuine respect for others is only one part of your measure as a complete person and as a complete Taekwondoist. Beyond that, you need to show yourself worthy of the trust others place in you. Taekwondo values those who represent themselves as they are, who do not fear the consequences of telling the truth when asked about something, and who keep promises that they make. This is how to show others that you are a person who is not false. In so doing, you will begin to earn the respect of others, including those who do not even know you well.

Representing yourself truthfully, and not being afraid to reveal your own thoughts and feelings about things, takes some courage. But if you do not do this, you will soon come to be seen as one whose actions and words do not correspond. In a sense, this principle is similar to the idea that one ought to treat others the way one wishes to be treated by them. If you seek to maximize the well-being of those around you, and you are forthright in your dealings with them, it will be apparent that you deserve respect, and you will be esteemed.

The pursuit of honor has an ultimate reward that lies beyond the level of others' esteem. If you know that you have earned the trust of others, and that you have worked to deserve the trust of others; if you perform with courage, and know that others can depend on you and others know that they can depend on you, then you will acquire self-respect. Self-respect is a grail that some pursue throughout their lives.

By being a student with whom others want to train, you become trust-worthy. By upholding your end of obligations, by speaking your mind, by showing respect to others, and by being courageous, you achieve honor. And in making yourself an honorable person, you make yourself worthy of your own respect. This is one of the fundamental values of Taekwondo.

Im Jeon Moo Tae

COURAGE IN BATTLE. The hwarang were warriors, and their exploits produced the kind of heroes of which legends are made. It was not through faint-heartedness that Silla prevailed time and again against its immediate neighbors as well as against foreign imperialists and succeeded in unifying the entire Korean peninsula. At this point in history, you probably will not find yourself facing situations like these, but there are other tests of courage. Even the resolve to live by *Kyo Woo Yi Shin,* the injunction to remain trustworthy to your friends, can require courage, both in its implication that honesty is required of you and in its implication that you will respond to others' need, no matter the risk to yourself.

Living courageously requires the ability to distinguish the reckless from the risky, and to decide upon a course of action that will achieve results. Little is ever gained from a total aversion to risk, just as little is ever gained from a complete disregard for danger. The key to turning risk into triumph lies first in the belief that victory is assured, and, second, belief in one's own capabilities and resources. Belief in one's own capabilities and resources requires the capacity to assess oneself unflinchingly, to determine where one's strengths and weaknesses lie, and to do everything possible to maintain strengths and correct weaknesses. In the course of Taekwondo training, this is ever the goal. Seek to perceive obstacles and overcome them, to enhance your abilities, and to face risks and dangers with the self-confidence you have earned. Discover your own indomitable spirit—which you can read more about on pages 21–22.

Sal Saeng Yoo Taek

DO NOT TAKE LIFE UNJUSTLY. Most martial artists these days are not in the business of taking lives or even of being in a position to take lives. That is left to the authorities—police, military, the courts, and so on. The relevance of this tenet to our lives is in its emphasis on justice. It is important to do what is right. That is implicit also in *Kyo Woo Yi Shin,* of course. Earning the trust of your friends, your colleagues, and your partners requires that they be able to depend upon your judgment. *Sal Saeng Yoo Taek* refers to the place of Taekwondo in one's life, and what one is to do with the knowledge and skills that come with diligent practice. When is it acceptable to strike someone else? Or, to put it another way, when is it right to defend yourself with Taekwondo techniques? What place does the physical, forceful aspect of Taekwondo have in our lives?

The usage of Taekwondo's powerful techniques requires considerable judgment. Taekwondo is not to be trivialized by showing off, boasting, or bragging. To begin with, bragging about one's ability is foolish—you never know what you will come up against in an actual fight. Just because you have a strong kick does not mean that you cannot be clocked by a wild hook punch to the face. But beyond this basic truth of conflict, bragging about one's Taekwondo skills or showing off in order to impress others cheapens your own accomplishments. Your ability is a treasure, and it has been gained as neither a free gift nor an impulsive purchase but through your own hard work and dedication. Show the greatest respect for what you have achieved by remaining satisfied in your own knowledge of it. Feel free to invite others to watch a class, if you want to show them Taekwondo, or take them to a tournament. Those may be the best ways to expose someone to the thrill of this martial art.

In addition to the need to maintain a respectful attitude toward Taekwondo as well as to your own achievements in Taekwondo, you must keep in mind that you really can do some serious damage to another person with what you have learned. A side kick is very powerful; before you aim it at someone's knee, you must be quite certain that you are in danger of physical harm, or that someone under your protection is in danger of physical harm, and that violence is necessary to nullify the situation. Responding violently to taunts or insults is improper. Attacking someone because they have insulted you is not self-defense; it is a surrender to provocation. It signals a willingness to relinquish the power to decide the course of your own fate. Instead, always seek to find an alternative to violence. Try talking. Keep walking. Look for crowds, storefronts, restaurants, or other safe environments in which you might take refuge. Increase your distance from your antagonist. Avoiding conflict is no sign of cowardice. It is a sign of wisdom. Indeed, it is the first rule of self-defense. By avoiding conflict, you avoid injuring another person as well as the danger of harm to yourself. If you keep a calm mind, without fear and full of quiet self-confidence, you will find it surprisingly easy to avoid violence except under the most extreme circumstances.

However, *Sal Saeng Yoo Taek* by no means forbids force. Once it becomes clear that you are in danger, or that someone who depends on you for safety is in danger, you must fight as if your life itself depends on it.

Indomitable Spirit

Indomitable spirit is the wellspring of the martial artist's courage. More important, it is the foundation of the martial attitude that nothing is impossible. Will every student become a master? Will every tournament fighter win a place on the Olympic team? Will every violent confrontation end peacefully or without injury? Obviously not. But indomitable spirit does not require victory every time. It requires the belief that victory is possible. It requires a refusal to surrender, to give up, to collapse, to believe in shortcomings. A Taekwondo workout should be demanding. It should be difficult. It should pose challenges that students do not think they can meet. It should even, from time to time, seem impossible. Beginners often feel that a given drill cannot be done properly—and they are right. But the determination to try is what matters most. Taekwondo values a gritty commitment to do the impossible, and to push one's limits at all times. Eventually, students discover that determination brings its own rich rewards in the form of accomplishment and enormous satisfaction.

Attaining difficult and worthwhile goals requires discipline. Discipline is the imposition of your own will to do that which needs to be done. Sometimes, the word "discipline" carries a punitive tone. "Discipline" can serve as a euphemism for punishment. Punishment is radically different from the will to do that which is necessary. Discipline should not be a mold applied by a master or one's superior. True discipline is discipline of the self. Self-discipline requires the heart to unite the mind and body in order to accomplish that which is not easy. Understanding what must be done, resolving to do it, and then achieving it is a victory of the self over resistance, whether that resistance comes from others or from one's own mind or body. Self-discipline reflects an awareness of oneself and the surrounding world; in this regard, discipline can be thought of as a form of enlightenment coupled with perseverance.

When should a student listen to the inner voice that says "I can't"? We have sometimes heard that response to a command in class, and our response is that those words are not in our vocabulary. An instructor does not expect perfection from students; that is patently impossible. But an instructor does expect students to have high expectations of themselves, and to strive for perfection with every step, every block, every kick. The physical goals of Taekwondo are relatively simple and obvious. Achieving them is neither. It requires a tough, resilient will to vanquish inflexibility, exhaustion, clumsiness, ignorance, and fear. In fact, every practitioner of Taekwondo suffers these limitations—but they do not all suffer limitations of the spirit. There is always a way to win. To do your very best to see the way and achieve it, and to do that always, whether or not your belt is tied around your waist, reflects the indomitability of your spirit.

Three-Way Unification

In the pursuit of excellence as martial artists, students' ultimate goal is a lofty one, beyond the perfection of technique itself. Ultimately, the goal of training is to strengthen the fiber of one's character, the elements that make up oneself. In part, this can be achieved by doing one's best to live by the precepts described above. On another level, the improvement of oneself can be achieved through striving to strengthen and unify the triumvirate of entities that compose an individual: the mind, body, and spirit. Each of these entities plays a critical role in training, and without any one of them, becoming a true Taekwondoist will prove impossible.

The mind is the intellectual faculty—that part of the whole that is responsible for absorbing and assimilating information. The mind is also responsible for making information useful. Just as memorizing lists of words does not mean that one's vocabulary expands, memorizing various techniques and lessons does not mean that they will become useful parts of one's Taekwondo education. Information includes how techniques should be executed, what the positions of the arms, legs, and body should be, how to throw every kick, the patterns of the poomse, and the strategic principles of sparring and self-defense. But simply remembering all this information is not sufficient. When a student responds to the teacher's instruction to throw a down block, it is the mind that interprets the command and transmits that information to the limbs. Beginners frequently respond with the wrong block or kick; communication between their minds and their bodies is still incomplete. The links that allow them to act have not yet been forged. Learning new techniques, poomse, or strategies requires intense concentration. Responding instantaneously to commands in class or sparring events requires instinctive reactions ingrained through rigorous training and practice. Consistent practice will improve students' concentration and sharpen their thoughts, and help lead to correct action.

Beyond the constant sharpening of the mind's ability to receive and retrieve new information, Taekwondo training should also stress a student's ability to respond creatively and intelligently to new situations. It is not the dictionary or the calculator that is gifted with intelligence; it is the writer or the physicist who displays intelligence in seeking to apply the mechanical laws of words or mathematics to a larger problem. The warrior's mind is a potent weapon. Keep it sharp.

The role of the body is rather self-evident. Without a body, after all, it would be quite impossible to do anything remotely resembling Taekwondo—or anything else, for that matter. But training the body is different from the simple business of living and breathing. Becoming able-bodied has become an extremely popular goal. Lately it seems that everyone wants to be trim, sleek, strong, and fast, like a professional athlete, or they want to look physically perfect, toned, and beautiful, thanks to the influence of advertising and the advent of super-models. Health clubs are cropping up everywhere. Among adults in the larger cities, it seems unusual not to be involved in some kind of exercise routine like running, weight lifting, cardio machines, or aerobics.

Thankfully, strengthening the body confers not only cosmetic benefits but tremendous health benefits as well: it reduces body fat, strengthens the heart, makes the lungs more efficient, tones the muscles, and regulates the metabolism. Exercise also promotes mental health. It reduces stress, promotes relaxation, and improves sleep. The anecdotal evidence for the mentally healthful aspects of exercise is perhaps as voluminous as the quantity of people who exercise regularly. Taekwondo training values the health and strength of the body in part because it is through one's body that one experiences and inter-acts with the world at large. But physical training, especially in the martial arts, also tends to increase the general level of alertness to one's surroundings. Few things contribute as much to an overall sense of well-being as a strong, healthy body. It really is the temple in which you reside in this physical world. Its health has a direct impact on your mental and spiritual well-being. Through your Taekwondo training, treat your body with respect, maintain its integrity, and improve its strength and ability.

Perhaps the most significant goal of Taekwondo training with respect to the mind and the body is the attempt to eliminate the gap separating the two. The mind and body must learn to act together, without a gap between them. Through practice, thought and action can become unified as one, and the thought of a technique can become that technique in reality. How else do skilled black belts learn new techniques so easily?

When we talk about developing a strong spirit, we are referring to a strengthening of the will to do what seems difficult, and the resolve to over-come obstacles, objections, and barriers. This puts the principle of indomit-able spirit into a new context, that of its relationship to a strong mind and strong body. Taken this way, "spirit" can also be read as "heart." It is this qual-ity that pushes the mind to remember, assimilate, and analyze; it is heart or spirit that pushes the body to throw twenty more kicks, to run another mile, or to go through the poomse one more time; it is the spirit that does not refuse and does not give in. It is the spirit that helps the mind to overcome fear. Accomplished athletes often say that conditioning plays a part secondary to the role of heart in achieving the seemingly impossible. The top sparring coaches in the country, like nine-time U.S. champion Master Dae Sung Lee, or Master Han Won Lee at the Olympic Training Center, know that it is a com-petitor's spirit that ultimately makes him or her a winner, not just blinding speed and dynamite kicks. Resolve, focus, determination, and courage are things of the heart, not the mind or the body, and without heart, neither the mind nor the body will come to its full potential.

Taekwondo training is rigorous. The constant challenge of meeting the demands of training, of taking full advantage of the mind, body, and spirit, will sharpen all three of these areas. And not only will it sharpen them, it will lead to their conjoining. And by channeling this strengthening through the *Hwarang Ae O Gae,* you will become more able, better rounded, and a more complete person. This begins to be the essence of *do,* the "way."

The Dojang

Everyone knows that the dojang is not quite like any other place. The standard of behavior is unusually high. Not only is the standard of behavior high, but the form of behavior differs as well. In the dojang, we bow to our instructors, colleagues, and friends, rather than merely wave or shake hands. When we do shake hands, we do it with the left hand supporting the right arm, essentially offering the right hand with the left, treating the offering of the hand as one would the offering of something precious. Respect for each other is not only valued, but its demonstration is insisted upon. Somehow, all the rules here look different from a Western perspective, and, significantly, the vast majority of students come to value that difference as much as they value the physical benefits of Taekwondo practice. Without the substantial differences in teaching method, clothing, and behavior toward one another, learning Taekwondo would be much like learning any other difficult sport.

Aside from the bowing, the special form of handshake, and the dobok, one huge difference between training in a dojang and training in a gym becomes immediately obvious to any beginner. That difference is the relationship between respect and the concept of obedience. Respect and obedience are mentioned in the translation of *Sa Chin Yi Hyo* ("fidelity, respect, and obedience to parents and elders"). Once class begins, a student is expected to stay in it and do everything asked. There is no other option, except in cases of illness or injury. It does not matter whether what the instructor asks is possible, or whether a student feels like doing that particular drill or not. In response to a command, the only proper response is "Yes, sir" or "Yes, ma'am." Students do not have the option of deciding that they do not want to practice reverse ilbo-jeonjin step that day. In joining class, a student agrees to be taught. That means that the student agrees to respect and abide by kyobunim's judgment and kyobunim's decisions. To do otherwise would clearly represent a disrespectful attitude toward the instructor. Absolute respect takes on the form of something deeper—a willingness to obey.

An observer might find this element surprising. Does that unquestioning obedience not make students resemble automatons rather than adults— adults who are paying for a service? What of individualism? What about the "enlightened warrior" aspect of martial arts? And in the case of child students, how does this contribute to maturity?

Obedience as it applies in the dojang should not be confused with the ideas of obedience that normally spring to mind, which, for many people, include slavelike submission of the will, childlike acquiescence, or maybe the tricks of a well-trained pet. The common understanding of obedience frequently includes humiliation and surrender, a loss of the self. Obedience in the dojang does require the student to give up something, but it isn't the self. Rather, it is the ego, the *idea* of the self. This concept is not as abstract as it sounds. One of the reasons students return to the dojang and tend to stick with their training is that they often find that training brings them great peace of mind. Practice has a way of washing away negative thoughts, fatigue, stress, and depression. Day-to-day life can exert tremendous pressure. We go from one engagement to the next while still thinking about the last one, all the while worrying about the future as well. We are busier than ever, spending less time with our families, more time working, and less time alone or in contemplation. By the end of the day, the mind has become cluttered with a cornucopia of scattered thoughts and worries, all of which clamor for attention. The mundane concerns of routine living cling tenaciously to the consciousness, becoming part of how we define ourselves. We become spiritually *heavier* somehow. Rarely do we go anyplace where these things can be forgotten or easily put aside.

The dojang, however, can be such a place. Its formalized environment becomes a sort of sanctuary from the baggage and burdens of the self, where the accomplishments that matter are only those that can be physically demonstrated, and where the differences between students are solely those reflected in training. In surrendering the cares of the world, acknowledging sabomnim with a respectful bow, and throwing mind, body, and spirit into practice, the external world can, for a time, vanish. It is possible, however briefly, to attain freedom from one's own ego.

Obviously, with so much emphasis on performance, pridefulness may result from one's training successes. As moralists have said for millennia, however, pride is a thing to be wary of. Fortunately, Taekwondo has a way of helping students to manage it, and that, too, has to do with the place of respect. We do our best to show respect for each other at all times, but respect can be difficult to come by without a measure of humility to go along with it. We owe it to ourselves to surpass our own expectations and to focus on further limits to overcome, greater goals to achieve. When we enter the dojang, we enter it as Taekwondoists—people devoted to making themselves better through the improvement of their abilities. To achieve the difficult goals we set for ourselves, we essentially surrender our resistance to difficulty, or, in other words, our ideas regarding what we can and cannot do—the clamorous shouts of the ego.

The Dobok

The dobok, or the uniform, may be thought of as the clothing of the "way," the *do*. It is a simple, functional white garment that in its appearance emphasizes the absence of ego. In its simplicity and uniformity, the dobok erases boundaries: all students, rich and poor, young and old, wear the same kind of garment. Its whiteness is a symbol of the purity of the wearer, who should be unsullied by notions of personal grandeur, and who instead should constantly seek ways to improve upon his or her achievements. Its whiteness also symbolizes the blankness of one open to new knowledge, whose mind stands ready to receive, like a clean slate. A black belt's dobok differs only in that it often has black trim around the collar. This black trim emphasizes the dignity that black belts should cultivate within themselves and the honor that is owed them for their own perseverance, discipline, and accomplishment.

Because it is the only clothing permitted to be worn during Taekwondo practice, the dobok itself serves as a symbol of training and of the martial art. Outside the dojang, the dobok is a reminder of what you strive to be and of the values of the dojang. Keep it clean and unwrinkled. Take care of it as you would take care of any precious thing.

Rank

Traditionally, the belt served no other purpose than the utilitarian one of keeping the training clothing on the body. Today, the belt also symbolizes rank. Some students wonder why we bother with rank. Promotional tests are stressful and cannot always determine someone's ability. It is possible to miss a test and feel left behind. It is possible to feel unfairly graded, or feel that someone else was not graded strictly enough. And it is possible to feel that Taekwondo is about going up the ranks and getting a new belt rather than one's own personal improvement.

Yet rank serves several useful purposes. From an instructor's point of view, it is a convenient way to determine, roughly, what the levels of ability, or at least of training experience, are in any given group of students. That can help the instructor plan classes and figure out what needs to be taught to that particular group. It also offers a means of structuring a student's overall Taekwondo education; for every rank level, there is a body of appropriate material to be covered, usually starting with the most basic techniques and forms and progressing from there.

From a student's point of view, rank often serves as a motivation. Although students are usually tested in groups, promotion tests are subjective tests of the individual. No student of a given rank is expected to perform the same way others of that rank perform. Factors other than experience—age, for example—play an important role. It is natural to expect different kinds of ability from a student of twelve versus a student of sixty. The test is meant to encourage students to realize their greatest potential with respect to their level of experience. It provides concrete goals, apart from the desire to perfect the spinning hook kick or break a pile of boards with a palm heel. Each promotion is a milestone that seems achievable. Imagine starting as a white belt and not testing for four years, then suddenly being asked to test for black belt. Many students would find such a prospect daunting, to say the least.

In addition, rank provides public recognition of a student's achievement, and a sense of validation. Rank also provides students with a group of peers in skill and experience with whom they can train and discuss their own experiences. It establishes a baseline of expectations—all green belts (6th gups), for example, can be expected to know Taegeuk Sam Jang, and should be accountable for it.

Finally, because rank is a reliable way to determine what a student ought to know, it provides a framework of mutual expectations. Remember *Sa Chin Yi Hyo*? Senior ranks are obliged to teach junior ranks new forms and give them help when they need it. With rank comes responsibility, both to the holder of the rank and to those junior to that rank. This emphasis on responsibility is one of the greatest differences between martial arts and other forms of exercise. You can lift weights or play tennis for ten years and never be expected to help others do it, but if you've done Taekwondo for ten years, you can be sure that with your knowledge comes a debt to your juniors.

Promotional tests provide a chance for students to demonstrate that they have mastered the material appropriate to the new ranks they wish to earn. It can be difficult, of course, to rely on a typical test to show a student's worthiness of any given rank. He or she can be having an off day, just as everyone has off classes from time to time. Or he or she can be injured or sick, or be grappling with difficulties at home. Sabomnim takes factors like these into account. After all, it would be improper to permit students to test who have not already demonstrated a basic readiness to take the test. But promotional tests serve another purpose, outside of a proof of skills. Fundamentally, the promotional test is psychological, not physical. Most classes are more difficult than the average promotional test. They last longer, include more variety, and are designed to offer new and challenging material. But they do not place as much of a premium on poise and confidence. The promotional test stresses the student's ability to listen carefully, to recover gracefully from mistakes, and to offer absolute effort—all while being watched by a crowd of onlookers and a table full of masters and instructors. To succeed on a promotional test is to defeat the demons of one's fears.

The Black Belt

Strangers to the martial arts sometimes take the black belt to signify the acquisition of some remarkable abilities: levitation, perhaps, or the ability to bend steel bars or leap twenty feet straight up into the air. These misconceptions are popularized through celluloid images, the products of Hollywood and Hong Kong—such is the legacy of Bruce Lee and Jackie Chan. Martial artists, however, have fewer illusions about what a black belt symbolizes, and to Taekwondoists, the black belt has a very specific and very special meaning.

The award of the black belt signifies mastery of the most basic skills of Taekwondo *to that student's fullest potential*. A black belt candidate must also demonstrate mastery of all the requisite poomse and other formal matters unique to particular dojangs. Not all students have the capacity to become perfect athletes. Physical limitations should not prevent them from realizing the best possible results, however. There is more to being a black belt than being able to whip out a perfect spinning hook kick. The black belt also signifies the wearer's maturity as a student of martial arts, and preparedness to undertake training on a more serious level. It is perhaps more important to demonstrate an understanding of the deeper values underlying Taekwondo training than it is to embody perfect technique or be able to do a thousand push-ups. A student's respect, indomitable spirit, sense of compassion and justice, loyalty, and trustworthiness all matter when a sabomnim deliberates upon that student's readiness to take the black belt test. After all, nothing reflects so much upon a master's ability as the quality of his students. When sabomnim permits a student to take the black belt test, technical excellence is only one of the qualities that student is expected to display. Stamina, self-assurance, and courage must also be evident. The test ought to be difficult, and rightly so: it must provide the student an opportunity to demonstrate more than quality kicks and sharp hand techniques—strength and resilient mettle must also shine. A student who has been permitted to take the test has already proven readiness in the course of training. Now it is time to display prowess and composure, together.

Older students are natural candidates for the black belt, once thay have sufficient training. A fifty-year-old will usually have much more trouble mastering the techniques, especially those that require flexibility, than will younger students, and if such a student has also neglected his or her physical health, then that student will have farther to go than others in achieving a satisfactory level of fitness. But as we have said, physical and technical perfection are not the sole criteria determining one's readiness to test for black belt. Character also matters. And older students have a great deal to offer a dojang in terms of their experience and their leadership ability.

Little matters more to the entire persona and character of a dojang than the quality of its black belts. They are its representatives to the public and to the martial arts community. Far more than their juniors, they stand for what that dojang and the sabomnim of that dojang are able to achieve. Black belts must always maintain a sense of dignity, composure, and tact. It is up to them to set a standard of behavior in the dojang; others will follow their example. When their senior walks in, they should stand—as should everyone else. They take care to bow properly, to shake hands properly, and to help perform whatever tasks are necessary to make running the dojang easier. To whatever extent is possible, they should seek to remain active in the affairs of the dojang and, if they have a chance, to be active on a larger level in the Taekwondo world.

At the same time, they must strive to improve their skills—achieving the rank of black belt is a substantial goal, but it is not an end in itself, nor is it the end of one's Taekwondo education. In fact, the opposite is true. The black belt is like a bachelor's degree: the culmination of intensive study that prepares the student to undertake deeper studies. Black belts need to train even more assiduously than they had before, if possible, and they need to focus their energies toward understanding and applying techniques in new ways, expanding the boundaries of their abilities. If they are tournament competitors, this is the level where their careers become more serious. All black belts should attempt to improve their sparring and their poomse, as well as begin to learn the poomse appropriate to their next dan requirement.

With the honor of the black belt comes another responsibility as well. The principle of *Sa Chin Yi Hyo* ("fidelity, respect, and obedience to parents and elders") entails the concept of responsibility to junior students in the dojang. For black belts, that responsibility is fulfilled by teaching. All students are obliged to assist their juniors, but black belts must do more. At this point, it is important that they make every effort to help others with their Taekwondo education. Junior students look up to black belts as the leaders of the dojang. Everything that a black belt student has gained needs to be repaid, and it is repaid to junior students who need the help of experts. Black belts need to share their experience, their knowledge, their inspiring advice, all those things that make them leaders. Being a black belt is a humbling experience. It is one thing to tie a belt around one's waist and work out. It is a very different thing to re-earn the right to wear that belt, and everything the belt symbolizes, every time one steps onto the mat. Of all things in Taekwondo, the right to wear the black belt is the last to be taken for granted.

Combat and Competition:
Martial Arts and Sports

Throughout recorded history, people have felt the impulse to prove their skills in sporting contests that establish dominance of one kind or another. Dominance can be attempted in the realms of aesthetics, endurance, strength, skill, agility, and strategy, to name a few. The motives for individuals who attempt the difficult feat of prevailing against all challengers in a given arena have probably been as numerous as the heroes themselves, and they range from personal glory to material gain to national pride, encompassing infinite variety along the way. The effort to excel frequently demands much sacrifice in terms of time, energy, social or familial commitments, or simply the opportunity to do something else with one's life. The historical question of what drives a player to the lengths often necessary to achieve the highest goals is further complicated by the historical legacy of sports.

Many cultures have left us records of games in which the stakes were quite high. At high levels of competition, losers of some games lost their equipment, their holdings, their freedom, and, sometimes, their lives. The gladiators of ancient Rome had little choice but to fight each other to the death before the cheering crowds of the Circus. For a select few, repeated victory could mean freedom. For others, victory merely assured that they would live to fight another day. History has left us ample record, of course, of jousting in medieval Europe, where cadres of knights and retainers would clash in organized combat with blunted weapons. Sometimes these tournaments were held with battle-ready weaponry as a true test of mettle. Injuries, often fatal, were common, even with points and blades dulled. Medieval tournaments were enormously expensive, and the costs of entertainment and lodging for visiting lords, not to mention the outfitting of fighters and the replacement of equipment lost to the victors, were passed directly on to a grudging populace. Victory was sweet, however, with treasure and glory in the offing, as well as fruitful political alliances and even the arrangement of advantageous marriages.

In other cultures, the winners were the ones to lose their heads or have their brave hearts torn out in gestures of appeasement to the gods, notably among the Aztecs. Although the stakes in some of these games could not have been higher, not all such contests were military or martial in nature. Some of the more innocent-seeming games have included polo and the great games of the Central American ball courts. In modern American society, two popular sports have taken the place of sanctioned mock-combat for public entertainment. Boxing, obviously, is one, and the other is football, with its staged battles for territory and the crushing collisions of offensive and defensive players. In both sports, success can bring great fame and wealth.

Regardless of stakes or motive, sporting competition explicitly pits opponents against one another for the purpose of proving superiority in the given event. Taekwondo competition is no different. Taekwondo competition for the most part is still amateur, and, with little corporate sponsorship as yet, brings little hope of material gain. Competitive poomse is about doing a form better than any other competitor does it, according to the judges' determination. Competitive sparring provides an opportunity to show one's superior technique, speed, and power in controlled combat with an opponent.

For a number of years, a debate has gone on within the Taekwondo world, as well as within the larger martial arts community, regarding the place of sparring competition. Opponents of competitive martial arts events generally criticize sports adaptation of martial arts on two grounds. The first is that training for competitive sparring requires that athletes adapt their practice to prepare them to spar within the guidelines established by the rules governing the sport. Rules limit what techniques may be used and what zones of the body are legal to strike, among other things. Training to spar under these conditions inevitably leads to some limitations on the overall ability of the martial artist, which, in turn, subverts the central purpose of martial arts training, which is self-defense by whatever means necessary, including the use of lethal force if circumstances warrant it. Some even say that Taekwondo, with its highly specific sparring rules, has become overly specialized and has lost much of its usefulness as a viable martial art.

It is true that many of the more obscure techniques originally included within the Taekwondo repertoire have faded from practice in many dojangs, perhaps partly owing to their exclusion from the tournament ring. It can be argued equally, however, that while techniques such as the spear hand, the ox jaw, the chicken beak, and various other hand strikes can be useful, they require far too much specialized training to harden fingertips and other hand surfaces, and that today's martial artists are better served by basic fist and knife-hand techniques. In this regard, there has been some movement toward an overall simplification of the traditional Taekwondo canon.

Yet the increasing popularity of Taekwondo competition has had another significant effect on our martial art. As competitors and coaches have sought for more effective ways to win matches, the very techniques that have been retained through the filtering process mentioned above have evolved. The turning kick is not the same kick it was twenty years ago. Nor are the back kick or the spinning hook kick. The principles of footwork have changed. All of these changes have made modern Taekwondo faster and more powerful than the methods traditionally passed on from antiquity. Indeed, one of the things that sets Taekwondo apart from more traditional martial arts is its interest in the improvement and evolution of all of its techniques. While tournament rules may limit the targets one may hit as well as the kinds of techniques allowed, Taekwondo has nonetheless become even more powerful.

Another factor to consider in this debate is that under self-defense circumstances, a trained fighter with a modest degree of self-defense training will strike to the legs and other "illegal" targets just as well as one who has forsaken competition training—and probably a good deal faster and harder. Most self-defense training simply does not emphasize speed and power to the same degree that competition training does.

Finally, competition training teaches an important lesson for any student interested in self-defense. That lesson has to do with actually being hit. Many students have a fear of physical contact when they begin their training, or feel that being hit would somehow cripple or destroy them. But once they have been exposed to sparring, they learn that being hit is not the end; they learn that they can take it, and survive, and learn to strike back. In this lesson there is a tremendous sense of security and self-assurance, and it is a critical lesson in martial arts education.

The other ground for debate about competitive sparring focuses on a somewhat more abstract issue. This has to do with the appropriateness of bringing a discipline advanced largely for the purpose of self-improvement into the competitive arena. As has been discussed throughout this chapter, Taekwondo training is ultimately about finding a way to improve the quality of one's own character. It is not about proving one's superiority over others as a martial artist or as an athlete. The urge to establish and demonstrate one's excellence in public smacks of the tantrum of the ego. How can the adaptation of Taekwondo to the tournament ring possibly mesh with the much loftier goals of personal discipline, respect, courage, indomitable spirit, and peaceful, nonviolent character?

Concern about the competitive aspect of tournament sparring tends to obscure the deeper relationship between tournament training and the interplay between the Taekwondoist and the ring. Yes, tournament sparring is competitive. It is full contact and it invites injury, in spite of padding and hogus and watchful referees. One person wins and the other loses, sometimes by knockout. Winning is considered to be good and losing is considered to be bad, or, at the least, unfortunate. Attendant to these matters are the appearance of anger, vengeance, frustration, elitism, disappointment, vanity, and a host of other difficult emotions all too commonly displayed by athletes one can watch on television at any time.

Clearly, all of that negativism is undesirable, and to anyone who has witnessed or participated in a Taekwondo tournament, it is all too familiar. But that in and of itself does not mean that competition is bad for Taekwondo or for Taekwondoists. On the contrary, it can be argued that competition can form some of the most important training experiences a martial artist can hope to undergo.

It is all well and good to form lofty philosophical principles about the meaning of one's training, to codify those principles, and to promote them. It is not too difficult to live by them in the rarefied atmosphere of the dojang. It is more difficult to take them out of the dojang and incorporate them into daily life. Most Taekwondoists probably do not even make a conscious effort to do so. Instead, they find the values that inform their training gradually seeping into their lives outside the dojang. This is the greatest result a sabom-nim can hope for, because it means that the values of Taekwondo have become integrated into the character of his or her students.

For those with the inclination to try sparring competitively, the ideals of Taekwondo acquire a new gloss. Circumstances as stressful or frightening as those of preparing for a match, eyeing one's opponent across the gym, and getting ready to step into the ring where a full-contact bout is imminent are exceedingly rare in daily life. To do it requires great courage and self-confidence. To do it well requires the utmost of one's character as a practitioner of Taekwondo: doing it well means always retaining composure, showing respect to one's opponent and to the officials, maintaining a sense of dignity, and never giving in to fear. Win or lose, elation can result from facing down such fear. Competition can be liberating.

Finally, there is the matter of violence between martial artists whose practice ideally contributes to a nonviolent nature. Some might argue that training to fight competitively emphasizes the wrong things, such as an aggressive attitude, when the emphasis of one's training ought to center on self-defense— ultimately a pacifistic attitude. Yet the more one deals with force, the more one understands it. The aim of training is not to breed killers with the instincts of killers. It is to train fighters who can analyze situations instantly and respond appropriately. In the ring, that means searching out ways to score points. In self-defense, that means searching out ways to avoid confrontation but then to act decisively when confrontation cannot be avoided. It is difficult to oppose a thing without first understanding it. It is easy to claim to oppose force or violence, but specious to do so without first trying to gain some insight into the nature of conflict. By training hard, a martial artist tries to understand force and conflict and, understanding it, learns to make peace. It helps to be aware of the alternatives.

As for what actually happens in the ring, well, it is violent. But at the same time, it is important to distinguish between random violence, accompanied by terror, fury, and ignorance, and the interaction of sparring contestants. Most competitors understand that by entering the ring, they sign a sort of contract. The terms of the contract are that *chung* and *hong* (the blue and red contestants) will fight each other to the best of their ability, each seeking to outscore the other, with the possibility of injury or loss by knockout. At the same time, they will abide by the rules, by the timer, and by the orders of the referee. Most important, they will behave toward each other with absolute respect. The emotional components of violence—rage, terror, hatred—are typically absent. If present, they are controlled. Sparring under these terms demonstrates a high degree of mental discipline and spiritual fortitude.

Naturally, tournament sparring is not for everyone. But for those with an interest in it, competition can be a richly rewarding experience. Few things can validate the self so well.

CHAPTER 3

Warming Up

General Loosening • Cardiovascular Warm-up • Stretching

Coaches, trainers, physical therapists, and athletes all recommend a solid warm-up before any type of workout; in a discipline like Taekwondo, warming up is critical, given the need for flexibility as well as cardiovascular endurance and muscular strength. A warm-up serves two basic purposes:

• It lubricates joints, preparing them for vigorous motion.
• It heats up muscles, relaxing them, making them more elastic, and charging them with oxygen by stimulating blood flow.

The joints themselves require as much consideration as the muscles and cardiovascular system when warming up. For example, warming up the knees gently prior to your workout will reduce wear and tear on these fragile components of the body. When setting out to practice footwork, throw kicks, spar, and generally move your legs through extreme extensions with speed and power, it's important to get the joints moving as smoothly as possible.

Most often, when we think about warming up we think about activating the muscles themselves through simple motions like jogging, jumping jacks, and stretching. While some researchers have claimed over the last few years that warming up prior to activity makes little if any difference to the integrity and health of the musculature, any athlete can tell you that warming up prior to a workout or competition makes, at the very least, a tremendous psychological difference. Also, because Taekwondo, like dance or gymnastics, requires tremendous range of motion, it's important to get the muscles relaxed and fully stretched out or tears may develop during practice.

We find it helpful to begin the warm-up by doing some gentle loosening exercises before moving on to the cardiovascular drills and complete stretch phase. This allows the body to become comfortable with each new stage of activity before being asked to do something more strenuous and, generally, allows it to adjust to increasingly difficult levels of exertion.

There are probably hundreds of stretches and calisthenic exercises that would be effective in Taekwondo practice. Generally speaking, the more stretches and calisthenics you know, the better. Strong and flexible legs, strong abdominals, a strong and flexible back, and a powerful chest and arms will all help improve your Taekwondo. Many of the stretches found in yoga can also be extremely beneficial in Taekwondo, both for stretching and for therapy to overused muscles.

You need to choose the exercises that suit you best and confer the most important general advantages: heightened respiration, a relaxed body, and strong muscles, especially the abdominals, the pectorals, and the lower back (the techniques of Taekwondo will strengthen the legs and arms). Determine what kind of regimen works best for you and stick with it. Add variety to keep your routine interesting and to round out your training. Generally, we find it most useful to begin at the top, with the neck, and work down the body. Here's how we do it.

General Loosening

Neck Rotation

Your body will spin and twist a great deal doing Taekwondo. Back kicks, spinning hook kicks, narabams, and even the reverse step can cause neck strain. Loosening up the neck before you proceed will help to prevent this. Begin by standing with your feet spread about a shoulder's width apart and your hands on your hips. Look to one side, then the other, holding your head at each position for a beat before turning to the other side. Keep your body and especially your shoulders relaxed and don't rush the process. Repeat the motion at least four times on each side.

Next, drop your ear to your shoulder, keeping your eyes focused straight ahead. Hold your head in that position for a beat, then switch to the other side. Again, repeat the motion at least four times per side. If you wish, pull down gently with your hand.

Now drop your chin to your chest. If your neck is relaxed enough, reach up with your hands, grab the back of your head, and apply gentle pressure downward. Hold for a beat, then tilt your head all the way back. Keep your jaw closed; otherwise, the front of your neck won't be adequately stretched. Repeat at least four times in both directions. Note that if you have any neck problems, you should avoid allowing the head to tilt all the way back.

Last, move your head in a slow rotation all the way around. You don't need to drop it completely back as you pass through the back side of the circle. Again, if you have any neck problems, it's best not to allow your neck to move through the rear part of the rotation. Instead, when your head reaches one shoulder, switch to the other one before repeating the motion. Rotate at least four times in one direction, then switch to the other.

Shoulder Rotation

Loose shoulders mean fast and powerful blocks and punches. Let your hands hang at your sides and pull your shoulders back, up to a full hunch, and around until they've traveled a complete circle. Repeat this motion, without hurrying, eight times, then switch direction and do it backward.

Shoulder Stretch

Cross one arm in front of your body. Place the other hand in front of it, just above the elbow, and pull the arm inward, stretching the back of the shoulder. Switch and stretch the other shoulder.

Now bend one arm fully and lift it straight up in front with the hand reaching down behind you as if to scratch your back. Use the other hand to push the elbow behind the head. Once there, you can use the head to help push the bent arm farther back.

Arm Rotation

Swing your arms in full, relaxed circles, eight times forward and eight times backward. For a strengthening variation, after the first eight forward rotations, hold your arms straight out to the sides and continue rotating them in small circles for at least another eight, then switch direction, keeping the circles very small until you complete eight more. Then switch to full reverse circles until you finish the eight-count.

Chest Stretch

Some people call these "chainbreakers." Hold your arms loosely in front of you, elbows bent. Pull both arms straight back, keeping the elbows bent and the body relaxed. Allow them to swing forward, then straighten the arms and swing them straight back and swing forward. Continue the motion, allowing the arms to alternate between bent and straight on each swing. If your shoulders are flexible enough, try to clap your hands together when you swing your straightened arms back. Repeat this motion at least eight times.

Trunk Twist

Sometimes these are called "washing machines." Hold your arms up loosely in front with the elbows bent. Twist in one direction until you're looking behind yourself. This is a very relaxed motion, and you shouldn't feel any tension anywhere. To help keep it loose, allow the heel of the opposite foot to lift off the floor as you twist. Swing around to the other side, again allowing the heel of the opposite foot to lift from the floor. Repeat the motion at least eight times.

Side Stretch

There are several ways to do this common stretch. This is the most basic. Hold one hand on your hip and reach over your head with the other. Bend sideways, toward the hip with the hand resting on it. Extend the raised hand until you are reaching fully to the opposite side, over your head. Keep your eyes and shoulders facing squarely ahead of you. Hold the position for a count of four, then switch to the other side. Once you've completed both sides, repeat the motion, this time linking your fingers over your head instead of keeping one hand on your hip. Use the hand on the side you're leaning toward to pull the other arm farther. You should really feel the stretch along your extended side. Hold the position for a count of eight, then repeat on the opposite side.

Hip Rotation

This is one of the most basic relaxation movements in Taekwondo, because it's so useful in helping to keep the hips and lower back relaxed. Keep your feet about a shoulder width apart. Place your hands on your hips. Swing your hips around in a complete circle (think hula hoop), keeping your head level. Do this at least four times, then switch direction.

Upper-Body Rotation

This time, keep your hands on your hips and spread your feet slightly wider apart. Keep your legs straight and drop down in front. Move your upper body through a large circle, bending all the way to one side, arching back, moving to the other side, and dropping again in front. Repeat this motion at least four times, then switch direction.

Knee Rotations

Place your hands on your knees. Bend your knees and move them in a circle slowly. Circle eight times to one side and eight times to the other. Now move them in independent circles, both going to the outside (right knee moving clockwise, left knee moving counterclockwise) simultaneously. Repeat this motion eight times, then reverse it, moving your knees in simultaneous inside circles.

Knee Bends

Keep your legs straight and place your hands on your knees. Keep your back straight. Crouch for a count of two, bending your knees fully, then straighten your legs and bend forward, stretching your hamstrings for a count of two. Repeat these motions eight times.

Cardiovascular Warm-up

The purpose here is to stimulate the heart and lungs and heat up the muscles preparatory to stretching and practice, rather than to provide a full conditioning workout. There are a number of ways to do this: running, jumping jacks, jumping, knee lifts, and a host of others. All of them work, but we like to emphasize those that develop skills or reflexes especially useful in Taekwondo. For a basic warm-up, continue reading. For more extensive drills, skip to the Extended Warm-up section that follows.

Basic Warm-up

Jumping jacks. Do fifty jumping jacks. Continue with some variations: slide the feet forward and backward, without jumping off the ground. Do twenty of these. Then do twenty more, moving the feet side to side and crossing them in front and behind each other. Finish with twenty regular jumping jacks, but twice as fast.

Running in place. Jog lightly in place. Then run in place with high knees, lifting them at least as high as your belt for ten seconds. Return to a light jog for a moment, then run in place again, this time kicking your heels up as high behind you as you can. This will help loosen your knees and quadriceps and will help warm up the hamstrings. Repeat the cycle three or four times.

Knee lifts. Bounce lightly on your toes, feet moving together. On each count, for a count of ten, lift your knee swiftly to your chest, then drop your foot back down to the floor. Do this rhythmically, and keep up the bounce with the other foot. (This means that for every lift of the knee, you will bounce twice on the other foot.) After the first ten, switch sides and repeat the process with the other leg. Then do it again, this time lifting your knee and setting the foot down as fast as you can. Repeat on the other side. Try some variations: two knee lifts per side, then switch; alternating knees; and knee lifts without setting the foot down.

You should be well warmed up now and ready for some real stretching. For a stretch regimen, turn to the Stretching section on page 44.

Extended Warm-up

Running is one of the best exercises you can do for Taekwondo training. In the chapter on sparring, we'll talk about running—both distance and track work—as effective cross-training for competitors. Meanwhile, there arc a number of methods you can use in the dojang to improve conditioning, strength, and agility.

Jog. After you finish with the basic loosening-up exercises, jog around the room. Concentrate at first on relaxing the upper body and shoulders and

Running with high knees is an excellent way to increase respiration and will also help improve the power and elasticity of the muscles that raise the legs. Speed and power in those muscles will be critical in sparring drills and practice.

maintaining a light pace. Gradually pick up the pace until you're moving at a good speed. Keep this up for two to three minutes.

Crisscross. Turn so that one side is facing forward. Continue running by crossing one foot first in front of the other, then behind. Step quickly. Concentrate on taking many small steps rather than fewer large ones. Swing your hips freely back and forth with each step. The ends of your belt should whip from side to side with the motion of your hips every time you step. Switch so that you lead with the other side and continue. Done properly, this drill will help your hips turn more fluidly.

Run backward. Turn around and run backward for a couple of laps.

Fighting stance. Slide or skip forward in a relaxed fighting stance, leading continually with one side. Make sure you keep your hands up in a good guard position. Continue for a lap or two, then switch to the other side. After you finish laps with both sides, continue in fighting stance, this time switching every two steps so that you alternate sides as you move down the room. Kihap each time you switch.

Knee lifts. Lift one knee as you move down the long sides of the dojang, not running but rather hopping forward every time your knee comes up. Maintain an even rhythm. You will take two hops as the knee comes up and down. As with the knee raises described earlier, make sure you lift your knee as high as you can, touching your chest if possible. Note that this is not a running motion, with only one foot on the floor at a time. In between each knee raise, both of your feet will be on the floor. Switch to the other knee on the way back. After you've done both sides, try the same thing but moving backward. When you've completed the backward circuits, move forward again, this time alternating your knees. Do this once around the dojang forward and once backward.

Bowling. Every three steps, so that you alternate sides, bend your knees and sweep your hand along the floor on one side as if you're releasing a bowling ball. Relax your body completely as you do this.

Standing jump. Run two or three steps, stop, and jump with both feet as high as you can, reaching for the ceiling. Repeat this down the long sides of the dojang, then use the following variations:

Variations:
Lift both your knees as high as you can on each jump.
Jump and reach back over your head, arching your back and kicking your heels back
    as you do. Be careful not to overarch on this one.

Lift both your legs straight out in front of you. Try to touch your toes.

Lift your legs in a split to the sides.

Finally, every time you stop, jump three times: 1) lift both knees; 2) lift your legs in a split; 3) arch your back.

Jump shot. Every two steps, jump off both feet and make an imaginary jump shot with one hand. Alternate hands each time, and keep your arms relaxed.

Spike. Every two steps, jump up, raise your arms, and strike downward with one hand as if you're spiking a volleyball. Stay loose and alternate sides.

Head the ball. Every two steps, jump up and thrust your head to one side as if you're heading a soccer ball. Alternate sides and be careful not to throw your head too hard.

Sprints. Sprint down the long sides of the dojang, jog lightly around the short end, and sprint down again. Repeat four times.

Shuttle run. Shuttle runs strengthen the legs, develop anaerobic capacity, and improve agility, or the ability to start and stop on a dime. Sprint halfway down the dojang, touch the mat, sprint back to your starting line, touch the mat, and sprint all the way down to the end. Repeat.

If you have a large room, shuttle back and forth at intervals of a quarter, a half, three quarters, and the whole room.

Finish up. Jog lightly for a few laps around the dojang to loosen up everything.

Stretching

Few physical attributes are as important in Taekwondo practice as flexibility. While it may be perfectly easy to throw kicks to the legs, knees, and groin without developing great reach, Taekwondo goes far beyond these basic defensive targets, extending its range of targets to the midsection and head. Most of the kicks we practice are in fact not aimed at the target areas of the lower body but instead at the head, kidneys, and abdomen. In competition, kicks below the belt are illegal, while kicks that strike the head almost always score a point. Some scoring systems award multiple points for kicks that reach the head, while those that reach the body typically score one point.

Of all the potential barriers to fine technique, stiffness is one of the most easily overcome as long as you take care to stretch properly and frequently. Students coming to Taekwondo later in life may have more difficulty gaining flexibility, but even they learn that it's possible to throw high-section kicks with grace, speed, and power. Frequent stretching is the key, and correct positioning combined with regular practice will be far more effective in producing long, supple muscle fiber than will sporadic stretching sessions or incorrect method. If at all possible, try to stretch regularly outside of the dojang. It's one of the easiest workouts to do on your own, and it has the added benefits of being truly relaxing, therapeutic to the body and mind, and possible to continue well into old age.

In the dojang, it is generally helpful—as well as in the interests of a rigorous workout—to precede the stretch with a thorough warm-up. Many students feel that they can't stretch properly without being well warmed up beforehand. However, it is possible to stretch well even without a complete warm-up as long as you take care to stretch lightly and patiently, giving the muscles time to relax, unknot themselves, and lengthen out. You should also try to find time to stretch at home, even if briefly.

During our years of teaching Taekwondo, we've learned and taught virtually countless stretching exercises and picked up numerous tips from students who have come to us with backgrounds in arts martial and otherwise, such as dance, gymnastics, yoga, karate, and others, and we find that the more stretches you know and do, the better. On the following pages, we'll list some of the most basic and most effective stretches we know.

Probably the single most important thing to remember in order to stretch properly is to keep a straight, flat back, except in cases where the stretch specifically calls for an arched or twisted back. There are two reasons for this. First, students will often find themselves reaching to touch their toes, for instance, and bending their backs to help them get there. You'll hear coaches say things like "Touch your head to your knee." That advice doesn't do any good as far as stretching the hamstring is concerned, because it emphasizes bending the back and neck. If you allow your back to bend, then your pelvis will not rotate in the direction of the stretch as much as it ought to, which, in turn, will prevent the leg muscles anchored to it from extending fully. Instead of trying to touch your head to your knee, think of reaching toward your feet with your chin and touching your chest or belly to your knee. That way, your back will stay flat and the pelvis will rotate. *Rotation of the pelvis is key to a proper, healthy stretch.*

Master Dae Sung Lee says that a fifteen-minute stretch first thing in the morning, when the body is still stiff from sleep, can do wonders for the flexibility, even if it isn't possible to reach full extension.

The second reason for keeping a flat back is that students who have trouble with their flexibility and bow their backs to compensate for a lack of reach sometimes find themselves developing sore backs or actual vertebral separation from bowing their spines too far. These students wind up not only remaining inflexible but battling back trouble as well. Remember that it's okay if you can't fall into a full split effortlessly, or if you can't lay your palms on the floor while standing or even touch your toes. It's more important to learn the correct technique; that way your flexibility is guaranteed to improve, however gradually, and your body will remain strong and healthy. Be patient.

If you choose to bypass the warm-up routines, be sure to begin your stretch with the exercises listed in the General Loosening section on page 38. It isn't necessary to do these stretches in any particular order. However, we find it useful to follow a pattern proceeding from less to more rigorous, hamstrings to hips to groin, and then to gluteus and calves. Also, some stretches logically follow others, and we find it best to follow that order, whether stretching alone or leading a class.

Also, remember to breathe evenly. Stretching is about mental relaxation as well as muscle elongation, and even breathing will help in both areas. Take a deep breath before lowering yourself into a stretch and exhale slowly as you go down or reach out. Try to inhale through your nose and exhale through your mouth—this helps to relax your diaphragm and abdominal region.

One final note on technique: Fitness professionals and researchers differ on the value or danger posed by bouncing or rocking in a stretch rather than holding steady in a position. We feel that whether to bounce or hold steady is largely a matter of individual preference, although it may be more helpful to beginners to hold steady, thus reducing the chance of pulling a muscle accidentally. More experienced practitioners may choose to bounce, especially in the first few seconds of a given stretch, and then to hold steady. We recommend that you hold steady or, at the most, bounce lightly, and never while fully extended.

Touch the Toes

Stand with your feet directly under your hips. Relax, straighten your back and knees, and bend forward, dropping your hands down to your toes. Stay there for a count of ten. Make sure your knees are straight—many people tend to let them bend—and let gravity do the work. A flat back is critical, as mentioned above. Slowly straighten up by uncurling your body, allowing your knees to bend and your back to uncurl one vertebrae at a time until you are standing upright. Then repeat the stretch, this time pulling yourself as far down as you can go, either by grasping your ankles or by placing your palms on the floor behind your feet and pulling backward.

Variations:

Cross one foot in front of the other and repeat the stretch as above. Cross to the other side after a count of ten.

Spread your feet to one shoulder width. Turn one foot so that the toes point straight out to the side. Straighten that leg and flex the ankle so that the toes are lifted off the mat. Allow the other leg to bend slightly, and lower your body over the straightened leg, keeping your back flat. Hold, then switch to the other side.

Back Arch

This is an exception to the flat-back rule. Note, however, that the back is arched backward, not bowed forward. Place your hands against the small of your back or behind your hips, whichever is more comfortable, and arch backward, pushing your hips forward. Hold for four, then release. This is particularly useful in combination with toe touches to loosen the hips and lower back.

Standing Groin Stretch

Spread your feet two shoulder widths apart, flatten your back, straighten your legs, and hang straight down. If you are flexible enough, grab your ankles and pull yourself farther down, or reach through your legs, place your palms flat on the floor behind you, and pull down. Hold for a count of ten and release. Then reach with one hand to the opposite ankle, again with a flat back and straight legs. Hold for ten and switch to the other side. Continue to alternate from the middle to each side and back to the middle for two sets.

Variations:

Windmills. Keeping your feet spread, reach to one side with the opposite hand, then to the other. Do this fast twenty times.

Pointed toes. Turn the toes of one foot straight out to one side. Keeping a flat back, reach out and down on that side to the ankle or farther for a count of ten, then switch sides.

Lifted toes. Point the toes of one foot out to the side and flex the ankle so the toes are lifted off the mat. This extends the hamstring. Keeping the toes up, your legs straight, and your back flat, reach out and down to the lifted toes or farther for a count of ten, then switch sides.

Hip Stretch

Two positions are given here. It's important to do both.

Side kick position. Spread your feet two shoulder widths apart. Turn to face one side. Lower yourself by bending the front knee while you keep the back knee straight. Your hips should be facing the same direction you are. Keep the rear heel on the floor and hold your torso upright. Concentrate on pushing your hips down. Pushing them down while keeping your body upright will stretch out the muscles in front of the hip. This stretch will also develop isometric strength in the quadriceps of the bent leg.

Front stance position. This is basically the same as above, but lift the heel of the rear foot off the mat, letting the ball of the foot support the leg. This change alters the angle of the back leg and results in a slightly different stretch.

Quadriceps Stretch

From the hip stretch described above, allow the back knee to bend and rest on the floor. Support your weight with the hand opposite that of the forward foot. Keeping the rear knee on the floor, lift the rear foot, reach behind with the opposite hand, and grab the foot. Pull it toward you, bending the knee fully. Now drop your hips toward the floor. Hold for a count of ten, then switch to the other side.

Hip and Hamstring

Keep your feet spread two shoulder widths apart and face forward. Turn the toes of one leg so that they point straight up. Bend the other knee halfway. Keep the bent knee pointing directly ahead; don't let it turn toward the straight leg. Hold for four, then switch, bending the other knee. Hold for four. Repeat if desired. Then begin again. This time, bend one knee completely, until you're nearly sitting with the toes of the other foot pointing straight toward the ceiling. Keep your body weight forward, between your knees. Support yourself on the flat foot of your bent leg, being careful to keep the heel of the foot flat on the mat. The temptation is to lift the heel and rest on the ball of your foot. If you lift the heel, your hips won't open up and you'll allow your hamstring some slack. Hold the position for ten and switch. *Note:* If this position doesn't seem to do anything for you, place your hand or elbow against the bent knee and push the knee out.

Groin Stretch

Keep your feet spread two shoulder widths apart. Lower your hands to the floor and slowly allow your feet to slide apart until they've spread as far as possible. Don't sit down. If you're flexible, you'll be in a straddle split or nearly in one. If you can, use your hands to walk your hips forward and back. Keep them pressed down to the mat; this way you'll stretch them through a range of motion. Now try dropping your chest to the floor and doing the same thing. Walk the hips back and forth several times, then *gently* sit down, keeping your feet spread wide apart.

Groin, Hamstring, and Hip Stretch/Straddle Split

This is one of the most basic stretches for any Taekwondoist, and one of the most difficult for beginners to do. Sit with the back straight and your feet spread as far to the sides as possible. Make sure your knees and toes are pointing straight up, not back. There are several variations to perform while sitting with the feet spread out to the sides. Try to do all of them, and repeat the front stretch and the front stretch to the sides.

Rotate pelvis. Place your hands on your hips. Now try to rotate your pelvis back and forth by rocking gently. You should feel your legs roll forward and back. The rest of your body won't move, and for most people the pelvis will move only two or three inches. Still, this is a surprisingly effective motion.

Side stretch. Place the back of one hand on the floor in front of you. Keep it there while you reach over your head with your other hand and stretch toward the opposite foot. Keep your shoulders square as with the side stretch on page 40. Hold the position for at least a count of four, then switch slowly. Keeping the back of your hand against the floor will help you align your body sideways. If you're flexible enough not to need to do this, then try clasping your hands behind your neck while you stretch sideways.

Front stretch. Reach out directly in front of yourself. Keep your back flat and feel your hips rotate forward. If they don't, then you're pulling the muscles of your back rather than stretching the muscles of the hip and groin area. It's much more important to feel the forward rotation of your hips than to be able to touch your head to the floor. If you find this stretch easy, then put your palms flat on the ground and pull your chest forward and down. Hold the position for a count of ten, then relax.

Front stretch to the sides. Now turn your torso so that you're facing one side. Reach out toward your foot, pulling your body down as you go. Try to bring your chest to your knee. Hold for ten, then switch sides.

Front Splits

Remain in the straddle stretch position. Lift yourself up on your hands high enough so that you can pivot your hips completely to one side. One leg should now be straight in front of you and one straight behind you. Most people will need to position the inside of the rear foot against the mat in order to brace themselves. Be cautious when you do this—you're placing a lateral stress against the back knee and it's possible to damage the knee this way. People with more flexibility should place the top of the rear foot flat against the floor. Either way, lower hips as close to the ground as possible. Hold the stretch for ten, then lower your body and lie along the length of the outstretched front leg for another count of ten. Then switch sides and repeat.

When you finish with the straddle and front splits, slowly sit up and straighten your legs in front of you. Draw your feet in, holding your knees together, and rock them from side to side.

Butterfly Stretch

An ideal stretch to follow the splits, the butterfly stretch relies on flexion—joints, in this case the knees, fully bent—rather than extension to stretch out the muscles. Sit straight up with your knees out to the sides, and pull your feet, soles touching, as close to your body as you can. Stretch with the following three variations:

Variations:
Clasping your feet, sit with your back perfectly straight, your feet pulled in close to your body, and your knees as low to the ground as possible. Hold for ten.
Clasping your ankles, push down on the insides of your knees with your elbows. Push the knees as far down as they will go. Hold for ten.
Clasping your feet, pull your body down—with a flat back as always—and try to touch your chest to the floor. Hold for ten.

Single Hamstring Stretch

Sit down and straighten one leg in front of you. Tuck the other foot in against your crotch. Reach out toward the foot of the straightened leg and, if you can, bring your chest to your knee. Hold for ten, then switch legs. Once you've done both, switch back to the first leg. This time, extend your body out and down to the middle, rather than toward the foot of the extended leg. You may need to grab the arch of your foot with your hand in order to keep your hips down. Hold the position for ten, then switch sides.

Hurdle Stretch

Most people who have run track or done some other form of exercise involving stretches are familiar with this position. Some fitness professionals and doctors advise against using this stretch, as it strains the knees. However, it's so effective at stretching muscles important for Taekwondo techniques that we have chosen to include it here. If you have a history of knee problems, you may choose not to use this stretch.

Sit on the floor with one leg extended straight in front of you as in the previous stretch. Curl the other leg behind you, with the knee fully bent. You have a choice of two positions for the foot of the curled leg: the ankle may be either straightened or flexed. Use whichever is more comfortable. Reach out to the foot of the extended leg and try to bring your chest to your knee. Hold the position for a count of ten, relax, and repeat.

Now stretch out to the middle, between your knees. Try not to let your hips lift from the floor. This can be difficult, and you might find it helpful to grasp your foot by the arch to anchor yourself. Hold for a count of ten, relax, and repeat.

Now lie straight back as far as you can while keeping your bent knee on the floor. Do not lie back any farther than you can with your knee on the floor. To stretch the quadriceps, the muscle group on the front of the thigh, you need to keep that knee down.

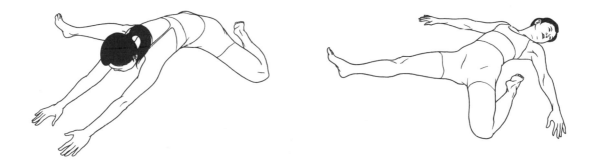

Gluteus Stretch

Sit with one leg extended straight in front of you. Grab the other foot and pull it in to your chest, letting the knee fall out to the side. Keep your back straight. If necessary, support the bent knee in the crook of your elbow. Hold the position for ten.

Now lie straight back, still holding the foot against your chest. Flex the opposite ankle and keep the knee straight. Hold for ten, then switch legs.

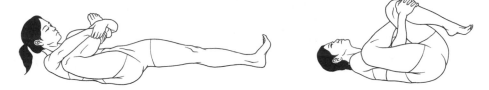

Gluteus/Hamstring Stretch

This is the perfect stretch to follow the two or three exercises described above. Sit with one leg extended straight in front of you. Bend the other knee and place the foot on top of the extended leg, just above the knee. Reach straight out to the foot of the extended leg. Hold for ten, then switch.

Double Hamstring Stretch

Sit straight up with both feet out in front of you. Keep your knees straight. Reach as far forward as you can, grab hold of the sides of your feet, and pull your head toward your toes. If this is easy, lace your fingers, turn your hands palms out, and reach over the tops of your feet, using your hands to form a stirrup. Pull yourself forward and hold for ten.

Double Hamstring/Calf Stretch

Sit straight up with both feet out in front of you. Reach forward and over the tops of your toes, grabbing the balls of your feet. Pull back on the balls of your feet and lift your heels off the ground. Now bend your elbows. Hold for ten and release.

Final Hamstring/Groin Stretch

Here are two variations of an excellent finishing stretch.

Sit straight up with your legs out in front of you. Pull one knee in to your chest. Form a stirrup with your hands, place your foot in it, and straighten the knee. Lift the foot as high as you can for a count of ten, then switch.

Now pull one knee in to your chest and grab the foot by the arch, using the hand corresponding to the stretching leg. Straighten the knee and pull the foot back and to the side, leaning back on the opposite elbow. Hold for ten and release.

CHAPTER 4
Stances

*Joon Bi • Horse Stance • Walking Stance • Front Stance •
Back Stance • Cat Stance • Twist Stance • Fighting Stance*

All technique begins with the feet and their position, the distribution of the body weight, and the mobility of the legs. Therefore, we concern ourselves first with stance.

In general classifications of martial arts, Taekwondo has often been grouped with "hard styles" like shotokan, as opposed to "soft styles" like aikido or tai chi. Hard styles concentrate on blocking powerfully and striking in retaliation, often in direct opposition to an attacker's motion. Soft styles concentrate on evasion and redirection, minimizing the impact of blocks and often focusing on the redirection of an attacker's force and body weight. Taekwondo merits the hard-style appellation insofar as we concentrate much of our training on developing fast and powerful kicks, and our blocks, when done properly, not only deflect blows but also seek to damage the attacker's limbs. However, we also place much emphasis on graceful, fluid motion and quick, evasive footwork; if our movements are not as purely circular as those of aikido or wu shu, they still rely greatly on flowing lines and avoidance. Beginners in Taekwondo frequently seek to maximize the power of their hand techniques by overexerting their shoulders and upper bodies, resulting in tense, jerky motions. Watching a novice go through Taegeuk Il Jang, one might easily conclude that Taekwondo is an upper-body form built on rock-solid right angles. But an expert going through the same form will make such greater use of the body's suppleness and the movement of the legs that one could not rightly call Taekwondo a hard style. Taekwondo, it turns out, falls much more easily into the middle range of hard-soft styles like its sister art, Hapkido.

Taekwondo's hard-soft nature shines in the proper practice of basic stances and footwork. Stances probably constitute the single most important element of good technique. How you move from one position to another, from block to punch, from front to back or to the side, all depends on your stability and balance. If your stances are strong, power will virtually rise from the earth and course through your body until it explodes as a block, kick, or hand strike. If your stance is unstable, you provide no foundation for your hands or your legs. Your movements will look weak, your balance will falter, and your techniques, whether they be blocks or strikes, will lack power. Strong stances ground your legs and hips; the solidity of the earth itself will bolster all your movements.

In blocks and in hand strikes of all kinds, power comes from the motion of your legs channeled through your hips and torso into your shoulders and arms. Correct usage of the legs allows your upper body to remain relaxed, loose, and fast. The power of your kicks will depend not only on strong and flexible legs but also on your control of your balance and your command of the ground beneath you.

In actual sparring situations, practitioners of styles more traditional than modern Taekwondo often employ a greater variety of stances than we do. Karate and kung fu fighters often use the back stance and a variety of others that we find rather eclectic—T-stances, cat stances, crane stances, and so forth. Taekwondo sparring relies heavily on its standard fighting stance, although many fighters also use a back stance, even if they've never trained to use it. The fighting stance is the most versatile position and the position most amenable to Taekwondo technique, but sparring situations will sometimes call for a shift of body weight to the back foot, particularly when one falls into defensive mode (see Chapter 9, "Sparring," for details on sparring footwork and offensive/defensive/trapping modes). Other traditional Taekwondo stances are not left out of an agile fighter's repertoire, however. Stances like the front stance, back stance, and cat stance all allow the recapture of balance and a means of attacking and defending. Able footwork distinguishes a competent Taekwondoist in the tournament ring every bit as much as swift kicks, and perfecting the basic stances will help guarantee steady balance and responsiveness in any situation.

Whatever your own sparring and self-defense preferences may be, weak stances will make poomse look sloppy and hesitant. Also, exacting attention to stance during basic drills aids your powers of focus, concentration, and body awareness, and will substantially increase the strength of your legs.

Joon Bi

Joon bi is the basic "ready" position from which all drills begin. Assume the joon bi position after bowing to the instructor or your partner before proceeding to the next drill or technique.

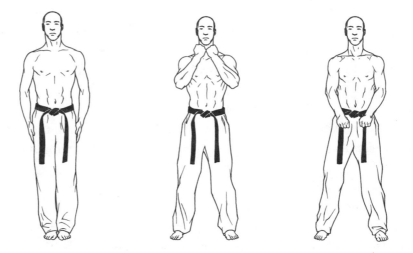

Slide the left foot to the left by a distance equal to one shoulder width. At the same time, raise your fists to a point just below your chin, outer edges touching, palms facing in. Once you have moved your left foot to its position, thrust the fists down in front of your belt and hold them there, about one fist's width apart from each other. Keep your eyes straight ahead and your posture straight, firm, and relaxed.

Feel free to modify this position according to the practices of your own dojang.

Horse Stance *(Joo choom-seogi)*

Sometimes called "horseback stance" or "horseback riding stance," horse stance is the most basic training position in Taekwondo. It does not often appear in sparring situations because it distributes the weight too evenly onto both feet, does not offer much mobility, and presents a full frontal target with an exposed groin to an opponent. However, powerful hand strikes based on the horse stance are possible, and strikes to the side, with the side of the body facing the opponent, are potent. It is an excellent position from which to practice blocks and punches, because it helps a student gain the ability to generate power without relying on throwing the body weight around, and it is also an excellent way to build the leg strength required for solid front and back stances.

Begin with the feet spread apart about two shoulder widths. The feet are pointing straight ahead, parallel to each other, and the knees are bent. Be careful not to lean forward or back; instead, lower the body weight straight down as if you are about to sit on a stool.

In this position you can practice the traditional punch as well as virtually any of the blocks. Practice all techniques both straight ahead and to the sides.

Blocks and strikes thrown to the sides are useful in combination with sideways steps. Turn your body so that one side faces your opponent or the direction in which you intend to move. Turn your head to face your direction of travel. To step, bring the rear foot forward in a straight line. Do not swing

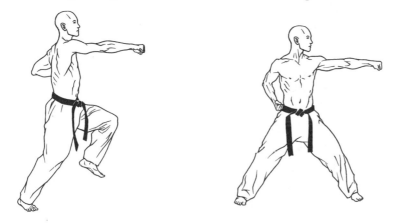

the foot around in a circle or crescent. Slide it so that it just passes the front foot and continue to slide it straight ahead until it has reached its stopping point. Keep your head at approximately the same height throughout the step.

While you step, hold your torso back rather than allow it to swing with your leg. At the last possible moment, quickly turn your hips and shoulders into the step. This delayed motion of the hips and body will give your blocks and punches real power. As the hips whip into position and your lead foot settles on the ground, power will flow into your shoulders and arms with the movement of your body weight.

The sudden motion of the hips, and the power that you can develop with that motion, illustrates an important point in the overall mechanics of Taekwondo technique. Many of the techniques, both offensive and defensive, are powerful because of their whiplike speed. A whip slashes through the air because the long coil amplifies every movement of the handle, until the end of the whip is moving many times faster than the hand that gave it motion. Think of your hands and feet the same way, and use your stance as the handle of the whip.

Walking Stance (Ap-seogi)

The precursor of the fighting stance, walking stance allows you to move back and forth while maintaining a high center of gravity and thus greater mobility.

Proper walking stance is a relaxed position that does not call for any great strength from the legs. Place one foot forward at the distance equal to one natural pace. The toes of the lead foot point straight ahead and the toes of the rear foot angle slightly out to the side. The hips and shoulders face the front squarely.

To move in walking stance, simply take one relaxed step forward. To move forward with a block or punch, however, requires an important modification. As the rear foot comes forward and becomes the lead foot, hold the hip back slightly, as with the horse stance. As you complete the step and execute your technique, thrust the hip into position. This will increase power to your forward hand technique as your shoulder and arm follow the motion of the hip. For reverse hand techniques, allow the rear leg and hip to come forward while keeping the knee of the lead leg bent. As you step forward and the lead leg

Walk as you normally walk.

becomes the rear leg, straighten that leg suddenly, pushing the hip forward. This will increase the power to your reverse hand techniques, especially your punches.

To turn around in walking stance, sweep your rear foot across your line of travel behind you and pivot around. The rear foot is now your front foot. Execute the block, attack, or combination you've been practicing as you turn.

The most important thing to keep in mind is that you must use your legs to turn your hips into your techniques.

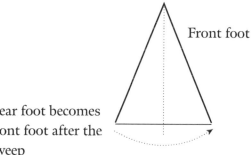

Front foot

Rear foot becomes front foot after the sweep

Front Stance *(Apkeubi)*

Long and low to the ground, the front stance enables you to execute blocks and strikes with great power by taking full advantage of body weight. It frequently appears in the poomse and is an excellent practice position.

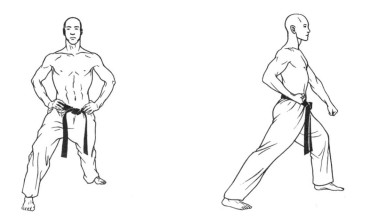

Take a long step forward so that the distance between your feet—the length of the stance—is approximately two shoulder widths. The width of the stance—the distance separating your feet if they were side by side—should be anywhere from one to one-and-a-half shoulder widths. When you move into front stance from joon bi position, the foot stepping forward or backward does not move into line with the stationary foot. Rather, it maintains its lateral distance, so that the stance, when completed, has both length and width. One way to achieve this position is to turn diagonally sideways in horse stance, straightening the rear leg and keeping the front leg bent.

In front stance, the front knee is sharply bent; the back leg is straight. You should just be able to see the toes of your front foot. The shin should be vertical or sloped slightly back. The front leg will support approximately 70 percent of your weight. Your hips and shoulders squarely face the front, not the side—a big temptation for beginners. The toes of your front foot point straight ahead. The toes of your rear foot are angled outward forty-five degrees.

Be careful to keep your body upright. Many students tend to lean forward in front stance. This skews their balance and makes it easy to fall or stumble forward. Depend on the deep bend of your front knee to make your front stance low. Keep your head and shoulders upright and look straight ahead.

When you move forward in front stance, keep your head at about the same level throughout. Some schools require the head to stay at precisely the same height when stepping; others don't. Either way, do not straighten up completely. Try to glide forward or back without stomping. Keep the moving foot close to the ground or even slide it.

Especially with reverse techniques, the front stance enables you to strike with great power because of its length. As with the walking stance, hold your lead hip back when moving forward until you make your move with your hand. Then thrust the hip into position so that its rotation will help speed your hand on its way. Likewise, with reverse techniques you should hold the rear hip back until the last moment. You have an advantage with reverse techniques, because you can keep the knee of your rear leg bent, your hips angled back, until the moment you strike. Then you can straighten the back leg so that it anchors into position and, meanwhile, propels your hand to its target.

Turn around the same way as in walking stance. First turn your head around in the direction of your rear leg. Then sweep your rear leg *across* behind you; do not bring it in to the front foot. Let it travel along a line perpendicular to your direction of travel. Now imagine a line extending through your front foot, from the heel to the toes, and continuing behind you. Sweep the rear foot until it has traveled to a point opposite the line extending through the front foot *equally distant* from its starting point. When it reaches that point, plant the toe and pivot around. Make sure your feet have resumed the correct angles (front toes straight ahead, rear toes out at forty-five degrees) and that your weight has shifted to what is now your front leg. Chamber your block, punch, or combination as you begin the turn, and finish the motion with power as you complete the turn, using the rotation from the turn to enhance your power.

You will also increase the power of your techniques as well as the overall grace of your movements by making sure you have relaxed shoulders. Concentrate on keeping the shoulders loose. Allow them to flow into and out of stances and to follow the motions of your hips. If your lead hip is cocked back in anticipation of a block with the lead hand or a front punch, allow the shoulder to hang back too; then it will move into position when you thrust the hip. Prevent your movements from being jerky and rigid. Concentrate on flowing smoothly from one position and technique into another.

Back Stance *(Dwitkeubi)*

The back stance appears a number of times in the poomse and often proves useful in sparring situations, especially when a quick flick of the front leg is required. It is a classically soft position, and with its low height from the ground, arched legs, and supple distribution of weight, it reveals all the grace of traditional Taekwondo.

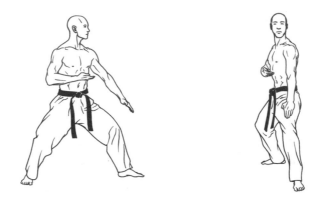

Like the front stance, the feet in back stance are separated by a distance of two shoulder widths. The front foot is placed directly in front of you, not out to the side, as in front stance. The toes point forward. The toes of the back foot point out ninety degrees. The heels of your two feet are directly in line with each other, so that if they were brought together they would form an L. Both your knees are bent, and 60 to 70 percent of your weight is supported by your back leg. Take care to ensure that the knee of your rear leg is turned out. Try not to let it turn inward or point to the front, which will make the stance look cramped and awkward. The front leg remains light, as if ready to lift in a defensive front kick or side kick. Your body is upright, and the front of your body faces the side, not the front. Be careful to keep your butt in.

This is the preferred stance for practicing knife-hand blocks. It can also be used to practice any of the others, of course, and is a powerful defensive sparring position, as it presents a minimal target to an opponent. It is also possible to launch stabbing jabs and traditional punches from back stance using the front hand.

To move forward, draw the rear foot forward in a straight line, not a crescent or curve, and slide it out ahead of you, changing the angles of your feet as you go. Try not to let your weight rise and fall too much, or you will end up stomping as you move into your new position. In back stance, your feet are especially gentle. Use the same motion to move backward, but begin by sliding the front foot back rather than by drawing the rear foot forward.

To turn around, first turn your head. Draw the rear foot slightly in to the front foot and change the angles of your feet so that the rear foot, which had pointed to the side, now points to the front, and the front foot, which had pointed straight ahead, now points to the side. Then smoothly slide the rear foot forward and execute the hand technique.

Cat Stance *(Beom-seogi)*

A defensive stance reminiscent of softer styles like kung fu, the cat stance is essentially a back stance modified so that the feet are close together. In cat stance, you can easily defend yourself from most strikes, although your mobility will be reduced. It is especially useful for quick front-leg kicks and for blocks using your arms and knees in combination. Place one foot just a few inches in front of the other. Rest the front foot on its ball and bend the knee slightly. Turn the rear foot so that the toes point somewhat less than ninety degrees out to the side and bend the knee of the rear leg. Adjust your body weight so that the back leg bears about 70 percent of your mass. Again, keep your body upright. The front of your body faces out to the side by about forty-five degrees.

Twist Stance *(Apkoa-seogi)*

The twist stance is best thought of as a transitional move and, like the cat stance, is associated with classical martial arts. It appears most conspicuously as the final move in Taegeuk O Jang (the fifth poomse) in combination with the backfist. It is useful as the most stable landing from a hopping attack; picture yourself jumping forward off one foot and landing on the other, attacking with the lead hand as you land. The toes of your lead foot angle slightly to the side. The rear leg crosses behind the lead leg and the ball of the rear foot rests lightly on the ground. Both knees are bent to maintain a light, springy position.

Fighting Stance *(Gyoroogi-seogi)*

The stance that distinguishes modern, Olympic-style Taekwondo from its predecessors and from other more traditional styles of martial arts, the fighting stance provides the greatest possible freedom of movement to the feet, whether they be used to kick; to step in, out, or to the side; to spin; or to jump. The fighting stance keeps a fighter's center of gravity high and mobile; lower stances, though quite stable, do not serve our needs as well. A good, light fighting stance guarantees quick footwork, the key to Taekwondo sparring.

Place one foot about one pace in front of the other and bend your knees

slightly. Shift more weight to the front foot than to the rear foot—anywhere from 55 to 60 percent of your weight should be on your front leg. Your body primarily faces the side with just a slight turn to the front, an angle that presents a small frontal target area to an opponent and provides the greatest power to kicks thrown with the rear leg. The lateral distance between your feet—the distance that would separate them if they were side by side—is small. Angle your front foot somewhat inward; the rear foot faces more toward the front than the front foot does. Your stance may be slightly pigeon-toed. Stay light on your feet, bouncing slightly on your toes and keeping your heels off the ground. Keep your fists raised in guard position, the lead hand out in front of you, the rear hand closer to your chin, in the manner of a boxer.

Moving around in fighting stance is a simple matter of stepping forward or backward. However, the art of movement while sparring is highly developed, and for more information on it, refer to Chapter 5, "Steps and Footwork," and to Chapter 9, "Sparring."

Steps and Footwork

Common Principles • Switching Stance • Moving Forward • Jeonjin Step • Ilbo-Jeonjin Step • Reverse Step •
Moving Backward • Hoojin-Step • Ilbo-Hoojin Step • Reverse Ilbo-Hoojin Step • Fake Step •
Moving Sideways • Basic Side Step • Yeop Step • Moving Diagonally • Diagonal Steps • Suggested Drills

Footwork occupies a supreme position in the list of necessary sparring and defensive skills. Footwork determines your distance from your opponent. Footwork determines whether you will be able to attack or defend yourself, and it determines what techniques you will be able to use, whether they be kicks or hand strikes. Good footwork will help you keep your balance in the most furious exchange, and it will ensure that every kick packs as much power as possible. Couple excellent footwork with strong stances and technique, and you will be able to maneuver in any sparring situation, ready to kick or punch at every opportunity.

Remember that once you have joined in conflict, the first battle is one for territory. You must learn to take command of the space between yourself and your opponent. Space is not a static thing; it changes constantly with your change of position and even with your change of attitude. If you are contemplating rushing in, then the space before you may seem small; if you wish to attack from a stationary position, then the space between you and your opponent may seem too great. This holds equally true in self-defense, in tournament sparring, or in the large-scale conflict of wars. In *The Art of War,* the ancient Chinese general Sunzi writes that any commander who wishes to prevail in battle must first understand and control the terrain in which he is to meet his enemy. Failing to do this, Sunzi explains, the general will be unable to exploit his force's greatest strengths, and he will expose himself to his enemy's most powerful attack under the circumstances. In a text written with large-scale conflict in mind, this lesson remains invaluable to the individual hoping to master Taekwondo.

Strong footwork is so essential to sparring skills that one cannot even begin to learn sparring techniques and strategies without establishing a solid foundation in the basic steps. Ten-time U.S. team member Master Dae Sung Lee includes steps in his list of the four vital areas of sparring, along with technique, agility, and timing. Footwork is equally important in self-defense. If you cannot move quickly, you will be caught stock-still, flat-footed, or off balance, and your opponent will almost certainly strike you or take you down. On the other hand, if you control the distance separating you, you will have a commanding advantage. Agility allows you to avoid harm and makes you a constant threat.

The stepping techniques of Taekwondo are very simple, but there is no shortcut to mastering them. Do your best to follow the basic guidelines, and practice constantly.

Common Principles

To maintain attack readiness, you need to maintain an agile fighting stance. Therefore, you must undertake motion in any direction with the aim of regaining fighting stance as quickly as possible. Keep this goal in mind while you apply the following principles to all your footwork:

- Relax the upper body and shoulders.
- Stay light on your feet. Use your toes, not your heels.
- When advancing, retreating, or evading, the hips and shoulders turn explosively with the step. This allows you to kick or punch easily as you move, and it also helps you to develop misleading feints (more on feints under "Trap Tactics" in Chapter 9, "Sparring").
- The stepping foot always moves in straight lines, sliding forward, backward, diagonally, or sideways, but never arcing or swinging.
- Come to a complete stop at the end of a step or series of steps, without staggering. If you stagger or dance at the end of your steps, your balance may be thrown and, in any case, you will not regain fighting position quickly enough to kick or punch at the proper moment. This will affect your timing. Learning to start explosively and stop on a dime are among the most difficult lessons, and require much leg strength.
- Keep your hands raised, especially the rear hand. The hands may drop to the down block position as necessary.
- It is probably impossible to devote too much time to the practice of

footwork. Begin every sparring session with footwork practice and integrate it into other workouts at every opportunity. Use it as a warm-up and as part of regular drills.

Footwork has a profound impact on your strategy from moment to moment, because it alone determines your distance from your opponent and also whether you face your opponent in open or closed stance (defined below). Open versus closed stance will dictate what options are available to you.

Open stance is that position in which two combatants stand with their opposite foot forward—that is, one stands with the left foot forward while the other stands with the right foot forward. This results in both practitioners' front or abdominal sides facing the same direction.

Closed stance is defined as that position in which two combatants stand with the same foot forward—for instance, both with the left foot forward. In this case, their front or abdominal sides will face opposite directions.

For more information on open versus closed stances, see Chapter 9, "Sparring."

Switching Stance

Before you learn to move in any direction, you must first learn to adapt your fighting stance to circumstances. That is, you must be able to switch smoothly from a left lead to a right lead and vice versa. This will enable you to keep yourself in either an open or a closed stance, as needed.

To switch stance, quickly slide the feet so that they take up each other's position. Try not to jump. Jumping will only slow the switch of stance. Instead, learn to slide the feet along the ground or as close to the ground as possible. Also avoid moving your feet along curved lines or crescents. They should scissor back and forth. Make sure the hips and shoulders turn with the change of stance.

You can also perform a reverse switch. In the regular switch, the rear foot passes by the toe side of the front foot as it slides forward and the front foot slides back. Likewise, the rear shoulder moves directly forward. In the reverse switch, the rear foot passes by the *heel* side of the front foot as the front foot moves back, and the rear shoulder moves along the plane of the back rather than the plane of the chest. This may sound awkward, but with practice the reverse switch can be a cunning feint.

The ideal switch is practically instantaneous. Practice making your single switch as fast as it can be. Also practice switching twice in a row. This can confuse your opponent and reveal opportunities to attack.

Moving Forward

Forward motion forms the basis of virtually any attack. Once you have begun your assault, you must continue to press your advantage, using the accumulation of momentum and speed to energize your attacks and overwhelm your opponent. At the same time, of course, you must ensure that you maintain your readiness to kick or punch with every step forward. There are three basic forward steps.

Jeonjin Step

Jeonjin step is the most basic of the forward motions. It is useful in covering forward distances ranging from short to relatively long. Because the rear foot does not pass the front foot, the lead foot remains the same in jeonjin step, leaving your position relative to your opponent—open or closed—unchanged.

Moving forward in the basic jeonjin step involves only two motions:

1. Slide the rear foot up to meet the front foot.
2. Slide the front foot forward. Stop *completely*, in fighting stance, with your weight properly distributed toward the front leg.

Slide quickly. With practice, the movements of the rear and front foot will become almost simultaneous. Most important, avoid jumping up as you move forward. Jumping will increase the time required to complete the step, and it must be remembered that it is during those transitional moments when your feet are engaged in a step that you are most vulnerable, able neither to kick nor to punch very easily.

There are two important variations to the jeonjin step. The first involves the same motions as the two listed above, but the rear foot passes the toe side of the front foot before the front foot moves forward. This skipping motion can cover a large distance quickly. Again, keep the feet as close to the ground as possible. The step is a slide, not a jump.

The other variation of the jeonjin step, and one that often requires a good deal of practice, is a small shuffle forward. To step forward this way, move both feet simultaneously, using them to propel yourself forward. The distance between your feet will remain the same throughout the step, unlike the basic jeonjin step or the skipping step, where the feet come together. This shuffle is highly useful in delivering a quick attack such as a jab or a cut kick. Each of these versions of the jeonjin step has its unique applications, depending on the circumstances.

Apart from its usefulness as a means of closing distance, the jeonjin step offers the most effective means of simultaneously delivering a front kick, turning kick, or side kick with the front leg. To kick with the front leg while advancing toward your opponent, slide the rear foot forward while chambering the

You can feint using the jeonjin step simply by lifting the front foot slightly and stomping. This can distract the opponent long enough for you to strike with a rear-leg turning kick.

kick. Unleash the kick, then step down in front. This technique can be performed with any of the three jeonjin steps described—the basic slide forward, the skip forward, or the shuffle forward. Of those, the most challenging is the kick off the shuffle step. However, the front-leg kick off the shuffle step is also one of the quickest and most subtle means of attacking or defending. Remember that the shuffle step requires you to lift the lead foot before pushing with the rear; that means that to throw a front-leg kick with this step, you must chamber the front leg while moving the rear foot, or you will lose the advantage of surprise.

Beware that you will face two possible counterattack scenarios when stepping forward with the jeonjin step. Using the standard jeonjin step, you may be vulnerable to your opponent's turning kick as your rear leg slides forward. With the shuffle step, you may tempt your opponent to throw a front-leg axe kick. Remember this as you practice, and also practice using these techniques as counterattacks to your partner's advances.

Front-leg kicks using the jeonjin step are a potent means of initiating a combination of attacks—for more information on the applications of sliding-in front-leg kicks, see Chapter 9, "Sparring." Be sure to practice the step itself as well as the step in combination with front kicks, turning kicks, side kicks, and cut kicks.

Ilbo-Jeonjin Step

Ilbo-jeonjin step refers to forward motion with a change of lead. More simply put, it is a step forward, rather than a slide. While its motion would seem as natural as walking, it requires somewhat more attention than the jeonjin step to perform properly. It is useful as an aggressive forward motion when you wish to change your lead or when you wish to build momentum prior to throwing a rear-leg kick. You can also use the step to develop feints in order to mislead or trap your opponent.

While the ilbo-jeonjin step requires only one basic motion—a step forward with the rear foot—care must be taken to ensure that you maintain an agile fighting stance. Keep the following points in mind when advancing with ilbo-jeonjin step:

1. Burst forward with the rear foot. Make sure the rear foot moves forward in a straight line, passing just next to the front foot.

To feint with the ilbo-jeonjin step, lift the rear knee and partially chamber the leg as it comes forward, rather than keeping the foot low to the ground. Be sure to draw the rear knee straight forward, not out to the side. With this motion, you can fool your opponent into believing you are attacking.

2. Turn the rear hip and shoulder into the forward motion, so that the change of fighting stance is complete when the rear foot plants in front.
3. Come to a complete stop in fighting stance, with your body weight distributed toward the front leg.

The only time you won't want to come to a complete stop is, of course, when the step is but one of a series of steps or kicks. In such cases, it is still important to keep the weight forward, not back.

Reverse Step *(Bandae-jeonjin)*

Like the ilbo-jeonjin step, the reverse step (or reverse ilbo-jeonjin step, technically) combines forward motion with a change of lead. The reverse step can be perceived as an especially threatening motion, however, because it is easily mistaken for the prelude to a back kick, narabam, or spinning hook kick. Of the three basic forward steps, the reverse step requires the most practice to master.

The basic movements of the reverse step are:

1. Pivot on the ball of the lead foot so that your heel, rather than your toes, is pointing straight ahead.
2. Draw the rear foot up to and past the front foot in a straight line. Your back will momentarily face forward while this transition is completed.
3. Step forward with the rear foot and reassume fighting stance.

The most important element of the reverse step, and typically the most difficult, is the linear motion of the rear foot as it draws forward and assumes the lead. In principle, this motion doesn't differ from that of the ilbo-jeonjin step, but the spin of your body as you step forward will make the rear foot tend to sweep to the outside in a broad crescent. This will both slow your step and throw your balance off center, usually pitching your body to the side as you step forward. A quick opponent will be able to strike as you regain your balance. Concentrate on deliberately sliding the rear foot in a straight line.

Mastery of the reverse step will prove invaluable in developing strong spinning techniques such as the spinning hook kick, the back kick, the reverse step turning kick, and the narabam. It also provides a powerful delivery for hand techniques such as backfists and outside knife-hand strikes. Combined with ilbo-jeonjin step, the reverse step can dazzle an opponent while you advance, prepared to throw a battery of powerful attacks.

Moving Backward

Just as it is important to advance skillfully, and in such a way that the option of attack remains open, so it is important to retreat skillfully. It is all too easy to back up before an aggressive opponent, giving up ground and trying to avoid being hit. This almost always results in actually taking a blow. However, the practitioner with the ability to maintain a fighting stance even in retreat is far more likely to offer potent counterattacks and convert a retreat into an assault. Good footwork will allow you to pose as much of a threat in retreat as in headlong attack.

Many students tend to shift their weight to the back foot when they step or slide backward. Take extra care to retain the distribution of your body weight on the front leg as you retreat, or you will have difficulty regaining your fighting stance.

As with the forward steps, there are three primary means of retreat.

Hoojin Step

The opposite of the jeonjin step, the hoojin step is the basic retreat. It involves a slide and leaves the lead foot unchanged.

1. Slide the front foot back to meet the rear foot.
2. Slide the rear foot back to reassume fighting stance, coming to a *complete* stop with the body weight shifted to the front leg.

It is imperative to slide both feet as quickly as possible, and to bring the rear foot fully back into fighting stance. A common error is to allow the rear foot to lag in its backward slide. This usually has two unfortunate results: First, the feet get caught close together, which reduces your mobility. That often means that you present a frontal target, vulnerable to powerful techniques like side kicks and push kicks or even simple body punches. The second unfortunate result is that the legs tend to straighten and the body tends to rise. Should you stand up in midstep like this, you will be stuck like a pole in the ground, unable to move or kick.

You can apply the same variations found in the jeonjin step to the hoojin step. The first is the skip step; slide the lead foot behind the rear foot, then slide the rear foot back. This will cover greater distance than the regular hoojin step.

The other variation, the shuffle, requires that you push back with both feet simultaneously, resulting in a subtle slide backward. Perform a rapid series of small slides backward. This will preserve your fighting stance and prepare you to launch counterattacks at the first opportunity.

Ilbo-Hoojin Step

A plain step backward, just as the ilbo-jeonjin step is a plain step forward, the ilbo-hoojin step plays a key role in defensive footwork. A single retreating step may be all you need to evade a simple attack, such as the turning kick, and it puts you in a solid position from which to launch a counterstrike.

Keep in mind the importance of sticking with your fighting stance. When you step backward, be sure to rotate the hips and shoulders back. Take extra care to keep the weight forward, rather than letting it settle onto the rear leg as you complete the step. Think of using the leg stepping back as a stop to your backward motion, rather than as something to stand on. This will help you to keep your weight forward.

Reverse Ilbo-Hoojin Step *(Bandae Ilbo-Hoojin)*

The reverse ilbo-hoojin step is a tricky move that provides both a quick escape and a cunning means of setting up to retaliate. It is the perfect opposite of the reverse step. Instead of taking a step backward by drawing the forward shoulder and foot to the rear, draw the lead shoulder back by moving in the direction your abdomen faces. The lead foot will pass by the toes of the rear foot, rather than the heel of the rear foot.

The reverse ilbo-hoojin step will allow you to retreat with a change of stance, like the ilbo-hoojin step, and offers the possibility of using a retreating narabam, a back kick, or the spinning hook kick.

Fake Step

The fake step does not really fit into either category of forward or backward motion. It actually resembles more of a stance switch than anything else, but one that allows for the possibility of moving forward, attacking, or drawing a counterattack.

To initiate the fake step:

1. Step forward as you would the ilbo-jeonjin step, but exaggerate the motion of your rear shoulder as it moves forward.

2. Meanwhile, do not take a full step forward with your rear foot. Instead, place it down maybe a half step forward, and slide the rear foot back.

You will notice that with the yeop step (see pages 79–80), you might advance slightly, but the movement of the rear shoulder forward will often appear to an opponent to be the beginning of a kick. That can lure the opponent into throwing a counterkick, for which you will be ready and waiting in your fighting stance.

Moving Sideways

Sideways motion may be even more important to evasive footwork than backward motion. If all you can do is retreat, you will eventually be caught, no matter how good your footwork or your fighting position. There will come a time when you make a mistake, and an aggressive opponent will be able to take advantage of your retreat. Remember that with forward motion, all an attacker needs to do is press the advantage by continuing to advance. Keeping up a retreat will only help the attacker's aims. You must learn to use the space available to the sides as well, and to sidestep attacks rather than fall away from them. An agile sidestep will create openings that you would not otherwise be able to see, and it will prevent you from being driven back uncontrollably.

Basic Side Step

You can move sideways in two directions from fighting stance, either toward your open (abdominal) side or toward your closed (back) side. The basic idea to keep in mind is to prevent your feet from crossing each other. If they do, they may tie up each other and you will lose mobility.

To step to the open side, first slide the back foot perpendicularly in the open-side direction, then slide the front foot to reassume fighting stance. This will place you one pace off your previous line.

To step to the closed side, first slide the front foot perpendicularly toward the closed side, followed by the rear foot.

Try integrating these simple steps with the other basic footwork.

Yeop Step

"Yeop" means "side," and we use this term to distinguish a more sophisticated piece of footwork from the sidestep described above. The yeop step not only moves you slightly to the side but changes your angle with respect to your opponent. The change of angle makes the yeop step an especially useful means of evasion and preparation for counterattack.

There are two basic forms of the yeop step. Like the other steps, the first form of the yeop step consists of two basic motions:

1. Draw the rear foot to match the front foot.
2. Slide the front foot out to the reverse side and turn ninety degrees. Your front foot should now be your rear foot, and you will now face a new direction, perpendicular to your opponent.

The second version of the yeop step is simpler. Just pivot on your lead foot toward your closed (back) side, sweeping the rear foot ninety degrees.

Use the yeop step to avoid attacks to your open (abdominal) side. Practice this step extensively, so that the movements of your feet become nearly simultaneous. Because the yeop step aligns you perpendicularly to your previous orientation, it often reveals an unexpected vulnerability in your opponent. From your new position, it is comparatively easy to strike back. See Chapter 9, "Sparring," for further discussion of yeop step applications.

Moving Diagonally

To this point, we have described footwork that you can use to move in the four cardinal directions: straight ahead, straight back, to the right, and to the left. But by modifying the previous steps, you can increase your control of the territory by commanding the directions in between as well.

Diagonal motion combines the principles of all the above steps. Moving diagonally, you can simultaneously move in or out of your attacker's range, as you do with forward or backward motion, and you can remove yourself from your attacker's sights altogether. By moving into and out of the "crosshairs," you can seize control of the skirmish and dictate who attacks when. Note that if you move only straight ahead or straight back, you are, in essence, always in the line of fire, even if you are too far away to be hit easily. But distance does not always guarantee safety: some fighters have surprisingly long reach, while others can catapult their kicks from a seemingly unbridgeable distance. Likewise, a side step can take you out of the path of an incoming back kick but may leave you without an inviting counterattack.

Diagonal steps can be broken down into two categories: open side and closed side. Open-side diagonal steps are those where you move toward the direction your abdomen faces; closed-side diagonal steps are those where you move toward the direction your back faces. Practice moving at forty-five degrees but also learn to vary the angle so that you can adapt to circumstances.

Open-Side Diagonal Steps

A basic and cunning defensive maneuver, the *diagonal hoojin step* will neatly take you out of range and out of the path of attacks to your closed, kidney side, and set you up nicely for a counter turning kick (see "Turning Kick" section in Chapter 9, "Sparring"). Simply slide your rear foot back and forty-five degrees to the side (if your right foot is back, slide it back and to the right; if the left foot is back, slide it back and to the left). The front foot will follow directly, as with a shuffle step, but will not step sideways. This motion will draw you back and pivot you forty-five degrees off of your attacker's line. Try to counterattack immediately with a rear-leg turning kick.

The *diagonal ilbo-jeonjin step* will take you out of the path of attacks to your closed side and simultaneously put you *inside* your attacker's range, making it almost impossible for you to be struck by a follow-up kick. This involves an ilbo-jeonjin step, but instead of stepping straight ahead, step ahead and forty-five degrees or less out to the side. The best time to use this step is simultaneously with your opponent's attack. Often, you will have the pleasure of watching his or her foot shoot right past you as you step in and to the side. As you close the distance and evade the attack, you can punch, adjust your distance, and counterattack. The diagonal ilbo-jeonjin step is an excellent means of dodging incoming back kicks, spinning hook kicks, and narabams to the closed side.

Closed-Side Diagonal Steps

Just as the open-side diagonal steps offer effective means of avoiding attacks to the closed side, the closed-side diagonal steps offer effective means of avoiding attacks to the open side. The first to consider is the *diagonal ilbo-hoojin step.* As your opponent attacks, step back as you would with ilbo-hoojin, but instead of moving your forward foot straight behind yourself, step back and forty-five degrees out to the side. You will have evaded your opponent's attack while lining yourself up to counterattack with a rear-leg turning kick or a back kick.

Likewise, you can move forward diagonally as well, and this move bears the same simplicity as the jeonjin step. The closed-side forward diagonal step is the *diagonal jeonjin step*. As with the diagonal hoojin step, this is based on the shuffle variety of the jeonjin step, where the lead foot moves first, followed by the rear foot. First, push your front foot forward and forty-five degrees toward the closed side. Quickly draw the rear foot to follow it. This is a neat way to avoid a turning kick coming in toward your abdominal side, and, like the diagonal ilbo-jeonjin step, positions you to punch immediately, then adjust your distance and kick.

Suggested Drills

In keeping with the idea that the constant practice of footwork is critical to maneuverability and freedom to apply appropriate techniques, do your best to combine the previous steps in any number of ways, learning to move in any direction and to change your heading with agility. We list here several combinations to get you started.

Jeonjin/ilbo-jeonjin
Ilbo-jeonjin/reverse step
Ilbo-jeonjin/side step
Jeonjin/yeop step
Ilbo-jeonjin/reverse step/switch stance
Ilbo-jeonjin/ilbo-jeonjin/ilbo-hoojin

Hoojin/ilbo-hoojin
Ilbo-hoojin/reverse ilbo-hoojin
Ilbo-hoojin/switch stance
Ilbo-hoojin/hoojin/ilbo-jeonjin

This is only a tiny sample of all the possible combinations of steps, and uses only the most basic forward and reverse steps. Use your imagination and string all kinds of steps together. Include stance switches. You don't need to master every combination; instead, try to train yourself to move instinctively. Practice steps in every workout. You can achieve instinctive movement by practicing every different kind of step in small combinations with one or two others. Move backward, forward, to the sides, and diagonally. Combine changes of direction—remember that your footwork can be the deciding factor in a match, whether you are fighting for a medal or fighting for your life. You need to be able to move backward, then instantly forward, or forward, to the side, and forward again. The more you practice, the stronger your legs will become, the greater your speed, and the surer your footing.

Also practice your steps with a partner who mirrors your movements. For example, one partner steps forward with ilbo-jeonjin; the other retreats with ilbo-hoojin. Build up the number and variety of steps, moving back and forth.

Once you have begun to move comfortably, combine the steps with kicks. Remember that every time you step forward, you could throw a kick with that motion. Every time you switch, you can kick; every time you step backward, you can kick. Every reverse step, forward or backward, can be a back kick, a spinning hook kick, or narabam.

For further discussion of footwork and the concept of agility, see Chapter 9, "Sparring."

CHAPTER 6

Blocks

Down Block • Inside Block • Outside Block • High Block • Outside Forearm Block •
Double-Fist Block • Reinforced Outside Block • X Block • Double Knife-Hand Block •
Single Knife-Hand Block • Crossing Palm Block • Pressing-Down Block

Self-defense begins with the concept of self-protection. Taekwondo defense stresses simple motions, with an emphasis on blocks and evasion. Only after such concepts are taught does the time arrive for the development of attacks and counterattacks, which serve largely as measures to ensure that an attacker won't have another chance to cause harm. Some styles use highly sophisticated and complex defensive maneuvers designed to trap an opponent and provide an opportunity either to strike from there or control him. In many of these systems, a block is quickly followed by an attempt to control the attacker's limb and either immobilize it (and therefore the attacker himself) or keep it out of the way while delivering a counterattack. As practitioners of a striking style, our philosophy is different. In general, Taekwondoists would prefer either to avoid an attack altogether through quick, evasive steps followed by a counterattack, or to parry attacks with simple movements of the arms and retaliate with swift, well-placed kicks and hand strikes, making the most of our expertise in delivering powerful blows.

Basic differences in defensive tactics reveal a great deal about various martial arts and their overall philosophies. For example, most styles use a basic down block, but that doesn't mean that they all favor a straightforward punch for self-defense—many, in fact, would likely make little use of that most simple Taekwondo technique.

Viewed purely in light of their approaches to self-defense, most martial arts fit somewhere along a range from almost purely defensive in technical development to almost purely offensive. Taekwondo's sister art, Hapkido, provides an example of an art that lies closer to the defensive extreme. It employs relatively few strikes compared with Taekwondo. Instead, the Hapkido artist waits for the attack and then controls the attacker's body and energy through redirection, finishing with a jointlock, a throw, or a choke.

Taekwondo probably lies near the opposite end of the self-defense spectrum. A great deal of the Taekwondo artist's training focuses on learning to strike with terrific speed and power. The Taekwondoist's defensive goal is to create an impenetrable sphere of protection around his or her body, off of which blows may only glance while footwork provides the opportunity for a counterstrike. Because of our emphasis on speed and power, many see Taekwondo as a highly aggressive style, extroverted rather than introverted, and not particularly defensive.

It is useless to struggle with arguments about the superiority of one martial art over another in terms of their self-defensive capabilities. In the case of the examples of Taekwondo and Hapkido, both employ techniques that, if performed well, will help the individual to prevail in violent confrontations. And, perhaps more important, both styles, as different from each other as they are, have much to offer one another. Once he or she has gained some mastery of a particular style, the student with a serious interest in martial arts should always seek to learn from other sources. No style is all-inclusive. In the much-fantasized-about contest between martial artists of different styles, it is usually the better-trained, more intelligent adversary who carries the day, not the one who practices the "superior" martial art.

Defensive training in Taekwondo has undoubtedly been influenced to some extent by the growth of competitive sparring. Tournament rules strictly forbid grabbing or the use of striking techniques other than kicks and punches. These rules have encouraged Taekwondo masters to develop the fastest and most powerful kicks. They have also encouraged masters and tacticians to conjure up new footwork and evasive steps. Whatever one may think of tournament restrictions as they relate to martial arts, stylists everywhere admire Taekwondo's results. It is now up to all masters and teachers to ensure that their students have the skills they need to defend themselves if they cannot avoid a confrontation.

Common Principles

We use our limbs to create a sphere of protection, using them as a first line of defense to protect the head and vital areas of the body. Hands, arms, and feet all do their part to safeguard the vital center of the sphere.

Divert Blows

Blocks are not usually intended to stop a punch or kick. Instead, the goal is to divert the blow from hitting you. In movies, you often see someone catching a punch in his hand and hitting back while holding on to his opponent. Don't even think of doing that in an actual martial arts setting, or a real combative one, either. It poses too many dangers to your own hand and offers no real advantage; it only keeps one of your hands occupied without providing effective control over your opponent. Instead, you should seek to block in such a way that the blow is directed to the space beside your body.

Blocking Surface

Use your wrist or forearm to make contact with the attacking arm. The forearm will bruise less easily than the wrist because of its thicker muscle mass. On the other hand, if you restrict your blocking surface to the thickest part of the forearm, that nearest the elbow, you'll limit the effective blocking surface and make it more difficult to combine your block with jointlocks, if you are learning them (they will not be discussed in this book), and other hand techniques. Note that we do not advise the use of forearms in defense against knife attacks, because of the substantial risk to muscle tissue and blood vessels. If you must use your limbs to defend yourself from a knife attack, use the wrist area.

The Block as a Weapon

Generate as much power as you can when you block. Think of the block as a strike against your opponent's arm or leg. When you block an attack, seek to damage your opponent's arm or leg and make him think twice about attacking again.

Snap the Wrist

As with traditional punches, all blocks involve a snap of the wrist at the last moment before contact. This adds to the pushing force of the block and also distributes the force of impact over a greater surface area of your forearm and wrist, which helps to reduce bruising and injury.

Chamber and Reaction

All basic blocks include the reaction of the retracting arm, as with the traditional punch. Also, the closed hand blocks all use of the same fist as that used for punching, including the straight wrist. (See Chapter 7, "Hand Strikes," for details.)

Proper blocking requires careful attention to the chamber position. This is equally true of punching. However, punches all start from the same chambered position, whereas the blocks each have their own starting point. Proper chambering is critical to powerful blocks and is critical in good poomse. It should be noted that chamber positions is one area where individual schools differ the most widely. In the interest of simplicity, the reaction arm in all of the basic blocks will be pointed straight toward the center target, as if it had just completed a punch. Modify the following blocks as necessary according to the doctrine of your school.

Practice each of the blocks in horse stance and also moving forward and backward in walking stance, front stance, and back stance. (Some blocks won't be suitable for practice in all stances, and will be so noted.) Generally, block with the lead hand when you practice in the moving stances. This is not a hard-and-fast rule, however, as several blocks in the poomse are executed with the reverse hand, or the hand corresponding to the trailing leg. As you become more comfortable, vary the blocks you practice with. Try doing two or more blocks per step. Also try block/punch combinations and block/kick combinations.

The Five Basic Blocks

In Taekwondo, five basic techniques serve as the essential "building blocks" for all the defensive techniques that follow. These five blocks—down block, inside block, outside block, high block, and outside forearm block—are characterized by closed fists, and the reverse hand always returns to standard chamber by the belt. They are most often practiced in front stance, but they work easily with all Taekwondo stances, making them the most versatile of all the blocking techniques.

Once students have mastered these simple motions, they'll be ready to move on to some of the more advanced positions.

Down Block (*Arae-Makki*)

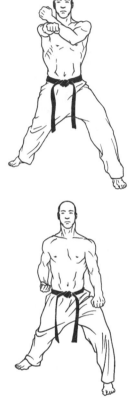

Meant to protect the lower abdomen and groin, the down block begins with the blocking hand balled into a fist and crossed in front of the face, elbow down. The wrist is turned beyond the point that the back of the hand faces outward. If you are blocking with the right arm, then the right hand will be positioned by the left side of your face, the back of the right hand facing toward the left. The left arm (the reaction arm, in this case) points diagonally inward from the shoulder and is aimed at the center target. As you block, the reaction arm and the blocking arm will move simultaneously. The blocking arm begins its sweep downward with the elbow bent until the upper arm becomes vertical. Then the forearm whips down. The palm of your fist will be facing upward for most of its journey. The block ends just in front of your leg, not to the outside. You don't need to send your block farther than this; at this point, you have done all you need to do to deflect a blow. Moving farther would be inefficient.

Just as your arm reaches the end of its motion, snap the wrist over so that the back of the fist faces straight ahead. This final motion will increase the power of your block and will also help distribute the impact of the block against the punch or kick around your wrist or forearm, whichever has made contact.

Practice the block in horse stance, alternating arms each time. Also practice the block moving forward and backward in walking stance, front stance, and back stance.

Inside Block (*An-Makki*)

This is one of three basic blocks meant to protect the upper body. Many beginners find the inside block to be one of the most challenging. Chamber the blocking hand by placing the fist upside down near your ear, palm facing ahead. The elbow is lifted up so that it points straight out to the side. The opposite arm, as always, points diagonally inward toward the center target. As you block, bring the elbow in and across the front of your body. The block finishes with the fist in front of the opposite shoulder and at the same height as the shoulder, with the elbow bent at ninety degrees and the upper arm at an angle of about forty-five degrees from the body. The palm of the fist faces out for as long as possible but at the end of the block snaps over so that the back of the fist faces straight ahead. When you finish, the blocking arm is reaching across the body to protect the whole of your chest and solar plexus region. When done properly, this is a powerful block.

Practice in horse stance and then moving forward and backward in walking stance, front stance, and back stance. Note that when you turn around in walking, front, or back stance and inside-block simultaneously, it is easiest, especially for beginners, to chamber the block before beginning the turn. The temptation is to block with the reverse hand when turning so that the blocking arm moves with the direction of the turn, but with the inside block this will not be the case. Take care to block with the front hand once the turn is completed, unless specifically drilling with the reverse hand.

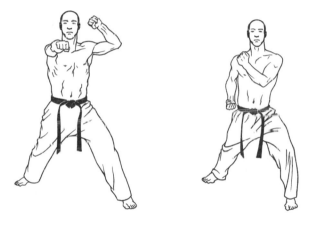

Outside Block (*Bakkat-Makki*)

The opposite of the inside block, the outside block also effectively protects the upper body. After the down block, it is probably the easiest of the basic blocks. Chamber with the blocking hand reaching straight across your abdomen, elbow bent at ninety degrees, palm of fist facing down. The blocking arm should reach across to the opposite side of the torso at about the height of your diaphragm. The reaction arm points at the center target.

Block by bringing the blocking arm up sharply across the body, using the elbow as a pivot point. The elbow itself does not need to move at all, except to rotate. The block finishes in front of its shoulder with the palm of the fist facing your body. Be sure to snap the wrist over at the last moment before stopping the motion of the block. When the block is finished, the elbow is bent at

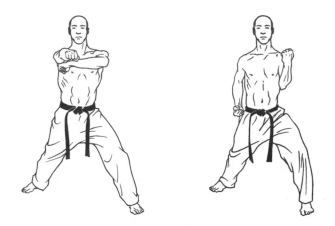

ninety degrees and the upper arm is at about forty-five degrees from the body. The fist is directly in front of its shoulder, neither above nor outside it.

As with the others, practice first in horse stance and then in walking stance, front stance, and back stance, moving forward and backward.

High Block (*Olgul-Makki*)

The high block is meant to protect your head from something coming down from above, or to divert something coming straight at your face. To chamber the block, reach across your body with your fist, palm facing up. The elbow is bent, and your arm should extend to the opposite side of the rib cage. The opposite arm, as always, points at the center target. Block by retracting the reaction arm and simultaneously raising the blocking arm straight up until it is one fist's width above your head. Snap the wrist over at the last possible

moment. Be careful not to pull the block too far above you; your arm should finish not directly above your head but slightly in front of it; otherwise, if you throw your arm too far back, you'll expose your forehead and face to the blow you are trying to stop.

It takes a fair amount of practice to execute this block with real snap and power. Work with it in horse stance and then in walking stance, front stance, and back stance, moving forward and backward.

Outside Forearm Block
(Bakkat Palmok Bakkat Momtong-Makki)

The outside forearm block is the last of the five basic blocks and the most difficult to perform, although it is a simple technique. The chamber position is the same as for the down block: the fist is raised across the face, with the palm facing, but not touching, the cheek. Maintaining angle of the elbow at ninety degrees, swing the block out and away from the face so that, like the inside and outside blocks, it protects your upper midsection. The block stops in front of its shoulder, as with the outside block, and the fist snaps around at the last moment so that the palm faces out. In the final position, the forearm is vertical with the elbow down. The elbow is bent at ninety degrees, the upper arm forms a forty-five-degree angle to the body (as with both of the other midsection blocks), and the fist is aligned directly in front of its shoulder, neither outside it nor above it.

Many students find it difficult to resist lifting the elbow, straightening the elbow, or both. Try to avoid these pitfalls as you practice the block in horse stance and moving forward and backward in walking stance, front stance, and back stance.

Other Fist Blocks

Double-Fist Block *(Bakkat Palnok Momtong-Makki)*

Essentially the same as the double knife-hand block, whether high or low, and the single knife-hand block, except that the hands are closed into fists rather than open in knife hands.

Reinforced Outside Block
(Kodureo Anpalmok Momtong-Makki)

The same as the outside block, but the reverse hand supports the blocking hand by turning the fist palm up and placing its first two knuckles against the inside of the elbow of the blocking hand. The chamber for this block, however, is completely different from that for the outside block. Chamber by extending

the reaction arm, or in this case, the supporting arm, straight out behind yourself as you would for a double knife-hand block, fist closed and palm facing down. Chamber the blocking hand, fist closed and palm facing down, near the opposite shoulder with the elbow bent. Practice this block in front stance.

X Block *(Otgoreo-Makki)*

The X block is especially useful for trapping an attacker's limb. Chamber the block with both hands stationed at the belt, fists closed and palms facing up. For lower X block (*otgoreo arae-makki*), thrust both hands out and down, crossing the arms just above the wrists and turning the hands over at the last moment so that the palms face down. The hand on top corresponds to the leading leg. Likewise, for high X block (*otgoreo olgul-makki*), thrust the hands from chamber up and out until the arms are fully extended and the hands are at face level, crossing the arms just above the wrists and turning the fists over at the last moment. This is another block to practice in front stance.

Open-Hand Blocks

In some styles, open-hand blocks form the true foundation of defense due to their follow-through possibilities. The open hand makes it easy to follow through with grabs and jointlocks, and it also increases the effective blocking surface by making the edge of the hand available. Of Taekwondo's open-hand blocks, the double and single knife-hand blocks are the most common. From an aesthetic standpoint, the knife-hand blocks are among the most graceful movements in basic Taekwondo, with their flowing lines and strong back stance. The knife hand is also a potent striking weapon and is a favorite for breaking techniques.

The palm blocks find great usage in competitive sparring because of their speed and because many practitioners use them instinctively. Whether you find yourself using the knife-hand blocks or the palm blocks more regularly, be sure to keep proper form and technique in mind. Without correct form, it's easy to damage your fingers should they be struck by a punch or kick.

In both the knife hand and the palm block, the fingers are held tightly together with the thumb held firmly against the edge of the hand, neither sticking out nor tucked against the palm. Keeping your fingers together and the thumb in will protect them from splaying if hit edge-on, which is a common source of injury in sparring. To form a knife hand, hold your hand rigidly open, fingers together, thumb tucked tightly against the edge of the hand, wrist straight. To form a palm-block hand, hold the hand rigidly open, thumb tucked. The wrist is either bent up at ninety degrees (in the case of the crossing palm block) or kept straight (in the case of the pressing-down block).

Knife-hand blocks are most commonly practiced in back stance, while palm blocks appear most often in fighting stance, walking stance, and cat stance.

Double Knife-Hand Block (*Sonnal-Makki*)

Midsection (sonnal momtong-makki). This is the most common of the knife-hand blocks. Stand in back stance. Chamber the block by extending your arms behind you, with the rear arm straight out, palm down, and the lead arm bent, hand near your face, palm toward you. To bring the block into position, snap

the open lead hand, elbow at ninety degrees, out in front of you until the forearm is vertical, elbow down. The palm of the hand faces out at an angle of about forty-five degrees. The rear arm, extended straight behind you, comes to rest with the palm faceup directly in front of the solar plexus, protecting that area. The forearm should be parallel to the floor.

Lower section (sonnal arae-makki). The chamber is the same as that for the midsection block. The difference is that the blocking hand will move from chamber to extend down straight over the lead leg, finishing about a fist's width above the thigh, palm facing the leg. The other hand will finish in the same position as in the midsection block, palm up in front of the solar plexus. Be careful to keep the opposite hand in the correct position; many students find it tempting to let it drop from the solar plexus.

Double low-section block (kodureo sonnal arae-makki). In this variation, the lead hand protects the lower section above the leg, as described above, but the reverse hand comes to station at the groin level, palm facing forward and up so that its angle is parallel to that of the blocking hand. The chamber is the same as for double knife-hand blocks.

Practice each of these variations in back stance, moving forward and backward, remembering to chamber straight out each time. Remember to turn the wrist of the blocking hand over at the last possible moment. Also try two blocks in one stance, beginning, for instance, with midsection block and then, without moving your feet, rechambering and switching to low-section block, and vice versa.

Single Knife-Hand Block
(Hansonnal Bakkat-Momtong-Makki)

As with the double knife-hand block, the lead hand will block, palm facing out at forty-five degrees. However, the other hand, instead of resting open and palm up in front of the solar plexus, will come to the standard chamber position by the belt, fist closed, palm facing up.

Chamber this block by crossing the arms in front of your face. The blocking hand will be open, palm facing you, and the blocking arm will be on the inside. The other arm is on the outside and the fist is closed, palm facing out. As you block, bring the blocking hand sharply down to the level of your lead shoulder, keeping the elbow bent at ninety degrees. Keep the palm facing you until the last possible moment, then snap it over and into position. As you move the blocking hand, the other arm will simultaneously and sharply drop into its chamber position by the belt.

Low section (hansonnal arae-makki). This time bring the blocking hand to the low section, open, palm facing the leg about a fist's width above it. The reverse hand returns to the same chamber position by the belt, fist closed, palm facing up.

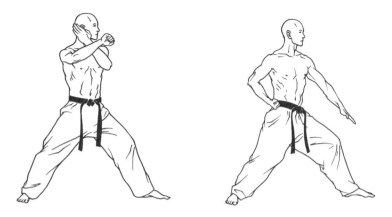

Crossing Palm Block
(Son Badak An Momtong-Makki)

Taekwondoists often use this block instinctively in sparring situations—it's often seen being used to defend against turning kicks to the kidney side of the midsection, when the lead hand stays up and the reverse hand drops down, palm open and pushing across the body to meet the kick. Be cautious using it this way, because the palm itself is the blocking surface and you don't want to damage your hand.

The crossing palm block also makes appearances in two of the poomse.

Chamber the block at belt level with the hand open, wrist bent back at ninety degrees, fingers pointing down. The reaction hand is closed in a fist and points straight at the center target. Block by sharply drawing the blocking hand across the body in front of your abdomen, keeping the fingers pointed down

until the hand reaches the other side of your body. At this point snap the hand over so that the fingers point up. Simultaneously with the motion of the block, retract the reaction arm until the fist is at chamber position. Practice this block in walking stance and front stance, moving forward and backward.

Pressing-Down Block
(Badangson Momtong Nullo-Makki)

A close cousin of the crossing palm block, the pressing-down block differs in that the wrist is held straight rather than bent and, as the name suggests, the motion of the block is downward rather than across the body. It is one of the simpler techniques in the repertoire.

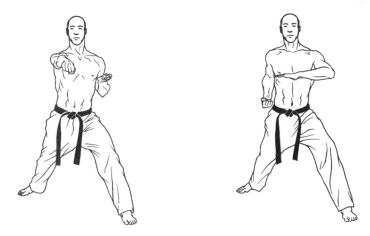

Chamber the block with the reaction arm pointing at the center target, fist closed. The blocking hand is held rigidly open at your side, elbow bent, with the palm facing up. To block, retract the reaction arm and swing the block down, using the elbow as a pivot, until the forearm is parallel to the floor and the palm is facing down. The block is held out about two fists' width from the body, not against the abdomen, and the elbow is kept at ninety degrees.

CHAPTER 7

Hand Strikes

The Kihap • The Fist • The Traditional Punch • Punches for Sparring and Self-Defense •
Back Fist • Hammer Strike • Elbow Strikes • Knife-Hand Strike • Spear Hand •
Ridge-Hand Strike • Palm-Heel Strike • Throat Strike

Taekwondo has won admiration for its repertoire of fast and powerful kicks, but no martial artist could be called complete without developing equally strong hand techniques. Taekwondo includes numerous strikes and blocks that will rival those of any other art for speed, power, and effectiveness, and many Taekwondo instructors have added jointlocks, escapes, throws, and falls to their programs, often borrowing from Taekwondo's sister art, Hapkido. We will limit our discussion here to the basic strikes and blocks that appear most commonly in traditional Taekwondo training and poomse, with the addition of punching techniques adopted from boxing along with a discussion of blocks and punches in tournament sparring.

The popularity of sport Taekwondo has had an impact on the way hand techniques are taught in many dojangs. By and large, it is kicks that are valued in the competition ring, rather than punches, because tournament judges have a bias in favor of kicks. The most effective tournament fighters, however, know better than to neglect their punches and hand techniques, because these can take a punishing toll on an opponent. Taekwondoists training for competition should take extra care to develop fast, powerful hands.

Generally, when you practice hand techniques, concentrate on breathing, relaxing (especially the shoulders), speed, hip rotation, and posture. When practicing traditional techniques such as the corkscrew punch or the down block, remember not to neglect reaction, the retraction of the opposite hand. Punches and blocks thrown in horse stance (or any other) will lose a great deal of power if you neglect to pull the opposite elbow back quickly. That's due to one of the laws of Newtonian physics: every reaction produces an equal and opposite reaction. Therefore, if you whip your elbow back quickly, your punch or block will be that much faster and more powerful.

Also remember that strong technique relies much more on speed and accuracy than on brute strength. This is true of punches, blocks, knife-hand strikes, kicks—any motion you can think of that involves one surface hitting another, whether offensively or defensively. Again, the reason depends on simple physics: the faster a mass moves, the more power it delivers. You can have hulking upper-body strength, but slow strikes are not only more likely to miss, they'll also lack real impact. This is why body weight matters. A heavy fist and arm moving quickly deliver a stronger blow than a light fist and arm moving at the same speed. A light martial artist can hit every bit as hard as a heavy one, provided the speed is proportionally higher. Therefore, do your best to develop fluid, whiplike motion.

You don't need to tense any muscles at all until the moment of impact. In fact, the more relaxed you are, the faster and more powerful you'll be. Tense muscles oppose each other, and any motion takes more effort and more time to accomplish. This applies to punches thrown during poomse or in a traditional horse stance, and it applies to punches you're trying to drive through your opponent's hogu with the referee looking on. Most important, it applies to that frightening situation when you hope that all your training comes into play—assault by someone with an intent to harm you. If you ever have to defend yourself, you must remain relaxed, focused, clearheaded, and fast.

The Kihap

One of the central techniques of Taekwondo, and of many other martial arts, is the yell, or kihap. Many beginners are reluctant to belt out a loud yell when they punch or kick, but the kihap serves a number of important purposes. Over time, it becomes automatically incorporated into all kinds of strikes—kicks, punches, hand strikes, even falls and jumps. Yell from the abdomen by tightening your diaphragm, rather than forcing the yell through your throat.

Among the advantages to the kihap are:

• It draws power—*ki*—from your belly and out into your strike.
• It tightens your abdominal muscles, which helps protect you from blows and falls and helps protect against having your wind knocked out.
• It helps you overcome your own fear.

• It can frighten your opponent.
• It can help you overcome any pain you might be feeling.

The Fist

It's virtually instinctive to strike with the fists. Unfortunately, it's easy to damage your hands delivering a punch if you don't use proper technique. Equally, it's easy to deliver a weak or impotent blow, no matter your strength, if you are hesitant, slow, or if you fail to form a tight fist firmly supported by the structure of your wrist and arm and delivered with all the power of your hips and body weight.

Start by closing your fingers with the tips curled to make firm contact with the center of your palm. Wrap the end of your thumb against the middle phalanges—to use the anatomical term—of the first and second fingers. That is, if you think of your fingers as having three bones each, and your thumb as having two, make sure you curl your thumb so that its top portion rests against the middle bones of your index and middle fingers. Your thumb is *not* inside your fingers. This leads to broken thumbs when you hit something. Nor does your thumb stick out from the side of your hand like a hook waiting to snag on something. With your thumb in the correct position, it is safe from impact and it helps to secure your fist.

Now straighten the back of your wrist. With your wrist straight, it won't bend as easily when you deliver a blow, and you should be safe from sprains or fractures of its delicate bones. This is the correct position for all punches and most blocks in Taekwondo.

Finally, when punching, make sure you strike with the *first two* knuckles of the fist—the large ones of your index and middle fingers. These are the sturdiest and least likely to fracture, and, when your wrist is straight, are aligned with the bones of the wrist and arm. When you punch with the first two knuckles, a tight fist, and a straight wrist, you'll strike with maximum impact and the least risk to your hand, fingers, and wrist.

The Traditional Punch (*Chirugi*)

For traditional punching drills and in all poomse, Taekwondo uses one basic punch. Some styles call it the corkscrew punch because of the hand's motion as it travels to its target. Many Taekwondo masters have largely relegated this particular punching style to drills, because innovations in punching technique have resulted in other, faster methods. Nonetheless, we practice punching this way because it ingrains certain principles of movement and concentration that continue to be useful, even in competition and street situations. The standard punch is an excellent way to practice the development of great power with minimum body movement and, therefore, minimum loss of balance and control.

Begin in horse stance. Straighten your left arm and tighten your fist. Aim your hand directly at the solar plexus of an imaginary opponent of your own size. Your left arm should now be angled diagonally inward from your shoulder. The basic practice targets are along the centerline of the body: the solar plexus, the groin, and the upper jaw (punches to these targets are called, respectively, *momtong-chirugi, arae-chirugi,* and *olgul-chirugi*).

Form your right hand into a fist. Turn it upside down so that the palm is facing up. Now rest it lightly at your side against your belt. This is your punching hand. The extended arm is your pointing or reaction arm. You are now in chamber position for punching.

Lift your right hand until it is against the side of your rib cage. Now extend it straight toward the target, diagonally from your shoulder. The hand is still upside down, palm of the fist facing up. At the last possible moment before your elbow straightens and your fist reaches the target, snap your hand over. The snap of the wrist delivers one more bit of power and also helps to drive the knuckles into the target. At the same time that you punch, retract the opposite hand so that the fist rests upside down against the belt.

Finally, *kihap*!

This is the traditional Taekwondo punch. There are several things to remember:

• Exhale through your mouth—not a problem if you've given a good kihap.

- Draw the pointing, or reaction, arm back just as fast as the punch strikes out. This will keep you centered and will maximize the speed of your punch.
- Keep your shoulders square. This ensures that your balance is perfectly maintained. Remember to punch diagonally inward from your shoulder, not straight out.
- Sink your hips slightly with every strike. This helps center your balance and helps transmit power up through your hips into your punch. If you relax, this motion will happen automatically.
- Snap the punching fist over at the last possible moment, not before. This increases the overall speed of your fist and makes your punch that much more potent.

Suggested Drills

There are many ways to practice the traditional punch, and different drills will help you develop strength, speed, and accuracy. Ultimately, the kinds of drills you can do are limited only by your imagination. Here are some simple ones we like to use.

Half speed. Start by throwing ten punches at half speed in horse stance, alternating between left and right, without a kihap. Concentrate on loosening the arms, maintaining a solid stance with the knees bent, and punching directly into the target area. Be careful not to turn the fist over too early.

Full-speed single punch. After throwing the slower practice punches, do another set at full speed. Kihap with every one. Obviously, this is the primary punching drill: Settle down into a solid horse stance, zero in on your imaginary target, and do sets of punches. Bring the reaction arm back at full speed and keep those first two knuckles aimed straight at the target.

Double punch (Doo bon-chirugi). Now throw two punches at full speed, with a kihap after the second one. Make sure the first punch has as much power as the second, but don't exhale your full lungful of air on the first punch, or you won't have any air left for the kihap. Do a set of these punches, switch so that you're starting with the opposite arm, and do another set.

Triple punch (Sae bon-chirugi). As with the double punch, kihap on the third punch. Note that this time, because you're throwing an odd number of punches each time, you'll automatically alternate starting hands. Try punching toward a different target with each blow, first in order of low, middle, high for a number of sets, then reverse.

Twist punch. This is a modified triple punch. On the third punch, straighten the leg corresponding to your punching hand. Twist your shoulders and body about forty-five degrees as you punch. Punch at the same target you would have in horse stance, straight in front of you. As you twist, you'll end up in front stance with your arm extended not in the direction of your stance but to the side. At the end of the punch, your shoulders will be square to the direction you're facing but not to the punch; instead, they'll be nearly in line with the punching arm. Note that as you turn into the front stance, you should use the action of the rear leg as it straightens to propel your hip, and therefore your shoulder and punching arm, into position. With practice you can achieve great power this way. Use this drill to develop timing, leg strength, and coordination.

Calisthenic punch. This time, remain in horse stance and punch very slowly with the muscles of your upper body tightened as much as possible. Exhale slowly as you extend the punch to the target, then repeat, alternating arms.

Punches for Sparring and Self-Defense

As mentioned above, the traditional punch is an excellent way to practice generating power and speed by relying on the fundamentals of body mechanics instead of throwing the shoulder into the motion. Your chances to use this punch, however, will come rarely. More often, you'll find yourself facing an opponent in standard fighting position, with your hands in guard position, not chambered at your sides. Nor would you want to chamber your hands at your sides when you need to defend yourself. Remember the cardinal rule about self-defense: you will always seek to avoid harm. Never seek to harm another unless you have exhausted all other options. You will therefore keep your hands raised in guard position when in confrontation. Of course, this stance also enables you to strike back quickly should you have the misfortune of a fight.

Taekwondo acknowledges the Western art of boxing for its development of fast, basic, and powerful hands. Boxers have refined the simple jab, reverse punch, hook, and uppercut into quick and deadly weapons, admirable complements to the martial artist's store of knife hands, hammer strikes, backfists, and palm heels.

This is the time to apply some of the principles studied during practice of the corkscrew punch—how to develop power using the simple mechanics of breath, reaction, and the wrist. Now we'll move on to include the legs, hips, and shoulders.

Students of hand techniques stress the importance of leg mobility when punching. Just as we take full advantage of the strength in the legs when we throw our kicks, we try to take equal advantage of the legs when we punch. All punches start from the floor; the power flows from the push of the legs, through a twitch of the hips and into the shoulders, which remain loose and relaxed while the arm shoots out like the end of a whip.

Stance

Start in fighting stance, hands raised. Be sure to keep your fists tight and approximately at the level of your chin. This still allows you to protect your midsection while keeping your hands closest to that part of your body you need to protect the most: your head. Your lead hand is extended slightly out in front of you; the rear hand is next to your chin. Keep your elbows down.

Your stance for punching is a little different from the usual Taekwondo fighting stance. When you close in on your opponent and it looks as if your hands are going to come into play, square up your stance slightly. Most Taekwondoists maintain a fighting stance nearly parallel to their opponent. The feet are almost in line with each other and the knees are bent and often turned slightly inward. While this stance works beautifully for kicking quickly and ensures rapid footwork, it's not easy to punch from this position. It's especially awkward to use the rear hand, because the rear shoulder is "stuck" and doesn't rotate forward very easily. Therefore, the best position for punching is more square than the typical kicking stance. Instead of lining up your feet, place them on the opposite corners of an imaginary square.

The Jab

The jab is the fundamental punch of boxing, self-defense, and sparring. It's fast, it can be used to maintain an opponent's distance, it serves as an effective setup to more powerful blows, including kicks, and, if done properly, it can be quite powerful in its own right.

From your punching stance, the jab is a simple extension of the lead hand straight out in front of you. Aim at your opponent's chin. The wrist snaps over at the end of the punch, as in the traditional Taekwondo technique, and the striking surface is always the first two knuckles. Keep your elbow down during the punch. Your tendency will probably be to raise it. This slows the technique and makes your ribs vulnerable to a counterattack. When the punch is extended, tuck your chin down next to your shoulder. The rear hand stays close to the chin as protection against a counterattack to that side of the head. Finally, keep your chin down. Many students will lift their chins when they punch, presenting a nice clear target to their opponent for a counterattack. Keep the chin down and the head inclined forward rather than back.

Make sure that your shoulders are relaxed when you punch. Stay light on your feet. Use your lead hip to generate power for the punch. The power from the slight rotation of your lead hip will move through your torso and shoulder and help you snap your fist out. Your rear foot will lift slightly from the floor. Note that you do *not* pull the opposite arm back in reaction. Keep it at your chin and keep the punch light and fast.

Throw a set number of jabs, then switch stance and throw an equal number with the other side. While most Western-style fighters develop one side for power, usually reserving the side with the greatest dexterity for that purpose (usually the right), martial artists work on both. For a righty, jabbing with the left, or the secondary, hand will probably feel more natural at first than jabbing with the right, but with practice both will come to feel natural.

Reverse Punch

Also called the counterpunch, the reverse punch is the natural companion to the jab and the punch most typically used to deliver the powerful knockout blows you see in the boxing ring. In Taekwondo sparring application, the reverse punch is usually aimed at the opponent's solar plexus or the center of the chest, as are jabs, since under World Taekwondo Federation competition rules, punches to the head are illegal. The streetfighter's version of this punch is the big, sloppy roundhouse blow that swings around wide before connecting with the target. Properly speaking, this is a reverse hook, but the technique requires more development than it typically receives from the untrained fighter.

The reverse punch uses the rear hand rather than the forward hand. Most people can develop greater power with it than with the jab, because it affords the opportunity to use more body weight as the shoulders and hips swing into the blow.

As with the jab, the reverse punch comes straight out from the chin with the elbow down. Rotate your shoulders around completely when you throw this punch. At first, the motion might feel unnatural or clumsy. Make sure your hips are loose. Swivel them around when you throw the reverse punch and channel their strength through your shoulders and into the punching arm. It will help if you keep your rear heel off the floor while in your fighting stance. Snap the fist over at the end of the punch. Tuck your chin into the shoulder of your punching arm as the shoulder comes around and keep the lead hand poised beside your chin.

Be careful not to let the punch swing wide. It should dart forward and back, striking quickly with the power of your body weight behind it. This is another case of the principles of the traditional Taekwondo punch coming into play: Your body weight rotates around the vertical axis of your pelvis. Just as in horse stance, you never lose control of your center of gravity. When punch-

ing, imagine striking like a snake—stay fast and loose and fire your punches straight from your shoulder.

Throw a number of reverse punches, concentrating on speed, linearity, rotation of the shoulders, and relaxation of the upper body. Allow your legs to generate power.

Once you have the motion of the jab and reverse punches down, throw them in combination. Lead with the jab and follow through with the reverse punch. Throw twenty combinations, then switch stance and repeat.

Continue throwing punches in combination, increasing the number in each set. Finish with one hundred sets on each side. That will total four hundred punches. If you can do this, you'll be on your way to having solid, fast punches that won't miss when it counts.

Hook Punch

An excellent technique for close fighting and for follow-ups when your opponent's guard drops, the hook punch follows a tight arc with little motion from the body and, like the jab and reverse punch, requires little effort from the shoulder. Its technique differs from the others in that the elbow is lifted to the horizontal plane rather than kept down and the fist is turned vertical, perpendicular to the angle used in the other punches.

For a good hook punch, lift the elbow of your leading arm, turn your fist so that it is vertically aligned, and use a twitch of your leading hip to generate power. Let your arm swing in a small, tight hook with the elbow bent; lifting the elbow into the punch will help you swipe your fist through the punch's range of motion. Note that the hook punch does not travel very far either in front of you or to the side. The hook is an inside technique. You shouldn't find yourself reaching into it, although your lead shoulder will naturally swing slightly in with the motion.

Hips and shoulders are everything in the hook punch. The angle of the elbow barely changes at all. In fact, since your leading arm is already bent, simply maintain the angle of the elbow. If you lift your elbow straight up while preventing the fist from rising, and instead allow the fist to travel horizontally in front of your face, you'll come very close to the ideal form for this punch. The shoulder, meanwhile, should be perfectly relaxed. To some people, this seems awkward, but if you think of the shoulder as a hinge for the motion rather than as the source of strength for the punch, then it will be much easier to find the fluidity you need.

Practice first by throwing a number of hooks with your lead hand. Once the motion becomes comfortable, switch stance and try the other hand. Switch back and forth, throwing at least twenty punches with each lead hand.

Once you've settled into the hook punch, try it in combination with the jab/ reverse punch. Throw the punches with rhythm: jab, reverse, hook, jab, reverse, hook. Stay relaxed and gradually speed up the combination until you're able to snap the punches out with power. Then switch stance and try the same thing with the other side.

Also practice the hook punch with the reverse hand. Undisciplined fighters punch this way with a wide arc, beginning from a reverse hand drawn far back. This is rarely effective, especially against someone trained in defense. The big roundhouse punch is too slow, too obvious, gives up too much control, and makes it difficult to follow up with another strike. Try to keep the reverse hook punch as controlled as a jab. It should be a quick, tightly controlled motion that gets its power from a sharp twitch of the hips and shoulders, without overextending itself. As with the lead or front hook punch, the hand doesn't need to travel very far. Allow the shoulders and hips to do the work; the punch is just the end of the whip as your body uncoils into the motion. Keep the shoulders loose, especially the shoulder the punch hinges on.

Once you've become comfortable with the reverse hook, try it in combination with other punches. First throw consecutive hook punches, starting with the lead hand. Then try a four-punch sequence: jab, reverse punch, hook, reverse hook. Try twenty sets, then switch. The more combinations you throw, the more natural punching will feel.

The Uppercut

This is really a variation of the hook and is used to punch into an opponent's body or to slash up with a rising strike to the chin. It requires greater mobility of the upper body than the previous techniques, because, in keeping with the principle that effective punches are generated by the use of legs, hips, and shoulders, you'll have to change the level of your shoulders in order to drive your punches to their targets.

First try with your lead hand. Bend your legs so that your body dips down. Rotate your lead shoulder back slightly and pull the elbow back. Now rise up quickly, turning your fist palm up and keeping the elbow bent. Rotate your shoulder into the punch as your fist turns over and your legs drive the punch up. This attack should be effective against an opponent's ribs, kidney, or solar

plexus. If you don't dip down too far and pull your fist in tightly before driving up, you'll have an effective attack moving up into an opponent's chin.

The same motions apply for uppercuts with the reverse hand, except that you don't need to pull the reverse shoulder back as far.

Try combinations of uppercuts, beginning with the lead hand and finishing with the reverse hand. Then work them in with combinations of other punches.

The number of punch combinations is limited only by your imagination. Concentrate on combinations that work together and try to emphasize fluid connections between your attacks.

Suggested Drills for Punching

- Jab
- Jab/reverse punch
- Jab/reverse punch/jab
- Jab/jab/reverse punch
- Hook
- Hook/reverse punch
- Hook/reverse hook
- Jab/reverse punch/hook
- Jab/reverse punch/hook/reverse hook
- Jab/hook/reverse punch
- Uppercut
- Uppercut/reverse uppercut
- Reverse uppercut/uppercut
- Jab/reverse punch/uppercut
- Jab/reverse punch/uppercut/reverse uppercut
- Hook/reverse uppercut
- Jab/reverse hook/uppercut

In WTF-style tournament sparring, you have to keep in mind that punching to the head is illegal. Use the most effective punches for the midsection targets. These include a midsection jab, the reverse punch, and the uppercuts. It's enormously helpful to invest in a pair of bag gloves and practice your punches against a heavy bag. This will help you develop power, endurance, strong wrists, and a real sense of what it's like to strike an unyielding target. See Chapter 9, "Sparring," for suggestions on punch strategy in the ring and training methods.

Additional Fist Attacks

Apart from the fronts of the knuckles, the fist has two other useful striking surfaces: the back of the knuckles and the outer edge of the fist, below the pinkie. Taekwondo takes advantage of these surfaces with two techniques in particular. When practicing these techniques, as with the rest of the hand strikes, point the opposite arm directly at the target and retract it to chamber position by the belt as you deliver your blow.

Backfist *(Deung joomok)*

Using the back of the fist is nearly as common an instinct as using the front. The backfist is a versatile technique that can deliver a swift, stinging blow. With a big windup, it can pack a good deal of power.

There are two primary methods to using the backfist. Which one you use will depend upon the target you hope to strike. The two common targets of the backfist are the temple and the nose, although, as you'll see, the chin is another good option. Striking to the temple and striking to the nose require somewhat different deliveries. In any case, use the backs of the first two knuckles, the same as those used in standard punches.

To strike to the temple (*deung joomok bakkat-chigi*), chamber the fist of the striking hand—usually the lead hand—under the opposite armpit, palm facing down. Whip the fist out toward the target in an arc, using your shoulders to help propel it. Turn the fist over at the last possible moment so that it is vertical, back of the fist facing the side, as it meets the target. Remember to use the push from your hips and not your arms alone in delivering this blow.

In self-defense situations, you may not have the opportunity to chamber the backfist fully. In this case, treat the backfist with the lead hand like a jab. Be quick and step in slightly with the lead foot when you execute to help you achieve power.

The backfist to the nose (*deung joomok olgul-apchigi*) makes its formal appearance first in Taegeuk Sa Jang. It is a frontal attack, deceptively coming straight into an opponent's face from above, while the strike to the temple comes from the side. Chamber this strike above the opposite shoulder, palm down. Strike by swinging the backfist in a tight vertical arc, beginning at the opposite shoulder and ending directly in front of your face, palm facing you. The elbow is bent throughout the technique. Keep a tight fist but a loose wrist, and allow your hand to snap freely into the target, like the end of a whip.

Hammer Strike (*Maejoomok-chigi*)

The hammer strike typically uses a vertical fist, palm facing the side rather than down, and strikes directly down. But turned horizontal, it can also be used to strike to either side, using the same chamber positions that are used for the inside and outside knife-hand strikes or the inside block and outside forearm block. Note that the wrist is held straight for all hammer strikes.

To chamber the forward hammer strike (*maejoomok nae ryo-chigi*), hold your fist upside down by your ear as if about to throw a ball—the chamber is the same as that for the inside block. Bring your fist forward and down in an arc, palm forward until the last possible moment, when you snap your fist into the vertical position as your arm straightens. You can also use the hammer strike as it appears in Taegeuk O Jang, chambering your fist upside down,

striking surface facing up, at the opposite shoulder and sweeping a large circle above your head and down to a target beside you. In either case, the elbow is straight at the moment of completion.

You have two options if you wish to strike horizontally rather than vertically with the hammer fist. The first is the inside hammer strike (*maejoomok olgul an-chigi*). The chamber is identical to that of the forward hammer strike and the inside block, but instead of using an overhand throwing motion, use a sidearm throw; your striking arm will move to the outside and then circle in with your palm facing forward. When your fist reaches the strike point in front of you, snap it over so that the palm faces you. The elbow is bent at the moment of impact.

The outside hammer strike (*maejoomok olgul bakkat-chigi*) uses the same chamber as the down block or the outside forearm block, with the fist raised across the face, palm in. And, in fact, the motion of the attack is identical to that for the outside forearm block except that the arm is straight upon completion of the move, rather than bent at ninety degrees.

Practice all three hammer strikes—forward, inside, and outside—in walking stances, front stance, and back stance, and use all of them against targets to the front as well as to the side. You will find the hammer strike to be highly versatile.

Elbow Strikes

Taekwondo has also developed the use of the elbow as a powerful weapon and one of the best choices of technique for inside fighting, when you may be too close to an opponent even to throw a punch, much less a kick. It is comparatively easy to deliver a smashing blow with the elbow, provided the hand is turned the right way and you practice delivering the strike with speed.

Inside Elbow Strike (*Palkeup*)

The inside elbow strike is featured in Taegeuk O Jang and is probably the most common form of elbow attack. Because the elbow strike is best used in close quarters, you should take advantage of the possibilities offered by the circumstance. If the opponent's head is within reach of an elbow strike, it may well be possible to grab it with your other hand, assuring yourself that your opponent will not escape.

The striking surface is the end of the forearm, just below the point of the bent elbow. Bend the attacking elbow all the way, so that the hand is close to the body. Form a fist and keep the palm down—this will rotate the outer bone of the forearm—the ulna—to the front. Lift the elbow so that it is horizontal and swing it back. Open the opposite hand and reach forward, as if to grab the target, palm facing the side. Strike by using your legs and hips to help you swing the elbow as fast possible into the target; keep the opposite hand in position and smack the elbow into it.

Another common method of delivering the elbow strike is to form the strike the same way, but instead of reaching out to grab the target, the other hand wraps around the fist of the striking arm and supports it as the blow is delivered.

Outside Elbow Strike (*Palkeup Yeop-Chigi*)

Here, the point of the elbow strikes the target as you draw your arm from the inside to the outside, beginning with the fist of the striking arm near the opposite shoulder. As with the inside elbow strike, the palm of the fist faces down and the arm is fully bent during the entire motion of the strike. The outside elbow strike is most effective in attacking an opponent to the side or with the lead arm moving forward in back stance.

Vertical Elbow Strike (*Palkeup*)

With some spring from the knees, this uppercut technique can deliver a tremendous blow to an opponent's jaw or, if you start low enough, solar plexus. The elbow is fully bent with a vertical forearm. The fist is turned so that the palm faces inside throughout the entire motion. Chamber the block

with your fist by your side, palm facing the ribs. Use your hips to help catapult the elbow up in a sharp curve. Turn your face slightly to the side as your fist rises and finish with your fist next to your face.

Rear Elbow Strike (*Palkeup Dwiro-Chigi*)

This strike uses the motion from the reaction of a standard punch to hit an opponent behind you. Chamber with the striking arm pointed ahead, fist closed, palm down. Whip the arm back, bending it as you go and turning the hand over, palm up, at the last moment as your elbow reaches the target and your fist draws alongside your ribs. With a twist of the hips, this becomes an extremely powerful strike.

Open-Hand Strikes

When they are not equating martial arts with flashy flying and spinning kicks, people often think of exotic looking open-hand techniques like the famous karate chop, more properly known as the knife-hand strike. In truth, fists are far more commonly used than open-hand strikes, but the open-hand presents several advantages if used properly, such as a quick transition to grabs, more striking surfaces, and greater safety to the knuckles. If you foresee yourself using knife-hand strikes regularly, you may wish to strengthen your hands and fingers so that they may be injured less easily. It is probably because of this need for conditioning that many martial artists rely less on open-hand strikes than on closed fists; the knuckles, even though fragile if used improperly, nonetheless offer a solid striking surface without a lot of strengthening exercises.

The striking surfaces of the open hand are the outer ridge, the inner ridge (with thumb both tucked and extended), the fingertips, and the heel of the palm.

Form an open-hand by opening the hand and holding the fingers tightly together with the thumb pressed firmly against the edge of the hand. The fingers must never splay and the thumb must never protrude; either can easily result in broken fingers. Tense the fingers to harden the muscles along the outer edge of the hand as much as possible. The wrist is held straight for knife-hand blocks (see Chapter 6, "Blocks") and for outside knife-hand strikes. For inside knife-hand strikes, the wrist is allowed to bend back slightly.

Knife-Hand Strikes *(Sonnal Chigi)*

These classic attacks, so often seen in James Bond movies and karate films, actually do appear in martial arts practice. The knife hand uses the outer edge of the open hand to strike against vulnerable areas of the body, most notably the neck, although it is also effective against the jaw and the midsection. The knife-hand strike is also a favorite breaking technique. Some experts advocate hardening the edges of the hands either by repeatedly striking a hard surface, causing a buildup of tough scar tissue, or by exercising the hands extensively to thicken and harden the bulk of muscle tissue lining the hand. If you feel you must harden the ulnar ridges of your hands, we suggest the latter in the interest of health and safety.

INSIDE KNIFE-HAND STRIKE *(SONNAL MOK AN-CHIGI)*
Many students learn the inside knife-hand strike as they prepare to learn Taegeuk Sam Jang. Chamber the inside knife-hand strike by drawing the open hand back by the ear, palm facing out. The opposite arm points directly at the target, fist closed. Swing your hand forward in a sidearm motion like that used for the inside hammer strike while retracting the reaction arm. At the last moment, snap your hand around so that the open palm faces up as the outside edge makes contact with the target. The wrist and elbow are slightly bent and the hand is parallel with the floor.

OUTSIDE KNIFE-HAND STRIKE *(SONNAL MOK BAKKAT-CHIGI)*
The chamber position for the outside knife-hand strike is essentially the same as that for the single-hand knife-hand block, except that the striking hand is

extended farther in order to achieve a longer movement. Cross your open hand in front of your face, palm facing in. Extend the hand as far as the opposite shoulder. The opposite hand is chambered in one of two positions, depending on the stance. In walking stance, front stance, and cat stance, point the opposite arm directly at the target, fist closed. In back stance, cross the opposite arm in front of your body and slightly beneath the striking arm. The fist is closed, palm outward. Strike by whipping the hand forward, snapping the hand over, palm down, and, at the last moment, striking with the outside edge of the hand.

Spear Hand *(Pyonson Keut-Chirugi)*

The spear hand—another technique featured in Taegeuk Sa Jang—uses the fingertips to penetrate soft portions of an opponent's anatomy, such as the abdomen. It is not advisable to use it against a bony surface, as injury to the hand is likely.

Form the spear hand as you would a knife hand, but bend the middle finger slightly to make the ends of the middle three fingertips flush with each other. Chamber the spear hand by drawing it alongside the ribs, palm up. In this case, the opposite arm does not point at the target. Instead, it performs a pressing-down block and remains in the block position while the spear hand is executed. Thrust the spear hand forward to the target, turning the hand to the vertical position at the last moment. As you complete the move, the elbow should come to rest on top of the opposite hand, still in its pressing-down block. This technique is best practiced in front stance.

Ridge-Hand Strike (*Sonnal-Deung Chigi*)

The ridge hand is the inner edge of the open hand. To strike with the ridge hand, form a knife hand in the usual way but tuck your thumb in against your palm rather than against the edge of the hand. The primary contact point for this strike is the inner knuckle of the index finger and the lobe of muscle between it and the thumb joint.

Chamber the ridge hand with the opposite fist pointing toward the target. The striking hand is held behind you, palm up. Strike by withdrawing the reaction arm and throwing the striking arm out in a tight arc curving to the outside and then whipping in as the hand snaps over to strike, palm down.

A variation of the ridge hand involves stabbing the hand forward with almost no curve at all before turning the hand over at the end of the motion.

Palm-Heel Strike (*Son Badak Chigi*)

The heel of the palm, maybe the sturdiest part of the hand, allows you to strike with great force with little risk of harm to yourself. The greatest danger in using the heel of the palm is hitting the target too high on the palm rather than on the heel; this can result in a sprained wrist.

Form the palm heel by bending the wrist back almost as far as it will go. Tuck the thumb tightly against the edge of the hand and curl the fingers against their lower knuckles, but not against the palm itself. Point the opposite fist at the target. Chamber the strike with the striking hand balled into a fist at standard chamber position by your belt. As you retract the opposite arm, thrust forward with the striking hand. As the hand moves forward, open the fist just slightly so that the thumb and fingers are in the correct position. As you turn your hand over near the end of its motion, bend the wrist back so that the rotational snap amplifies the thrust of the palm heel.

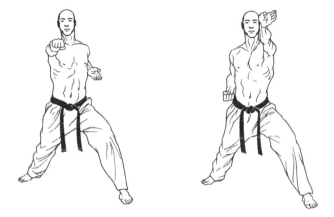

Note that at the end of the strike, the fingers do not point straight up. Instead, they point just slightly to the outside.

For an extremely effective groin strike, modify the palm heel by turning it upside down. In this case, chamber the striking hand in a fist with the palm facing down. As the strike reaches the target, snap it over so that the palm faces up with the fingers open. After striking, close the hand and pull back.

Throat Strike (*Khaljaebi*)

This technique goes by many names, most commonly tiger claw or tiger mouth. The Korean term for this hand position, *agwison*, translates as "arc hand." The term given above specifically denotes a strike to the throat, which is its most common usage. The technique appears in Koryo, the first dan form, as a throat strike (*khaljaebi*) and also as a strike to the knee (*mureupkeokki*). The throat strike is designed to deliver a quick shock to the opponent's trachea with the inside ridge of the hand.

The throat strike differs from the ridge hand in that the thumb is open and the strike moves linearly from its chamber to the target, like a punch. Form the strike by extending the thumb, partially curling it and the fingers as if holding a large can. Bend the wrist sideways so that the ridge of the hand points directly forward. Chamber the striking hand along the ribs with the hand in strike position. Point with the opposite fist. Strike as you would with a punch, accelerating the hand forward, holding it palm up until the last moment, then snapping it over, wrist turned to the outside, ridge of the hand thrusted into the target, fingers and thumb partially curled.

CHAPTER 8

Kicks

Front Kicks • Axe Kick • Crescent Kick • Turning Kick • Narabam • Side Kick •
Cut Kick • Back Kick • Hook Kick • Spinning Hook Kick • Flying Kicks

The kicks of Taekwondo set this martial art apart from all others—they are modern Taekwondo's heart and soul. The intense exploration of movement, power, and speed by countless masters and coaches has resulted in explosive and graceful techniques that have repeatedly proven themselves in self-defense and tournament sparring situations. The rigorous training required to master the kicks commonly bestows agility, flexibility, power, and extension on Taekwondo athletes. And the style of sparring practiced by the World Taekwondo Federation, with its realistic full-contact timed rounds coupled with rules aimed at enhancing the development of kicking techniques, has created a sport style fully worthy of its new Olympic status.

The evolution of Taekwondo's kicks illustrates a significant aspect of Taekwondo as a martial art. Many of the martial arts encountered today lay claim, with rightful pride, to their ancient roots as methods of warfare, and cling to the techniques as handed down from master to master through countless generations. Other modern martial arts separate themselves from the claims of history and culture, declaring that their superiority results from the freely borrowed techniques of other styles, often while failing to credit their sources—sometimes dismissing their roots altogether.

Taekwondo has largely succeeded in negotiating a fine line between these two worlds. Taekwondo instructors have taken full advantage of techniques developed centuries ago in the art's native Korea, but, in modern times, have also striven to modify the methods of Taekwondo according to the newest discoveries about biomechanics as well as insights offered by other martial arts such as Hapkido, jujitsu, and boxing. And in spite of the objections raised by some self-defense purists, the rising popularity of Taekwondo as a sport has had a profound impact on the power and efficiency of our techniques.

Fundamentally, Taekwondo relies on kicks as its bedrock techniques because of the great strength and range available in the legs. In previous chapters, we have stressed the importance of using the legs to provide power to all sorts of hand techniques. In this chapter, we will explore the use of the legs themselves to deliver blows of unparalleled effectiveness.

Common Principles

Taekwondo's kicks revolve around a common set of biomechanical principles, all of which emphasize speed, power, and extension. Many of these principles differ substantially from those employed by the kicking techniques of other martial arts.

The most important concept to master is that of the *open hip*. From the open hip comes power and range of motion. Another important concept is the knee-up or straight chamber—a real revolution in martial arts technique that makes kicks both faster and subtler. To control your motion toward or away from your opponent, and to allow your body weight to function as an effective boost to your power, keep your head in and upper body forward (in general) rather than allow them to fall back. Lastly, it is critical to develop the habit of rechambering the leg after any kick; otherwise, a kick is too easily grabbed and the balance will be thrown too far ahead or too far behind, making it difficult to regain fighting stance.

Several other concepts support these strategies, including a pivoting support foot, loose-turning shoulders, and thrust from the supporting leg. Here we'll discuss some of the basic ideas behind each of these key concepts. During the discussions of individual kicks we'll address the more specific requirements and modifications to these elements, as appropriate.

Open Hip

"Open hip" refers to the complete rotation of the hips into a kick. This is analogous to the rotation of a boxer's shoulders into a punch. When kicking from the back leg, for example, the rear hip will, whenever possible, turn completely with the action of the kick itself, so that at the moment of contact the kicking hip is aligned *just past* the target.

The open hip allows three important things to happen: 1) it maximizes power, owing to the movement of body weight into the technique; 2) it extends reach by approximately the width of the pelvis; 3) it allows the leg to reach higher, facilitating kicks to the head level and beyond.

Many martial artists of other styles argue that keeping the rear hip back rather than opening it up helps to retain balance and makes kicks speedier. However, kicks thrown with a restricted hip have only a fraction of the power delivered by those using an open hip and have less range as well. As for balance, Taekwondo's extensive development of footwork and mobility ensures that kicks, balance, and motion work together. Taekwondo kicks are not static; balance is a movable value.

PIVOTING FOOT

In order to open the hip completely, the supporting foot rotates a full 180 degrees in most kicks, so that the heel is pointed directly at the target. This is most common with the turning kick, the side kick, and the various spinning kicks, but less common in front and axe kicks.

ROTATED SHOULDERS

Along with the pivoting support foot, another key element in the delivery of power with the open hip is rotated shoulders. Moving the rear shoulder into the action of a kick further enhances the delivery of power by completing the transfer of body weight into the kick. This is particularly true of turning kicks, side kicks, and hook kicks, and can also come into play with back kicks.

Knee-up Chamber

After the opening of the hip, the knee-up, or straight chamber, is the most significant revision of leg technique Taekwondo has offered to the martial arts. "Knee-up chamber" refers to the position of the knee of the kicking leg prior to the release of the kick. In many kicks, even those where it wouldn't be expected—the turning kick is probably the most obvious example—the knee of the kicking leg lifts, fully bent, straight up in front, rather than out to the side. This is a clear departure from the traditional method, which called for the knee to be lifted to the outside to execute techniques like the turning kick.

We favor a straight chamber because it offers a great advantage in speed and versatility. The straight chamber allows the leg to move a shorter distance before hitting the target, which means a speedier kick. In terms of versatility, it means that the same chamber is used, for example, with the front snap kick, the front push kick, the turning kick, and bent-leg axe kicks. That makes it possible for you to make split-second changes during the course of an offensive, and it also increases the variety of available feints.

Thrust

While launching a kick, it often helps to push from the supporting leg, rather than allow it to remain passive. This is particularly useful if you need to cover distance to the target, and is a virtual necessity when using any of the linear kicks, such as the front push kick, the side kick, the cut kick, or the back kick. It is a key concept in the tournament ring, where controlling the distance between you and your opponent can make the difference between a solid point and a clean miss. Thrusting off the supporting leg can also help to prevent falling away from the target, or falling backward, when performing spinning hook kicks or combinations with spinning hook kicks.

Head In

In most kicks, the tendency of both beginners and seasoned practitioners is to allow the head to fall back, away from the target. Whether you are moving backward, forward, or just staying in one place, you should always try to keep your head forward, toward your target. Otherwise you will find yourself falling backward and not thrusting the power of your kick ahead, into the target. Keeping your head forward is also the safest way to protect yourself against blows aimed at your chin or face.

Rechamber

While there is nothing new in recommending a snappy rechamber of the leg after any kick, we mention it here because it plays an important technical and strategic role. Rechamber your leg fully after every kick in order to: 1) prevent your opponent from grabbing your leg; 2) regain the support of your fighting stance, allowing you to throw another kick as quickly as possible; 3) complete the turn in spinning techniques, whether they be back kicks, narabams, or spinning hook kicks. Concentrate on rechambering your leg as quickly as you throw the kick.

Keep all of these common principles in mind as you study and refine your kicking technique. Most of the time, when students need coaching on a specific technique or need to refine their approach, it's because one of these keys is missing.

For the sake of simplicity, all kicks are discussed from the point of view of fighting stance. Nevertheless it is possible to perform many, if not most, kicks from other traditional stances like front stance and back stance, and you should make an effort to master the kicks from these positions as well, particularly those that appear in the poomse.

Kicking Surfaces and Foot Positions

Just as there are a variety of surfaces available to the hands for use as striking surfaces, so there are with the feet. These are the ball of the foot; the top of the foot, or instep; the back of the heel; the bottom of the heel; the sole of the foot; and the inside and outside edges of the foot. When using the ball of the foot, the foot is pointed (in the case of the front snap kick) or flexed (in the case of some turning kicks), with the toes pulled back. To use the top of the foot, common in turning kicks and in kicks to the groin, point the foot and the toes. Keep the ankle relaxed to strike with the sole of the foot or the back of the heel, and flex the foot to strike with the bottom of the heel or with the back of the heel.

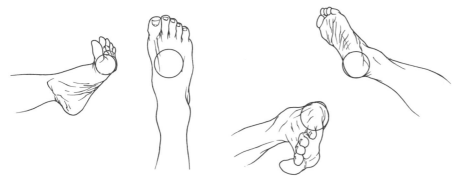

Individual kicks call for specific portions of the foot to be used. Pay attention to correct foot position at all times.

Front Kicks

The kick most easily learned by beginners, the front kick is an excellent standby technique both for self-defense and, in certain modifications, for tournament sparring. There are two common variations on the theme of the kick swinging straight in from the straight chamber: the front snap kick and the front push kick.

Front Snap Kick (*Ap-Chagi*)

The front snap kick rises straight up in front of you, chambered with a bent knee. The foot snaps out and back in as quickly as possible, and the ball of the pointed foot provides the striking surface. The toes must be pulled back or they'll be injured upon contact.

The front snap kick involves five basic movements:

1. Rear knee rises straight up, bent, into standard straight chamber position. The fully bent knee points at the target; where the knee points, the lower leg will follow.
2. The lower legs snaps out like the uncoiling of a whip. The foot is pointed and the toes are pulled back, exposing the ball of the foot as the kicking surface. If the toes are left relaxed, there is a danger of harming them upon contact with the target.

3. The hip rotates into the kick. The supporting foot simultaneously pivots on its ball, the heel of the foot moving to the inside. This allows the hip of the kicking leg to turn. The hips should move at least ninety degrees.

4. The leg rechambers and the hip and supporting foot return to starting position.

5. The kicking leg steps positively into position, either to the back or the front, depending on your direction of travel (to the back if you are stationary).

Try not to lean back when you kick. Instead, lean forward, keeping your head in rather than allowing it to fall back. If you allow your head and body weight to move backward, you will often find yourself falling away from your target rather than moving your body weight into it. You will also have difficulty moving forward, because your tendency will be to fall back.

To change the elevation of your kick, do not move the knee after the kick itself has been thrown—that is, after the knee has begun to straighten. You want to target your kick with your knee in the chamber position; to kick high, raise the knee high and aim it at the target. If your opponent's knee is your target, then keep your own chambered knee low. The exception to the general rule is found in the front push kick, discussed below.

Also keep in mind that if you intend to kick to the groin, you may want to use the top of your foot rather than the ball, in order to kick up into the target more easily. We highly recommend this technique for self-defense.

The above description applies to the rear leg front snap kick, but you can also throw the front snap kick with the front leg. The motions are essentially the same, except that the hips won't rotate as much, as they will already be close to the fully rotated position. To maximize your power with the front leg, you have to give a push with your supporting leg to throw your hip into the kick as much as possible.

Front Push Kick (*Meereo Chagi*)

One of the most useful sparring tactics, along with other linear kicks like the side kick and the closely related cut kick, the front push kick uses the strength of the legs to give an opponent a great shove. It's the kick seen on television police dramas, when a door needs to be kicked in. In actual confrontations or

in the tournament ring, it can be used offensively, thrown with the rear leg or with the front leg and a skip step. It allows the front leg to become a powerful defender, as it is possible to lift it quickly into position to fend off an opponent's hand or foot attack, and, chambered, it is a potent blocking method.

The push kick differs from the snap kick in that the knee is lifted as high as possible, regardless of target, and the striking surface may be either the ball of the pointed foot or, more commonly, the flat bottom of the foot, with the foot flexed. The movements are as follows:

1. Lift the attacking knee, fully bent, as high as possible.
2. Flex the foot to hit with the sole; if you need the additional range, point the foot with toes pulled back.
3. Allow the supporting foot to pivot on its ball as you rotate your hips into the kick.
4. Extend your kick straight out; the chambered knee will drop as the kick extends. Reach as far as possible. Lean in.
5. Rechamber the kick and set the foot down in front.

Make sure your recovery does not leave you off balance. It is tempting when throwing the front push kick to lean back. Avoid this impulse.

As with the front snap kick, this can be performed with either the front or the rear leg. Using the front leg, you can fend off most attacks. With a skip step, you can launch a powerful offensive that can move an opponent all the way across the ring or set yourself up for any of a number of follow-up kicks.

Axe Kick *(Naeryo-Chagi)*

The axe kick is meant to be lifted above an opponent's head and then brought down forcefully on the bridge of the nose or, conceivably, using the back of the heel, on the clavicle. Beginners learn the axe kick easily because it is so closely related to the stretch kick. Although the axe kick has to travel a fair distance before striking, it is surprisingly useful in sparring situations because it is easily confused with other kicks and infiltrates an opponent's defense with a fair amount of stealth.

Typically, the axe kick is delivered with the sole of the foot or the ball of the extended foot. These positions allow the foot to be extended with a pointed or relaxed ankle, both of which will contribute to flexibility and extension of the leg. However, the back of the heel is a hard and potent striking surface if you are limber enough to flex the foot fully and still lift it high over an opponent's head. The back of the heel has the advantage of delivering greater force; the sole and ball of the foot share the advantage of greater height and greater range, which make it easier to hit rather than miss.

The movements of the axe kick are simple.

1. Lift the kicking leg straight up, with the knee straight, as high as possible. Ideally, the leg, at the apex of the kick, will be high over your head.
2. Allow the supporting foot to pivot and the hips to turn into the kick.
3. Bring the kick down, knee straight, as hard as possible, concentrating your power at the head level. *Do not* allow your foot to slam into the ground. Lean forward, not backward. Control the descent of the kick after the delivery of power in the target zone.
4. Step either forward or backward positively, controlling your balance.

The axe kick can be especially effective with a push from the supporting leg. With practice, it is possible to slide several feet forward as the kick is raised, simultaneously allowing you to cover distance to the target and to close in while the kick is coming up. The axe kick makes a quick attack using the front foot or an effective counterattack or follow-up kick with either leg.

There are several variations of the axe kick that may be suitable under different circumstances. Try bringing the leg up with a straight chamber or bent knee, as with the front kick, and straightening the leg once the knee is fully raised. This bent-leg axe kick often surprises an opponent and grants you the option of throwing an axe kick, front kick, or turning kick before you have fully committed to any of them. In recent years, the bent-leg axe kick has become the preferred version of this technique.

You can also bring the leg up to the inside or the outside like a crescent kick, swinging it around in a circle in order to clear the opponent's shoulder, for instance, or to gain clearance if your bodies are too close to raise the kick straight in front of you. The kick is then unloaded as it crests over from the inside or outside. Try combining this technique with the bent-leg chamber rather than the straight leg.

Crescent Kick

The crescent kick is a close cousin of the axe kick, as it involves a straight leg and is meant to strike at the head level exclusively. The difference here is that the crescent kick strikes with the inside or outside of the foot as it sweeps through the target zone in a quick arc. Also like the axe kick, it is easily learned by beginners, as it derives directly from the crescent kicks commonly performed during warm-up. The movements necessary to perform the crescent kick are virtually identical to those used to perform the axe kick, with the exception of their circular motion. There are two types of crescent kicks: the outside crescent kick and the inside crescent kick.

Outside Crescent Kick (*Bakkat-Bandal Chagi*)

The outside crescent kick describes a circle—or, more properly, an ellipse—that begins by swinging the straight leg across the body, up, and over to the outside before bringing it down. The outside edge of the foot is used to strike the side of the opponent's head as you whip the kick across its highest point. You have the option of keeping the leg straight for a more traditional crescent kick or using the bent chamber for a snappier release.

Don't forget to allow the supporting foot to pivot and to use the full range of your hip's motion to propel your leg through the arc of the kick.

The motion of the outside crescent, and the motion of the inside crescent kick as well, also serves as an effective delivery for the axe kick, as already noted.

In sparring situations, we have noticed that the outside crescent kick is most often effective when thrown with the front leg. In closed stance, this has the advantage of arcing in over the opponent's lead shoulder and is thus hard to see or predict. In open stance, it is possible to attack with the outside crescent kick and often avoid the opponent's rear-leg turning kick attack, although against a speedy opponent with good timing you will have to beware of the underkick (see Chapter 5, "Steps and Footwork," and Chapter 9, "Sparring," for a discussion of closed and open stances and underkicks).

A potent variation of the outside crescent kick is to combine it with a reverse step, resulting in a spinning crescent kick. It is very quick and is especially useful—not to mention surprising—in close quarters, and should be practiced by students who lack the hip flexibility to throw effective spinning hook kicks.

Inside Crescent Kick (*An-Bandal Chagi*)

Somewhat more physically difficult to perform than the outside crescent kick, the inside crescent kick begins with the straight leg rising out to the side and curving in high across the head level. Use the inside of the foot as the striking surface and rely on the motion of the hips and the forward angle of your head to guarantee power. As with the outside crescent kick, you can also use this motion to deliver an axe kick. In fact, the inside crescent is commonly seen as a means of getting the foot into axe kick position—that is, over an opponent's head.

As the outside crescent kick is often seen to be more effective when thrown with the front leg, so the inside crescent kick finds its greatest usefulness when thrown with the rear leg. In closed stance, the rear-leg inside crescent approaches the opponent over the lead shoulder, and may be difficult for the opponent to see. In open stance, the outside crescent kick can easily be confused with push kicks or turning kicks. Used as a lead-in to the bent-leg axe kick in open stance, the inside crescent kick also allows you to cover distance easily because it lends itself to a forward slide.

Turning Kick *(Dollyo-Chagi)*

Frequently referred to as the roundhouse kick, the turning kick is the staple technique of every Taekwondoist's arsenal. ("Turning kick" is a more accurate translation of the Korean term for the kick than is "roundhouse," which is more figurative.) In tournaments from the local level to the international, turning kicks dominate the action. Faster and more versatile than any other kick, turning kicks combine easily with other techniques and are easily thrown in quick series. It would be difficult to exaggerate their importance in Taekwondo. Some would say that a competitor need only have excellent turning kicks, a good cut kick, and perhaps an effective axe kick to win consistently. But even those who favor a more diverse arsenal than this depend on the turning kick most of the time. It would not be surprising to discover that most competitors use at least four times as many turning kicks as any other. They are often the first choice of attack and the first choice of counterattack.

The turning kick is equally useful in self-defense applications. It can deliver a crippling blow to the knee or the groin as well as the midsection or even the head. And its versatility in combination with punches means that it is an ideal choice for following through after a combination of punches or other hand strikes.

Of all the kicks in Taekwondo, the turning kick takes greatest advantage of the modern development of the straight chamber. The combination of the straight chamber with the turned hips and horizontal motion of the kick makes the turning kick somewhat tricky for beginners to learn, even if it does later become the most preferred kick.

The turning kick's attack is angular; that is, it strikes at the side of the opponent rather than the front. The striking surface is the top of the foot, the instep. Its basic motions are as follows:

1. Chamber straight up. Lift the knee to point at the target, as with front snap kick.
2. Keeping the knee pointed at the target and the leg bent, pivot the supporting foot fully 180 degrees. The supporting heel will point directly at the target. The hips will turn over completely, with the hip of the kicking leg directly in line with the target or even slightly past it.
3. Snap the kick out with an extended foot. At the moment the top of the foot makes contact, there should be a nearly perfect straight line extending from the ankle of the kicking leg up through the leg, the hip, and the shoulder. The lower leg moves parallel to the ground as it snaps the kick.
4. Rechamber the leg with the knee up.
5. Step positively back or forward, depending on your direction of travel.

To throw turning kick to the high section, chamber the knee higher. Try not to lean back too much. Leaning back is a hard habit to break and all too common. It will prevent you from moving forward with your kick and sap power from the technique. Keep your head in.

There are a great number of drills you can do to make the turning kick more effective. Here are suggestions for some:

In place. The basic drill for turning kick. Perform a set of kicks with each leg, kicking with the back leg and returning the kicking leg to the rear after each kick.

Step forward. The ability to move forward in the course of an attack is critical. It increases power and enhances your ability to follow through with subsequent attacks. After the kick off the back leg, rechamber and step forward into a solid fighting stance. Concentrate on regaining your fighting position simultaneously with the step forward.

Double kicks. Throw two kicks, one with each leg, in rapid succession, stepping forward with each one. Try this combination kicking with the back leg first and with the front leg first. When you use this combination, don't worry about turning the hips completely into the first kick. Completely turned hips will actually make it difficult to throw the next kick in the series, and most Taekwondoists, competitors and noncompetitors alike, initiate the series with a turning kick that angles upward rather than one that is perfectly horizontal. However, it is important that the last kick in the series turn over all the way. You will find that the faster you can rechamber the first kick, the faster you can raise the second, so make sure you include a speedy rechamber in your development of this technique.

Double kicks, low/high. The same drill, but throw the first kick to the midsection, the second one to the high section.

Double kicks, airborne. Throw two kicks moving forward, but throw the second one before putting the foot down after the first. The second kick will be airborne. However, do not jump up when performing this combination. Try to shoot yourself forward rather than up. In order to throw a fast and powerful second kick, use your lead leg as a lever while it is still in the air after the first kick. Pull it back and down sharply; its leverage will turn your hips over and pull the second kick up.

Triple kicks. As with double kicks, but one more kick added. Try this one stepping forward and also airborne.

Performing the turning kick with the front leg is trickier than performing the front snap kick or front push kick with the front leg. Use the same chamber, but push more forcefully with the supporting foot to make the hips turn all the way into the kick. Don't let your butt stick out; push all the way through. Practice this kick a number of times. The front-leg turning kick is sometimes called the "quick kick" or "fast kick," because it can be thrown in a flash.

It is also important to practice a retreating turning kick. Turn to Chapter 9, "Sparring," for details and tips on this technique.

Narabam

The narabam is a common but tricky modification of the turning kick that can often prove useful in the ring and can add impressively to the turning kick's power. We don't recommend it to beginners until they become comfortable with the turning kick and the reverse step.

Sometimes referred to as a reverse 360-degree roundhouse or a spinning roundhouse kick, the narabam streamlines the reverse-step/turning kick combination (see Chapter 5, "Steps and Footwork," for a discussion of reverse step), making it quicker and more powerful. Begin with the basic reverse step motion: the lead foot pivots inward, heel toward the target. The rear foot slides directly ahead and steps out in front; however, in this variation, the foot does not step down. Use it as a lever while it is in the air to pull your hips around and throw the turning kick with the other leg. It is very important to pull the hips all the way over with this technique, or you will not gain all the range or the speed the kick can afford. Strive to spin quickly and kick parallel to the ground.

Experiment using the narabam in combination with other kicks, particularly other turning kick combinations. For a tricky combination, try it with the spinning hook kick, throwing the narabam first and then the spinning hook kick before stepping down after the narabam.

Side Kick *(Yeop-Chagi)*

The side kick is one of the best known of all kicks, owing to its graceful appearance and the strength of its impact. A sharp, well-executed side kick is the hallmark of a good Koryo and requires diligent practice. Of the three most basic kicks (front kick, turning kick, and side kick), side kick is the most difficult to master. However, it may be even more useful as a self-defense technique than the others, particularly when aimed at the knee, and can deliver a mighty blow to the midsection.

The side kick is also extremely useful in tournament sparring. Long-legged fighters often rely on it as a front-leg technique. Likewise, the front-leg side kick serves admirably as a defense against most attacks, along with the front push kick and the cut kick.

The side kick uses one of two striking surfaces: the bottom of the heel or the outside edge of the foot near the heel, also known as the blade of the foot. The motion of the side kick is linear, like the front push kick. Once chambered, the foot moves straight at a frontal target. The basic technique of the side kick is as follows:

1. Straight-chamber the rear leg, but modified so that the blade of the foot points directly at the target. This means the knee will drop somewhat to the side and your body will turn early so that the side corresponding to the kicking leg faces the target. Regardless of the height of the kick, chamber the leg as high as possible. The knee will drop into line as the kick is executed.
2. The supporting foot pivots 180 degrees, the blade of the foot pointing toward the target.
3. Extend the kick so that the striking surface extends straight into the target. It should neither curve nor dip. For many practitioners and most beginners, this is the most difficult element of the kick. Avoid the temptation to swing the foot. It travels in a precisely straight line.

4. At the moment of contact, the foot should be fully flexed with the toes pointed slightly down. The foot is tensed and the blade of the foot is extended into the target; the ankle should be pulled inward and back.

5. Rechamber the kick and step positively either backward or forward.

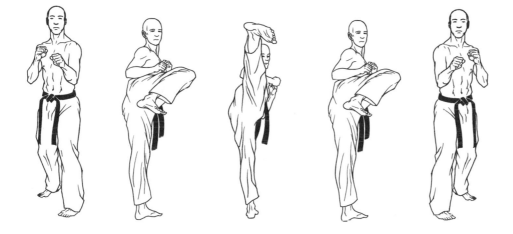

As with the turning kick, your body should be lined up from the ankle to the knee to the hip to the shoulder. It can be difficult not to turn the shoulders all the way over, exposing part of the back and turning the back partly forward, but you should try to avoid this.

Because the side kick is so useful in sparring situations, there are many drills and step combinations you can do to make the technique quick and effective, particularly to enhance the front leg's ability to rise and strike quickly. Try the following variations as you build up drills and combinations.

Front-Leg Side Kick (*Apbal Yeop-Chagi*)

Although the front-leg side kick does not differ from the rear-leg side kick in terms of technique, the footwork used to launch it can make the kick either subtle and quick or massively powerful. The kind of approach you use will be determined by circumstances—whether your opponent is near or far, for instance, and whether you are attacking or defending.

Execute a front-leg side kick simply by lifting the front knee into chamber position, pivoting the supporting foot as described, and kicking. You can build on this concept in two ways.

The first is to thrust with your supporting leg as you throw the kick.

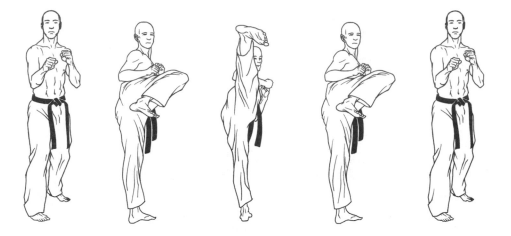

Thrust hard enough so that you slide forward. Your forward motion will increase the power of the kick and, more important, bring you into your opponent. This technique can be very quick and subtle. Be careful not to move the rear foot before chambering the front foot, or you will lose the advantage of surprise. The sliding side kick is very useful either as a quick attack or as a counterattack to an opponent closing in.

Perhaps the best way to maximize power with the side kick is to combine the front-leg side kick with a step forward. The movement forward when executing a side kick differs from the usual jeonjin step. Slide the rear foot behind and past the front foot with the heel pointing toward the target, anticipating the chamber position. Now chamber the front leg for side kick and strike. You will have covered the distance to the target with the step, moved your body weight into the target, and streamlined the chamber by combining the pivot of the supporting foot with the step forward. Concentrate on stepping smoothly and as quickly as possible when practicing this movement.

Cut Kick

The cut kick is a hybrid of the front push kick and the side kick, developed out of tournament sparring. It is another example of how the need for speed and efficient movement in the ring has affected Taekwondo method in recent years.

Often performed with the front leg, the cut kick requires simply that you chamber your front knee up high at an angle of about forty-five degrees and then kick straight out, push-kick style. The foot remains at a slanted angle, with the toes pointing diagonally upward, and the hips do not turn all the way around. If you need extra reach, the kicking foot can be extended, front-kick style, with the toes pulled back, and the ball of the foot rather than the whole sole used to push the opponent.

This kick does not have the power of either of its progenitors, but it is an excellent means of creating or maintaining distance between you and your opponent and is highly recommended both as a lead-in to further attacks and as a quick front-leg counter. It will be discussed in greater depth in Chapter 9, "Sparring."

Back Kick *(Dwi-Chagi)*

The back kick is another popular nominee for Taekwondo's most powerful kick. It is not uncommon to see knockouts in the ring scored by a back-kick blow to the body. With practice, it can be thrown extremely quickly. It's a natural combination with the turning kick and a natural counterattack to the turning kick. It can deliver a powerful blow even when retreating. With sufficient practice, the back kick is also one of the safer kicks to throw, because it does not offer your opponent any targets; the main thing to be wary of is the recovery phase of the kick, when you must keep your hands up and rechamber properly to regain a solid fighting position.

The most common image used to describe the back kick is that of a mule kicking backward. With your back turned to your opponent, the foot rises up and kicks straight behind you with the bottom of the heel. The motion takes full advantage of the largest muscle in the body, the gluteus maximus, to deliver the blow, as well as the energy of the spin as you turn into the kick.

Over the last few years, various forms of the back kick have emerged, each with their own benefits. The primary differences occur in the position of the shoulders and the position of the chamber. Both will be explained below. In any case, the striking surface is the bottom of the heel, with the foot fully flexed.

1. Pivot the lead foot so that the heel points directly at the target. Simultaneously turn the shoulders so that your back is turned to the opponent.
2. Bend slightly at the waist.
3. There is almost no chamber for this kick. Lift the kicking foot (not the

lead foot) so that the knee is bent. Do not lift the knee; it remains low and close to the other leg. Keep the supporting leg as straight as possible.

4. Kick straight behind you. The kicking motion is almost a flick; imagine the foot flicking up from the ground and flying straight back. You may look over your shoulder at the target; instructors differ as to the necessity of turning to see the target. The kick can be thrown accurately either way.

5. Rechamber fully after the kick and step down in front, completing the turn. Even though the chamber for the kick is minimal, rechamber with the knee raised. This will help you turn completely around quickly and regain a balanced, responsive fighting position. Be sure to keep your hands up in guard position.

At one time, the back kick was usually taught with the knee of the kicking leg rising, tucked under the midsection before releasing the kick. This method delivers great power; however, it may also slow the kick and it may contribute to difficulty in controlling the tendency of the knee to rise to the outside, resulting in a hooking motion that costs both accuracy and power.

Some schools teach that the shoulders should turn over fully as the kick is thrown so that the body aligns with the target, while others teach students to keep the shoulders facing squarely away from the target. Advocates of both positions rank among the world's best competitors and coaches. Beginners may learn the basic motion of the back kick more easily with the shoulders facing away from the target, which will help them keep the knees close together.

As you become more comfortable with the kick, allow the shoulders to rotate farther. This will increase the power of the kick. Note that if you reach out with the kick, striving to cover a greater distance, the shoulder will rotate automatically. Experiment with both techniques and identify which one works best for you.

Practice the back kick moving forward. To improve your accuracy, be sure to move forward in a straight line. Also practice in combination with an ilbo-junjin step. This move, also called the stepping-in back kick, can be a powerful attack. If you step forward without putting the foot down and then throw the back kick airborne, you will have executed a 360-degree back kick.

One of the best defensive techniques, apart from the back kick from a stationary position, is the back kick thrown simultaneously with a switch of stance, so that you will move backward with an incoming attack and meet the attacker with a powerful counter. For more information on sparring applications of the back kick, see Chapter 9.

Hook Kick *(Nakka-Chagi)*

The hook kick most closely resembles a backward turning kick, using the back of the heel or the sole of foot as the striking surface. It is the precursor to one of the most spectacular, powerful, and surprising Taekwondo techniques, the spinning hook kick.

You can often surprise an opponent with the hook kick, but it takes practice to get the hips to open up properly and to deliver real power. The hook kick is most effective at the extremes, either thrown to the head or thrown to the lower leg and used as a sweep.

1. Chamber the front knee as high as possible (except for the sweep, which requires a low chamber).
2. Pivot the supporting foot 180 degrees and drop the chambered knee sideways. This resembles the side-kick chamber.
3. Extend the foot straight out to one side of the target, with the hips turned around completely.
4. Snap the foot back, hooking it so that it travels along a path parallel to the floor. The kick ends with the knee fully bent.
5. Rechamber and set the foot down in front.

It is also possible to throw the hook kick from the rear leg, although it is slower and more difficult. Nonetheless, the hook kick from the rear leg can offer an excellent fake turning kick as the knee rises and your body turns to position the leg for the strike.

For greater effectiveness, combine the front-leg hook kick with the same step used for the stepping-in side kick, sliding the rear foot behind the front foot, then chambering and throwing the hook kick. Practice increasing the speed of this step so that it becomes a skip-in, with the kick chambering as you begin the skip and striking as you slide forward.

Spinning Hook Kick *(Dwi-Dollyo Chagi)*

Over the years, the spinning hook kick has become Taekwondo's premier kick in terms of flash and surprise. In tournament sparring, the spinning hook kick may be responsible for the greatest number of knockouts. It has cunning defensive applications and, if timed properly and thrown quickly, can be a devastating attack. As with the hook kick, fully realizing the spinning hook kick's potential requires a good degree of flexibility in the hips, as well as excellent balance and control of spin.

The spinning hook kick goes by many different names, including "back turning hook kick," "spinning heel kick," "wheel kick," and "turning back kick." Some of these names, such as "wheel kick," refer to a similar but different technique, while others refer to different aspects of the kick's motion. In addition to the numerous names by which it is known, there are numerous theories about the best way to throw the spinning hook kick, including differences in the chamber position, the angle of the kick, and at what point during the spin the kick begins. These differences, together with its basic mechanics, make the spinning hook kick one of Taekwondo's most difficult kicks to master.

Nevertheless, the spinning hook kick shares a fair amount of common ground with other techniques. At the most basic—and most traditional—level, the spinning hook kick combines a reverse turn with a traditional hook kick. Here is the method for the traditional spinning hook kick:

1. Pivot the lead foot so that the heel faces the target. Turn and look over your shoulder at the target.
2. Lift the knee of the rear leg, fully bent, up and to the outside as you would for a traditional hook kick.
3. Snap a hook kick to the head level target, striking with the back of the heel with a flexed foot or the sole of the extended foot. Bend at the waist as the kick rises. At the point of contact, the foot, knee, hip, and shoulder are in line with each other. Be sure that the kick sweeps horizontally through the target area. It should sweep neither up nor down.
4. Rechamber the kick and complete the turn, coming all the way back to the starting position.

The description probably makes the kick sound easier than it is. The difficulty for most students arises with the need to make the pivot, the chamber, and the kick itself flow smoothly and quickly enough that an opponent will not see the kick coming. Also, many students tend to fall backward when

throwing the spinning hook kick. To avoid this, concentrate on pushing your body weight forward, making the supporting leg active rather than passive.

It is not easy to avoid telegraphing your intention with this kick. Nonetheless, once you manage to weld the different parts together into one seamless technique, you will be able to strike with great speed and force.

Recently, masters have begun to eliminate the kick's chamber position with the knee lifted to the outside in much the same way that the chamber position for the back kick has largely disappeared. For the most part, this modification makes the kick faster and less visible; with a further modification to the kick, it becomes an extremely effective counterattack. Practice this version of the spinning hook kick with the chambered leg kept low rather than lifted to the outside. This motion somewhat resembles a back kick to the head, except of course that the kick extends to the side of the target and then sweeps through the target in a circular motion as you continue the spin instead of striking linearly. Note that because the chambered leg begins so low, this variation depends on the spin to pull the kick horizontally through the target; its motion is not truly circular by itself, as it would be with an outside chamber.

You should also practice stepping down in front as you complete the kick, instead of turning a full 360 degrees. This requires a speedy rechambering, and a push forward with the supporting leg is virtually critical, or you will not be able to step forward quickly.

You can use the spinning hook kick to launch a powerful attack by combining it with an ilbo-jeonjin step, taking a step forward before throwing the kick. We call this the stepping-in spinning hook kick. Apart from covering distance, the ilbo-jeonjin step will help you accelerate your spin. If you don't put your lead foot down after taking the ilbo-jeonjin step and launch the spinning hook kick while the lead foot is suspended a few inches off the floor, you'll have executed a 360-degree spinning hook kick even faster than the stepping-in spinning hook kick.

It is important to keep in mind that the higher your lead foot is suspended in the air, the higher your 360-degree kick will be, especially if you allow your head to drop when you throw the kick. If you seem to be having trouble zeroing in on your target, try lowering the lead foot.

To use the spinning hook kick defensively, as an opponent rushes in, the chamber vanishes altogether. Pivot and swing the kicking leg straight up behind you, allowing the knee to bend at the top of the arc as you finish the turn. The kick will strike diagonally upward through the target instead of horizontally. Try thinking of the kick as an upside-down axe kick, striking on its upward course.

Enhance the defensive spinning hook kick's effectiveness by switching the supporting foot backward simultaneously with the kick. This will allow you to retreat at the same time that you throw the kick, matching an opponent's advance, and it will also allow you to use the supporting leg as a lever to help you turn quickly and throw the kick up.

For more information about sparring use of the spinning hook kick, refer to Chapter 9, "Sparring."

Flying Kicks

Flying kicks belong to that family of techniques everyone has seen in the movies. In reality, relatively few flying versions of the standard Taekwondo kicks appear much in sparring situations, although they can be spectacular demonstration techniques and are great audience pleasers.

Just about any kick can be thrown while flying through the air; the limit is your imagination. We mention two of the most common here.

Flying Side Kick *(Twio Bakkuwo Yeop-Chagi)*

This is certainly the most famous of the flying kicks. The most important thing to remember when throwing the flying side kick is to lift both knees as high as possible and keep the opposite leg tucked tightly throughout the kick. Here is the method:

1. Get a good running start.
2. Jump off the nonkicking leg.
3. As you jump, rotate your body sideways, leading with the side you plan to kick with, and lean back slightly.
4. Lift both knees as high as you can.
5. Kick out with the leading leg, keeping your body sideways and your other leg tightly tucked.

The technique, as you can see, is fairly simple to describe, but throwing a good flying side kick requires much practice.

Flying Back Kick *(Twio On Mom Dollyo Dwi-Chagi)*

The flying back kick is basically the same as the 360-degree back kick, but with the addition of a running start. Be careful not to over-rotate while airborne.

CHAPTER 9

Sparring *(Gyoroogi)*

The Sparring Mind • Sparring and Taekwondo Values • Targets • Stance and Distance • The Four Abilities •
The Three Strategies • Sparring Drills • Tournament Rules • Ring Management • Coaching

Generally speaking, Taekwondo sparring reflects one of two scenarios: competitive and self-defense. The physical requirements of these two realms differ because of their inherent differences in purpose. Competitive sparring challenges you to display your superiority within a highly regulated environment. In the tournament ring, you can reasonably expect certain responses to your attacks and you can reasonably expect to offer certain defenses, all under the watchful eye of a referee or, in your dojang, your instructor. Significantly, competitive sparring pits you against a skilled adversary, where a mistake can mean taking a punishing blow that will leave you breathless or, in the worst case, unconscious. But when defending yourself from a violent assailant, on the other hand, you move in a far more random and unpredictable universe where you cannot reasonably anticipate your opponent's responses, although you may often assume that your opponent will rely on punches and grappling. However uneducated in fighting technique your attacker may be, it can be a terrible mistake to underestimate his abilities or his resources. Here there are no rules, no watchful referee to prevent you from being kicked when you're down or from being assaulted with a weapon.

The Sparring Mind

When we teach self-defense, we begin our lessons or seminars with a discussion about the role of your own psychology in violent situations. (This is especially true in women's self-defense, owing to the social conditioning most women experience, which tends to stress the traditionally feminine qualities of reserve and modesty, frequently at the cost of assertiveness and self-confidence.) You must be willing to commit yourself to protecting your body at all costs. That means that any attack you initiate must be carried through to its end, without hesitation or compromise, using every tool at your disposal.

We believe that this axiom applies to competitive sparring, as well (within the limits of the rules, of course). Serious training and the development of a serious and alert frame of mind will produce much of the psychology necessary to protect yourself outside the tournament setting. Likewise, the strategies described here will perform equally well under all circumstances, and Taekwondo technique, fast and powerful, will help you to prevail. As you train to spar, strive to be a complete martial artist, neglecting none of the wealth of technique that comprises Taekwondo.

Sparring and Taekwondo Values

Nowhere else in the practice of Taekwondo do your frame of mind and core attitude make as important a difference as in sparring practice or competition. This is where the value system ingrained by Taekwondo training, with its stress on mutual respect, a sense of justice, and indomitability of spirit, comes fully into play. Without maintaining a clear sense of your purpose and an absolute sense of respect for your partner or your opponent, you cannot hope to prevail in the ring or to grow through your class training.

Your physical growth as a martial artist will benefit through your sparring training as you refine your basic Taekwondo technique and adapt it to application, making your responses automatic and even instantaneous. At the same time, your strength and stamina will reach new levels.

Even more important than the physical growth you can expect, your mental growth will also benefit. There is no greater way to build a sense of self-confidence than to experience the challenges of rigorous sparring and to overcome all the obstacles you will encounter along the way, ranging from learning how to use your footwork and techniques when confronted with an actual opponent to learning how to defeat your opponent's strategy.

Targets

Sparring in the tournament ring demands a high degree of care and ability. In self-defense, a number of vital targets beckon. They include the eyes, the temples, the throat, the elbows, the solar plexus, the kidneys, the floating ribs, the groin, the outsides of the thighs, and the knees, to name a few. You don't need to have tremendous flexibility or athleticism to deliver a painful blow to many of these.

In the ring, however, you may strike only above the belt, you must avoid the neck, the spinal region, and the back of the head, and you may punch to the body but not to the head. While these limitations still leave a generous number of targets, you must consider your opponent's blocking ability and evasiveness as well. While the solar plexus is a tempting target, it can be very difficult to strike because the defender's elbows often interfere. Anyone who has accidentally smacked the point of an opponent's elbow with a turning kick can attest to the painfulness of the resulting swollen bruise in the top of the foot. Therefore, you should aim your midsection kicks at the level of the belt itself, just below your opponent's elbows. A strong kick to the gut can be just as effective as a blow to the solar plexus. Keep your kicks thrown to the kidney side below the elbows as well, although here you must be equally careful to avoid the rock-hard pelvic bone.

As far as self-defense is concerned, it should be noted that while a blow to the groin can have a crippling effect, it is not always an easy area to hit. Most men have a quick and instinctive reflex to cover the groin should it come under attack. For this reason, strike at the groin only when it is clearly undefended. Otherwise, use kicks to the legs and use knee strikes to the middle of the thigh or the abdomen.

Stance and Distance

Maintain an agile, comfortable fighting stance at all times. Most fighters have a particular way of standing based on the essential principles of the fighting stance (see Chapter 4, "Stances"). When moving around the ring, never twist your legs. For example, do not cross your front foot over your rear foot, or draw your rear foot across and behind the front foot, unless you are spinning.

Crossing your feet is a sure way to see that your opponent can strike you while you trip over your own feet. (This is not the same as allowing one foot to *pass* the other from front to back, or vice versa, which, of course, is necessary for stepping.) Also, never square up with someone within their striking range. When two fighters stand within each other's range, striking becomes a simple matter of which fighter is faster. This is a gamble you frequently cannot afford to take. It is much wiser to stand just out of range, outside the "hittable" distance. This will protect you from a faster opponent, and it will also allow you more time to see what your opponent is trying to do.

Standing outside of hittable distance will require you to plot out your attacks more carefully, since a single kick will not work—you will be too far away, unless you can slide forward quickly at the same time that you throw the kick. Maintaining proper and safe distance is a more sensible way to spar, but it also means that you will have to fight a smarter fight, something you should strive for anyway.

The Four Abilities

There are four particular areas of physical ability that you need to refine to a razor's sharpness in order to spar with excellence. They are technique, steps, agility, and timing. These stand apart from the realm of general physical fitness, which includes flexibility, strength, and both aerobic and anaerobic stamina. (See Chapter 3, "Warming Up," which discusses flexibility in some detail.) All students know that Taekwondo training strengthens the body substantially. But you can build on this strength in ways that are especially helpful to your sparring. Likewise, rigorous Taekwondo training profoundly affects a student's stamina levels, but here, too, there are exercises to practice outside the dojang that can have a radical effect on one's fighting trim. In the agility section of this chapter, you can read about what kind of cross-training you can do to improve your strength, speed, and aerobic and anaerobic capacities.

Technique

Broadly speaking, tournament sparring technique is no different from Taekwondo technique as commonly practiced. While some kicks appear far more commonly in the tournament ring than others, all have their time and place.

This is not true for hand strikes, which are strictly limited by the rules of WTF-style sparring. The modifications to basic Taekwondo technique for sparring applications all have to do with legal targets and control of distance to account for either offensive or defensive scenarios. (For a more comprehensive discussion of tournament rules and limitations on techniques, as well as a discussion of the purpose behind these innovations, please refer to the section called "Tournament Rules" on page 180.)

Controlling your distance from your target while attacking or defending will help guarantee that your target is actually in range, or "hittable." Explosive technique also plays a key role in sparring. Your opponent should not be able to anticipate your movements by watching you. That means that you need to avoid telegraphing your intentions. Often, you can give yourself away by initiating a kick too slowly, so that your opponent can see it coming and have plenty of time not only to avoid it but to launch a dangerous counterattack. Try to explode into every attack and into every step. That way you will achieve maximum power and maximum surprise, and you will give your opponent far less time to respond to your onslaught. When kicking with the rear leg, don't move the front foot first unless you are trying to close the distance.

Keep the principles of distance and explosiveness in mind as you practice the following techniques.

THE REAR-LEG KICKS

As a general rule, it is preferable to attack and counterattack with rear-leg kicks because, with few exceptions, they pack more power than the front-leg kicks. Kicking with the rear leg allows you to take full advantage of the rotation of the hips, which both vastly amplifies your power and helps you to move forward quickly.

The Turning Kick

The turning kick is the staple of any Taekwondoist's repertoire. It is more than an invaluable sparring tool; it is indispensable. The rear-leg turning kick should be your most versatile kick and among the fastest, and you should be able to use it in multiple series and in combination with any other kick.

Attacks

The various combinations of turning kicks and kicks and footwork are limited only by your imagination. But some have become so commonplace and have proven so effective in tournament situations from the local to the international level that we include them here. They are simple and direct. Two in particular, the double turning kick and the triple turning kick, have already been discussed in Chapter 8, "Kicks." Practice them in every sparring class, using a variety of targets including paddles, a heavy bag, a body shield, and a partner wearing a hogu (for more on hogu practice, see the "Sparring Drills" section in this chapter on page 173).

Keep your head in the fight, literally: except for special cases, it should be forward, not behind you.

Build on the double and triple turning kicks by combining them with each of the forward-moving steps: the jeonjin, ilbo-jeonjin, and reverse steps. Develop your ability to throw kicks prior to steps, after steps, and in between steps. Always concentrate on controlling your body weight. Keep it moving forward—don't allow your head to fall back. In addition to practicing turning kicks with reverse step, be sure to practice them in combination with narabams as well.

While you can achieve some of the most useful applications of the turning kick by using them in rapid combination, you also need to learn to exploit the hip rotation of the rear-leg turning kick. Once you throw the rear-leg turning kick, you can follow through with a spinning or reverse turn technique, such as reverse-step turning kick, narabam, back kick, or spinning hook kick. As with double and triple turning kicks, it is always important to rechamber as quickly as possible. In the case of turning kick/spinning kick combinations, the rechamber facilitates two things: First, it provides support by getting the foot back on the floor. Second, it actually contributes to the speed of your spin and gets you back into fighting stance more quickly. Think of a skater spinning on the ice. As she extends her leg, she slows; as she pulls it in, she spins faster and faster. The same principle applies to your kicks. (This phenomenon is referred to by physicists and engineers as conservation of angular momentum. The overall momentum of a rotating object or system remains the same regardless of changes in the system's radius. For instance, when you throw a spinning kick, your foot moves at a certain speed, or number of meters per second. That speed will remain the same whether your leg is extended at the peak of your kick or is pulled in while rechambering. Since the rate of meters per second remains constant, your spin will increase when the foot is closer to your body and slow when the foot is farther away.)

Defense

Combining the turning kick with retreating steps makes for some of the most effective defensive techniques Taekwondo has to offer. Notice that the turning kick in combination with any of the retreating steps results first in a retreat and then, as you kick, an advance. This offers terrific advantages in that it can turn a rout into a solid hit or a point. But it will not always be possible to advance upon an opponent who is also advancing, for the simple reason that you may not have adequate room in which to kick. You will, therefore, frequently need to counterattack while simultaneously retreating. The basic means of doing this relies not so much on any of the steps per se as on a switch of stance.

The stance switch performed simultaneously with a kick is important to master both as a skill and as a strategy. Practice the retreating turning kick (also known as the "switch kick" and "counter turning kick") by throwing a rear-leg turning kick and simultaneously sliding the supporting foot back, so that the supporting foot takes up the previous position of the rear foot. This will cause your body to pivot around the midpoint of your stance instead of pivoting around the axis of your front foot, which results in the kick being thrown virtually in place as the hips rotate into the kick. With a more energetic switch, you can slide back behind the original position of your kicking foot and actually retreat while kicking.

Once you have worked out the move, practice with a partner holding a target paddle. The paddle holder will advance; as the holder advances, you retreat, simultaneously kicking the paddle. Also practice with a partner holding a body shield. Develop the concept of the switch kick further by throwing two or three in a row, retreating each time.

In addition to the switch kick, another important defensive use of the turning kick combines the switch kick with the basic sidestep. Very simply, you step out to the open (abdominal) side with the back leg, and as you draw the front leg in to follow, you throw the rear-leg turning kick. This allows sideways evasion with a simultaneous counterattack.

Finally, you can offer a devious and effective counter to spinning hook kick and back kick attacks with a technique that has come to be known as the underkick. Practice this technique with an attacking partner. Begin in closed stance. The attacker throws a spinning hook kick. In response, throw a switch kick, but lean back at the same time so that the attacker's kick misses. As the attacker's body rotates with the spinning hook kick, your turning kick will find its target. This counterattack requires precise timing and judgment of distance. You don't want to take a kick to the head just so that you can respond with a kick to the midsection. With practice, however, the underkick will consistently allow you to evade and respond.

Once you have become comfortable with the spinning hook kick/under-kick combination, practice the underkick as a counter to the back kick. Because the back kick typically aims low, not to the head, you may find it necessary to use a sidestepping switch kick as you lean back in order to avoid the attack completely.

Back Kick

The back kick is a critical technique for effective and sophisticated fighters. As mentioned in the "Kicks" section in Chapter 8, "Kicks," it packs a tremendous blow, and it is one of the most potent defensive techniques in Taekwondo. But with strongly developed footwork and kick combinations, it can also provide you with a cannonlike offense.

Attacks

The back kick can form the basis for a powerful attack—so powerful, in fact, that knockout blows can result from a solid back-kick shot to the body, even with the hogu. While most competitors find that a back kick off the line (that is, when used as an initiating attack) rarely succeeds, they have also discovered that the back kick combines with other kicks, and with feints and traps, well enough to form a punishing attack.

First, strengthen your stepping-in back kick. The stepping-in back kick forms the basis for most other back-kick combinations. In some cases, one ilbo-jeonjin step forward will be all you need to close distance, create an opening, and build momentum for the back kick. You must make that initial step forward extremely quickly, or your opponent may retreat out of range or otherwise be prepared for your assault. Many instructors teach that the stepping foot should be placed down with the toes pointed backward and the heel of the foot pointing directly at the target, in order to get an early start on the spin. While this is a good way to learn the basic technique, we advise that you streamline the step further and eliminate the preliminary turn of the stepping foot. That turn can telegraph your intentions to a perceptive opponent and cost you the advantage of surprise.

You can further strengthen your offensive back kick by concentrating on the thrust of your supporting leg. The concept of supporting thrust is a principle common to all basic kicks, and is no less so in sparring situations. As you move forward with the back kick, drive in toward your target, reaching with your striking heel and pushing with the supporting leg.

Once you have mastered the basic mechanics of the stepping-in back kick, practice the turning kick/back kick combination, throwing the turning kick first, immediately followed by the back kick as you step forward after the turning kick. Then practice the same combination, but use the turning kick only as a feint to draw your opponent's guard to the side, opening up the frontal target for the back kick.

Build further on back-kick attacks by practicing them in combination with side kicks and with multiple-step footwork.

Defense

The back kick is a traditional counterattack to the open-stance turning kick, and this is probably the context in which it most frequently appears. You will find that as you initiate the back kick, you will be protected from the attacker's turning kick by your arm, which offers a natural down block, and your head will be lowered out of harm's way. At the same time, the attacker has presented a frontal target in the course of rotating to deliver the turning kick, and it is this you are aiming at as you flick the back kick up and in. With practice, your back kick will become a huge disincentive to an attacker who hopes to rely on a simple turning kick.

You can make your defensive back kick more versatile by combining it with a switch of stance, similar to that described for the retreating turning kick. Sometimes you will not have enough space to use your back kick, especially with an onrushing attacker, and you will need to retreat in order to obtain the necessary range. The stance switch will allow you to accomplish this. If you break the move down into its parts, you will see that the switch back kick is actually a combination of the back kick with a reverse ilbo-hoojin step. As you draw your lead foot back toward the toe side of the rear foot in reverse ilbo-hoojin step, throw the back kick. This retreat adds a powerful spin to the thrust of the back kick.

Practice these defensive maneuvers with a partner holding a body shield. The shield holder plays the role of the attacker, holding the shield out to the side. As the holder steps forward, he or she suddenly turns the shield to the front, offering a target for the back kick.

Spinning Hook Kick

This most flamboyant of Taekwondo techniques is often responsible for making Taekwondo competition the grand spectacle that it can be. It is likely that the majority of knockouts are scored with the spinning hook kick. Anyone who has seen one thrown with all the panache a trained fighter can muster will be impressed by its devious speed and power. You will learn to use the spinning hook kick like the back kick, exercising different kinds of footwork to take advantage of its offensive and defensive capabilities.

Attacks

Most Taekwondoists do not have the speed to make the spinning hook kick effective off the line. This is largely because the kicking foot itself must travel a fairly long distance before reaching its target, like a high-section turning kick, and that distance is further increased by the reverse spin, which takes a beat longer to execute than a forward hip rotation, and in fact has more distance to cover than a forward rotation of the hips. (Just look at the position of your hips in fighting stance: the rear hip is not directly behind the front hip, but slightly to the front side, not the rear.)

The extra time required to throw the spinning hook kick simply means that you must integrate this kick with footwork. Practice throwing the spinning hook kick in combination with turning kicks and with the ilbo-jeonjin step. Also practice attacking with the 360-degree spinning hook kick. You may want to double-check the coaching tips for this kick in Chapter 8, "Kicks."

Be as aggressive as possible when using the spinning hook kick offensively. Shying away from your attack with this kick will usually cause you to lose your balance or slow the kick enough to let your opponent get away. Commit yourself completely to this kick when you use it. Confidence in your technique and an accurate gauge of range will score points.

Defense

Defensively as well as offensively, the spinning hook kick is analogous to the back kick. This is basically because the reverse turn allows you to offer an effective and comparatively safe counterattack to the open-side turning kick, and you can also apply the stance-switching technique in retreat, as with the back kick, to help you control your range. However, the spinning hook kick also offers a counterattack to axe kicks that may be more technically feasible than the back kick, given some of the restrictions of tournament rules. (Naturally, tournament rule considerations do not apply to situations of self-defense.)

Use the spinning hook kick defense in the same situations where the back kick is effective: open-stance turning kick attacks, closed-stance front-leg turning kicks, and any time you retreat, especially during reverse ilbo-hoojin retreats. The spinning hook kick offers a cunning response to front-leg axe kicks that come in from behind your lead shoulder—a back kick thrown in this situation may easily strike the groin, which in tournaments is illegal, but the spinning hook kick usually won't (unless you have a flexibility limitation).

Front Push Kick

Rear-leg front push kicks can deliver a powerful wallop to the midsection, throw your opponent off balance, and drive him backward, allowing you to follow through with a coup de grâce such as a back kick, double turning kick, or spinning hook kick, any of which combinations may easily result in multiple potent blows landed and more than one point being awarded.

Attacks

The front push kick is a very safe technique to use, because your high-chambered knee will protect you against most attacks and because the kick delivers such a powerful shove that you will be safe from most counterattacks. Look for openings to use this kick, especially in open stance and any time your opponent presents a frontal target. You should always seek to follow your front push kick attack with another attack, because if the blow does not weaken your opponent by itself it will almost always give you an opportunity to strike again. Don't waste that chance.

Make an extra effort to thrust powerfully with your supporting leg when you attack with the push kick. That thrust will bring you closer, or, if you are already close enough, it will help drive your opponent back.

Defense

The front push kick is a handy and easy defense anytime your opponent presents that frontal target. Look for it during open-stance turning kick attacks.

Perhaps the trickiest and most useful defensive application of the push kick is as a counter to the back kick. As soon as your opponent begins the rotation, throw your push kick. Aim directly at the waist or slightly below it. You will usually force your opponent to stagger away, the back kick aborted. Follow through instantly with turning kicks to the opponent's ribs. This defense can also work against narabams and spinning hook kicks, although we recommend the underkick against the spinning hook kick.

THE FRONT-LEG KICKS

Front leg kicks can be used to initiate a sequence of attack moves quickly, generally with a rear-leg kick following the front-leg kick, and they can be used to great advantage as defensive maneuvers. A good front-leg fighter can be very difficult to hit, because the active front leg guarantees a safe distance from attacks by means of front push kicks or side kicks. At the same time, that front leg can be quickly raised with the knee bent in defense against turning kicks. Barking your shin against a raised defensive knee will make you think twice before using the same attack again. The turning kick, the cut kick (along with its close cousins, the push kick and the side kick), and the axe kick all make excellent front-leg weapons.

Turning Kick

As noted in Chapter 8, "Kicks," the front-leg turning kick is a bit more difficult to master than the more familiar rear-leg turning kick, but is well worth the effort. The front-leg turning kick is also called the "fast kick," because with it you can strike with lightning speed. Because it does not fend off an advancing opponent as a linear kick would, it is more useful in attack than in defense, and it works particularly well in concert with a quick rear-leg turning kick or a back kick. As you practice the kick, following the guidelines on pages 134–36, try to incorporate combinations of other turning kicks, back kicks, and spinning hook kicks.

Probably the most potent application of the front-leg turning kick is in combination with a jeonjin step, resulting in the skipping-in turning kick. This technique is actually easier to master than the standard fast kick. Begin the jeonjin step by sliding the rear foot forward to match the front foot. Then throw the fast kick, stepping down in front afterward. You will have advanced by the length of one step while simultaneously throwing a turning kick without changing your lead (jeonjin steps always result in the same lead). Practice the skipping-in turning kick in combination with other turning kicks. Start with a turning kick followed by a skipping-in turning kick. You will have kicked twice with the same foot. Then try throwing the skipping-in turning kick first, followed by the rear-leg turning kick.

A useful and subtle variation of the skipping-in turning kick is to chamber the kick without first moving the supporting foot and then thrust with the supporting leg as you throw the kick. The thrust will move you forward by as much as a foot, which gives you the advantages of surprise and advance, and will increase your power as well.

Cut Kick

In this discussion, we will use the term "cut kick" to refer to three linear kicks interchangeably: front push kick, side kick, and cut kick. Actually, the front push kick is probably more frequently launched from the rear leg, not the front leg, while in sparring situations the side kick and cut kick are often launched from the front leg rather than the rear leg.

Develop a fast cut kick and use it to counter an opponent's rear-leg kick. A quick shove to the opponent's midsection as his kick comes up can both prevent the kick from being fully launched and provide a chance to follow up with a variety of attacks, such as the front-leg axe kick, using the cut kick foot again, or the rear-leg turning kick. The back kick is another good follow-up from this position, especially if the cut kick has succeeded in driving the opponent back.

The cut kick, as will be discussed later in the section on offensive tactics, is also an excellent launch for an attack combination, because it creates the space you will need to stage further kicks and gives you an opportunity to chase an opponent. It is also a safe way to launch an attack, as your leg position allows you to cover your target areas. In a tournament setting, opportunities to chase are a critical consideration, as you will see in the discussion of ring management in this chapter.

The cut kick turned fully into side-kick position delivers a potent blow and can certainly be a point-scorer, particularly if performed as a stepping-in side kick.

Develop quick cut kicks and quick side kicks. If you have long legs, the front-leg kicks are especially effective in both attack and defense.

Axe Kick

The front-leg axe kick is another excellent means of initiating an attack. It is a deceptive technique, because as the leg rises it is easily mistaken for a turning kick or push kick (especially with a bent knee chamber, rather than a straight leg), both of which are more frequently aimed at the midsection level than the head level. The defender will, therefore, usually drop the defense to that area, leaving the head exposed. A favorite front-leg axe kick attack in closed stance is to bring the front leg up in an outside crescent kick motion, so that the foot rises in the opponent's blind spot behind his or her lead shoulder. Beware of the spinning hook kick or the under kick counter to this attack.

Try using the front-leg axe kick with a jeonjin step so that you slide forward into the attack. Also try it with a slide but without the jeonjin step. You can achieve this by raising the front leg bent and, as it rises, thrusting forward with the supporting foot so that you actually slide forward. This is a very subtle means of gaining ground without signaling your opponent by moving the rear foot that you are closing in.

PUNCHES

Taekwondo tournament judges are known to disregard punches when it comes down to awarding points for blows struck during a match, except in cases where punches are strong enough to knock someone down. Even when someone is being battered by powerful strikes to the midsection, judges almost always prefer to score kicks over punches. Do not let this fact of tournament life discourage you from using punches, however. Even if the judges never award you a point for landing a solid punch, strong body blows will take their toll on your opponent. Anytime you close within arm's reach, you should throw a flurry of punches, aiming for the solar plexus or the kidneys. You can also aim for your opponent's shoulders. This won't knock her wind out or knock her down, but anyone whose shoulders are being bruised will think twice before coming too close. Use your defensive jamming technique (see the "Stance and Distance" section on page 151) as a vehicle for your punches. Distance always plays a part in the options available to you, and when the distance is too small to throw a kick, use your hands. Remember: every moment in the ring counts, and every contact provides you an opportunity. Practice your basic punches regularly. Punches can make the difference between otherwise well-matched opponents as you plunge into the breach afforded by well-timed blocks and footwork.

Attacks

Although it is rare to do so, an attack may be launched with a lunging punch. Use the reverse punch, coupled with a lunging step into front stance, to knock your opponent back or shock his wind as you wind up for a follow-through with turning kicks or other attacks. If you have reached the point of exhaustion during your match, you can use lunge punches, followed by a clinch, to sap your opponent's energy while you recover.

Develop your ability to throw a down block with one arm while you punch with the other. This technique—the "cover punch"—will help protect you from turning kicks as you close in.

Defense

A punch can function as a perfectly suitable counterattack to a turning kick. Block the kick with a down block while you close in with a lunging punch, using the opposite hand. If you maintain solid footing, you may be able to throw multiple punches and leave your opponent gasping—a perfect time to follow through with a tough body blow, such as a solid turning kick, side kick, or back kick.

Steps

This is such an important area of sparring skill that it has its own chapter, as does the area of technique and kicks. We mention it here to emphasize its significance to the arsenal of winning tournament fighters.

As described in Chapter 5, "Steps and Footwork," there are two primary positions occupied by sparring partners: open stance and closed stance. In open stance, each fighter leads with an opposite foot (one right, the other left), so that their abdomens face the same direction. In this position, for example, each partner is vulnerable to the other's rear-leg turning kick. In closed stance, both partners lead with the same foot (right and right or left and left), so that their abdomens face opposite directions. In this position, both may be vulnerable to the other's front-leg turning kick. When sparring, you must constantly evaluate your position, whether open or closed, and how that position affects your ability to attack and to counter your opponent. You want to play to your own strengths, and to exploit any of your opponent's weaknesses that you may perceive. Additionally, you must also control the intervening distance, ensuring that it is neither too small nor too large for your strategy.

Both open stance and closed stance result from linear footwork—in-place stance switches and the jeonjin, ilbo-jeonjin, hoojin, and ilbo-hoojin steps, in addition to the reverse steps. In the open and closed stances, both partners move along the same line of travel, and those lines meet head-on. But the use of evasive yeop steps introduces two important secondary positions, where the paths do not meet head-on but rather intersect at right or oblique angles. This occurs when one partner advances and the other yeop steps. The partner who performed the yeop step will now be offset ninety degrees from the attacker's line of travel, and the partner who advanced will generally face the defender squarely, with full abdominal exposure, instead of presenting the narrow target normally afforded by the fighting stance.

Diligent practice of the basic steps will make you an above-average fighter all by itself. The ability to determine your distance from your opponent through judgment and action will help guarantee that you are close enough to hit and far away enough to avoid being hit. Many fighters find themselves missing their mark not because their opponents evade them but because they have not developed the ability to judge accurately when they are in kicking range. Review all your footwork carefully, and exploit your superior agility to see that you command a dominant position.

Agility

Agility is best described as a fighter's ability to explode off the mat into an attack. In its rawest form, agility bestows quickness, allowing a fighter to strike first in a race of techniques; for instance, two competitors facing each other in open stance will each look for a chance to deliver a turning kick to the open side, using the rear leg—the most effective and most commonly scored sparring tactic. Discounting the influence of sneaky trapping and other fakes, the fighter with greater agility can often win the race and be able to strike first. In tandem with excellent timing, agility will also allow a fighter to deliver counterattacks at just the right moment, beating an attacker's efforts to score points. Last, but by no means least, agility is what will permit a fighter to move around the mat quickly, always commanding a viable fighting position.

In recent years, coaches and masters have learned a great deal not only from their own accumulated experience but also from the coaching innovations developed in other sports. Currently, two particular cross-training methods have proved especially effective in increasing agility. These are running, including both distance and sprints, and plyometrics. Cross-training can also produce highly therapeutic results, helping sore or injured muscles regain their integrity and strength, and also helping in the prevention of injuries.

Ideally, a cross-training regimen aimed at improving agility and conditioning includes six days of workouts per week for elite athletes, apart from sparring practice and drills. It is important to keep one day aside for rest. Overtraining often results in injuries and exhaustion rather than improvement.

RUNNING

A combination of distance running and sprint workouts will make you a faster, stronger fighter in the tournament ring. The distance running will improve your aerobic capacity, which is the ability to sustain effort over a long period of time, and the sprints will build up your anaerobic capacity, or the ability to explode in short bursts of activity and to recover quickly. Anaerobic capacity is especially important to tournament fighters because sparring is primarily anaerobic, consisting of short, extreme bursts of energy with very short rest periods, rather than more sustained effort. Sprint workouts will ensure that you can last out a full match of three three-minute rounds without getting tired, and that you can reenter the ring after a rest period of a minute or less and feel refreshed.

Three days a week, on alternate days, go for a three- to five-mile run. Record your time and do your best to outperform yourself. As your condition improves, your runs should be closer to the five-mile mark, not the three.

Find yourself a running track on the nondistance days so that you can easily mark your distances for sprint workouts. Here's one track workout recommended for Olympic Taekwondoists:

Distance	Reps	Pace	Rests
880 yards	3	Beginners: 4 minutes per rep; Advanced: 3 minutes or faster for first rep; 3:15 or faster for each of the next two	Beginners: 2 minutes; Advanced: 1 minute
440 yards	3	1:15 per lap	1 minute
220 yards	4	Full speed sprint	Beginners jog ½ lap to recover; Advanced jog ¼ lap to recover
100 yards	5	Faster than 15 seconds	30 seconds
50 yards	7–10	5 seconds	Jog back

The paces indicated in the chart are not terribly fast by track racing standards. Look for improvement as your body strengthens. The important thing is to make yourself run faster than the minimum pace, and, more important still, to limit your rest periods. Limiting the rest periods improves your body's ability to recover quickly.

ADDITIONAL DRILLS

Mix in some other kinds of legwork to help you develop speed and power. On sprint days, do a set of speed drills using basic knee-up exercises. On distance days, do stairs, plyometrics, and speed kicks.

Sprint Days: Knee-ups

Begin in fighting stance. Lift the rear knee swiftly to your chest, then drop the foot back to its original position. As the knee comes up, bounce on the other foot; as the knee drops, bounce again. Keep bouncing rhythmically, once on the way up, once on the way down. Do thirty knee-ups as fast as you can, then switch legs and do thirty with the other knee. Do three sets each.

Do a set of knee-ups using two targets. Have a partner hold out both hands in front of you, about waist high. Lift the knee thirty times, hitting first one of the partner's hands, then the other. Again, do three sets of thirty with each leg.

Have a partner or the instructor time the sets of knee-ups, and strive to make every set faster than the last. You can also do ten-second drills, where you do knee-ups with one leg as fast as possible for ten seconds. Then switch legs and repeat the drill. Do this three times. Record the number of knee-ups you do, and try to do more in every ten-second period.

You can expand upon the knee-up drill and enhance your agility further by incorporating movement into the knee-up exercise. Move forward every time the knee comes up. Do this for both legs. Then move backward every time the knee comes up. Don't worry about how far you move with the knee-up; just concern yourself with the speed of the knee.

Distance Days

Stairs

Use a one-story flight of stairs, equal to about twenty steps. Run the steps three times without skipping steps. Your speed down is just as important as your speed up. Try to make each set as quick as the last. Once you've done the three sets, do three more, this time skipping steps.

Plyometrics

"Plyometrics" refers to exercises that are designed to improve your ability to explode off the mat with great speed. This in turn will improve your kick off the line. Here are five plyometric exercises.

Partner jumps. One partner sits on the floor with legs outstretched. The other partner jumps back and forth over the partner's legs with both feet together. Do not bounce between the jumps; jump directly from one side to the other. Jumping over once and back counts as one. Do thirty, then switch. Alternate back and forth with your partner. Do a total of three sets of thirty.

Partner hops. Now hop back and forth with one foot, the other foot held up in the air. Do three sets of fifteen, alternating with your partner.

Jackknives. Finally, do three sets of thirty jackknives. Jump up and lift both legs together straight out in front of you, reaching out to touch your toes.

Double box jumps. Find a pair of large, sturdy boxes or crates, or use a pair of sturdy tables for the next drill. The crates or tables should be about waist high. Start by standing on one. Jump down to the floor and bounce up onto the other one. Don't bounce up and down while you are on the floor; the idea is to bounce like a ball. Turn around and repeat. Do this thirty times.

Single box jumps. Next, use just one of the crates or tables and jump up onto it from the floor, then turn around and jump down. Do this thirty times.

If you do all these exercises with some regularity, you will find yourself becoming increasingly faster in the ring.

Timing

In between powerful technique and nimble agility lies timing, the ability to throw a kick or punch when a target is available. Inexperienced fighters often find themselves frustrated as they try to kick at what seemed to be an exposed abdomen or kidney, only to clash with a raised knee, have the attack blocked, miss completely, or, at worst, blunder right into a counterattack. Various remedies exist for each of these errors. Some involve improved technique; to avoid clashes with the opponent's legs, for instance, one might improve control, in order to be able to stop a kick when the target disappears or a defensive knee rises. To avoid a block, one might improve control so that the midsection kick becomes a high-section kick, or learn to feint to one area when actually attacking another. Some remedies involve agility; instead of missing a target completely, one adjusts range during attack or defense, controlling the intervening distance rather than being manipulated by it. Instead of staggering into a back kick, the agile fighter will sidestep or backstep and offer a counterattack.

No other aspect of sparring is as difficult to master or maintain as is timing, and no other aspect of sparring diminishes as rapidly with neglect. Sparring practice and timing drills are the only ways to improve and maintain a fine sense of timing. Raw speed may offer some compensation for weak timing, but even fighters without great speed can seem much faster than they actually are if they have the ability to strike at just the right moment, while fast fighters, if their timing is soft, may still find themselves at just the wrong range or pounded by counterattacks.

The Three Strategies

Once you have begun to develop the physical abilities you need to become a daunting opponent, you can begin to put them to use on a higher level. At this stage, you can kick hard and fast. You can change stance, move in and out with your opponent's motion, strike when your opponent is open, retreat, and generally move with a sense of control. Now you need to determine what strategies will help guarantee victory.

"Strategy" refers to the overall planning required to ensure the success of your objective. In the case of tournament sparring, the objective is to outscore your opponent, and, if the opportunity presents itself, to cut the match short by means of knockout. In the case of self-defense, the objective is to avoid injury and to protect those in your care. The objectives in these two cases differ drastically: the objective of tournament sparring encourages some risk-taking (and the rules of scoring, as well as the rules governing tiebreakers, favor those with an aggressive strategy), while the objective of self-defense suggests that avoidance of confrontation is the surest path. The strategies presented here apply to both tournament sparring and to self-defense situations once conflict becomes unavoidable.

Sparring situations present three different modes of action: offensive, defensive, and trap. Fighting offensively, you take the initiative and launch an aggressive attack sequence, driving into your opponent with combinations of techniques. Speed is critical. Defensive fighting requires you to respond to your attacker with evasion and counterattacks, taking advantage of the openings that every attack provides. Defensive fighting emphasizes split-second timing. Trap fighting requires you to masquerade as an offensive fighter in hopes of drawing a counterattack, to which you will respond with yet another counterattack.

You can see that the three strategies can be divided into levels of action, with offense at the first level (one action), defense at the second level (action/reaction), and trap at the third level (action/reaction/response). For a fighter with a sophisticated understanding of these three modes, no single mode is superior to the others. Each one provides unique opportunities, and to succeed, each one requires different kinds of ability. Offensive fighting, for example, requires terrific speed if blows are to land without incurring counterattacks, while defensive fighting requires excellent timing so that attacks are avoided while powerful blows are launched in response. Trap fighting requires a combination of these two, along with an ability to predict an opponent's counterattack.

Many students become strong in one of these areas at the expense of the others. For beginners, offensive fighting is the easiest and most obvious way to spar, especially as they haven't had sufficient practice at developing a sense of timing. Students with more experience understand the shortcomings of pure offensive fighting and learn that sometimes it is better to wait and counterattack. Defensive fighting is also the refuge of the exhausted. Students who have gained more substantial experience try to integrate offensive and defensive fighting into trap fighting, using feints to lure opponents into preset traps—forcing a back kick, for example, in order to strike with a push kick or turning kick.

A masterful fighter, however, understands the complete relationship of each of these strategies to the others, and smoothly switches modes in response to the opponent's actions. One need not be a master, however, to understand the triangular relationship among the three strategies·

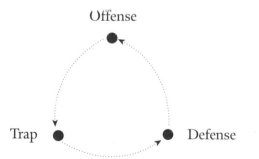

Offense

Trap   Defense

As you can see, an offensive fighter will prevail against a trap fighter, a trap fighter will prevail against a defensive fighter, and a defensive fighter will prevail against an offensive fighter. The offensive fighter will defeat the trap fighter because the trap fighter is essentially setting a bait, expecting a particular response. If you understand what response is expected, you can attack differently, in different combinations, or choose not to attack at all; you can, in essence, trap the trapper. The defensive fighter will defeat the offensive fighter because keen timing essentially makes counterattack simple; you can wait for your opponent to make an error or allow an opening, and respond instantly. The trap fighter will defeat the defensive fighter because the defensive fighter, stuck in counterattack mode, will respond to the trap fighter's lures. Use your ability to evaluate your opponent's mode and adjust your strategy accordingly.

Of course, you can't expect your opponent to rely on one set of tactics all the time. Be prepared to alter your own strategy instantly; if your opponent suddenly becomes highly aggressive, switch to defensive fighting. If your opponent starts trying to wait you out, set traps. And if your opponent starts using numerous feints, choose a moment between his false attacks and assail him with everything you have.

Tactics

"Tactics" are the specific means by which strategic goals are achieved. If your strategy calls for offensive action, then your tactics are those of offense and may include stepping-in kicks, double turning kicks, and so on. If your strategy calls for defensive action, then your tactics may include hoojin step followed by a switch-back kick.

Remember, an offensive fighter will prevail against a trap fighter, a trap fighter will prevail against a defensive fighter, and a defensive fighter will prevail against an offensive fighter. You must constantly evaluate your opponent's mode and adjust your strategy accordingly.

OFFENSIVE TACTICS

Three considerations must underlie all attacks. They are speed, vulnerability, and distance. Certain initial attacks, while popular, are not recommended because they leave you open to a counterattack either after delivery or, in some cases, before you can launch the kick. Some others are too slow, and some will not close the distance from your opponent sufficiently to afford a solid hit.

A single turning kick without any accompanying footwork will not usually score, because a smart fighter will be standing out of range of a single kick, and a competent fighter will be able to offer an effective counterattack to a single kick. Seek to throw multiple turning kicks. Double and triple turning kicks, as mentioned earlier, have become the dominant means of scoring in U.S. tournaments, a trend particularly noticeable at the national level. The best choice of offenses is determined primarily by a fighter's technical and physical strengths, but there are some strategic considerations to keep in mind.

Speed is absolutely essential in offensive fighting. Develop your speed using drills described under the "Agility" section in this chapter on page 164, so that you can feel confident in throwing kicks before receiving a counterattack.

You want to avoid attacks that invite simple counterattacks. For instance, in open stance, avoid throwing the front-leg cut kick. It is too easy for the defender to offer an outward-sliding switch turning kick and hit the open side. Also avoid attacking with a straightforward spinning hook kick, because for most people it is too slow and is too difficult to recover from—again, the switch turning kick is an effective counter. Lead into the spinning hook kick with a turning kick, a cut kick, or with other footwork to establish forward momentum and to drive the opponent back. Of course, if your opponent is foolish enough to stand in range of your spinning hook kick, and if you have the speed, then throw it for a quick point or a knockout. The same rule generally applies to the back kick. It is difficult to connect with the back kick straight off the line. Instead, lead into the back kick with a turning kick or with a cut kick. Note that if you choose to lead with a cut kick and you are in open stance, follow the guideline above and cut kick with the rear leg.

When using the front-leg cut kick or front-leg turning kick, be careful what kind of footwork you use to carry you into range. If you use jeonjin step, the initial movement of your rear leg may carry you into range of your opponent's turning kick before you can strike. Avoid this by using the shuffle jeonjin step—that way, the knee of your kicking leg will be raised in a defensive position before your opponent has a chance to strike at you.

Defensive Tactics

Taekwondo sparring proves the adage that the best defense is a strong offense. Many of the knockouts seen in the tournament ring result not from offensive maneuvers but from counterattacks. Attacking often leaves one vulnerable. Defensive fighting is the science of dissecting an attacker's tactics and taking advantage of every weakness. For every attack, there is an effective counterattack. Mastering those counterattacks requires three things: timing, so that the split-second instant of vulnerability is long enough, adaptability to changes in offensive tactics, and instinctive response to standard attacks.

There are no hard-and-fast rules to learning defense. Timing is the most important quality one must have, and to that end, practice of timing drills is the best medicine for one's defensive ability. Adaptability is the result of long training in offensive maneuvers, agility skills, and analysis of an opponent's strategy. Instinctive responses to standard attack patterns, however, are different. Use this chart to help yourself design drills to improve your defensive capability.

Attack	Defense	Footwork
In open stance, rear-leg turning kick to open side	Back kick Spinning hook kick	If attacker is charging, simultaneous switch. If not, footwork may not be necessary.
In closed stance, open-side fast kick	Short back kick	Short switch, at most. Opponent is very close if you are in range of open-side fast kick.
Cut kick, closed stance, rear leg moving first in jeonjin step	Axe kick	
Cut kick, closed stance, front leg moving first (shuffle jeonjin step)	Front-leg cut kick, pushing down attacker's cut kick, followed by back kick	Shuffle jeonjin step
Axe kick from open or closed stance	Spinning hook kick Jumping spinning hook kick	The jump lifts your body high enough so that the axe kick, even if it hits you during your kick, is ineffective.
Back kick, closed stance	Switch turning kick	Simultaneous slide to the open side
Spinning hook kick	Underkick (bada-chagi)	Simultaneous switch (in this case, drop your head back, not forward)
Cover punch	Axe kick or short turning kick	

TRAP TACTICS

Trap fighting requires the most sophisticated understanding of sparring exchange. As mentioned earlier, offensive and defensive strategies are respectively single- and double-layered, and trap fighting is triple-layered. It requires you to masquerade as an offensive fighter, while your true intent is to play as a defensive fighter by luring your opponent into a counterattack to which you can offer a response—if you are lucky, a premeditated response.

To trap most effectively, you need to be able to predict your opponent's counterattacks. Unless you have previously studied his or her fighting style, you won't have this information before you step into the ring. You will have to watch your opponent carefully to figure out his or her favorite counterattacks.

Then you can offer traps to lure the opponent into your counter.

The basic method of trap fighting is fairly well known. Generally, there are two kinds of traps: those using the front leg, and those using the rear leg. The shoulders also play an important role, especially for rear-leg traps.

Trapping is often called "checking." For the front-leg trap, lift the front knee slightly as if you were preparing to throw a cut kick or a fast kick. This is in the hopes of drawing your opponent's back kick, which will allow you to respond with the underkick (the switch turning kick), as listed above. Sometimes it helps to stomp slightly, to further the illusion that you are attacking or pressing forward. If your opponent offers a different counterattack—for example, an axe kick—you can respond with a spinning hook kick, as suggested in the chart.

Check with the rear leg by rotating your rear shoulder forward slightly, with a quick motion. This duplicates the upper-body motion of the rear-leg turning kick and can fool someone watching your shoulders. Enhance the illusion by lifting the rear knee slightly. If you draw the back kick or the spinning hook kick, you can, again, use the underkick.

Sometimes your opponent will not react at all to your traps. This indicates that he or she has switched from defensive fighting to offensive, and you will need to be careful in the moments between your trap efforts, or you may find yourself suddenly needing to counterattack a technique you had not anticipated. Other times, an opponent's response to your traps will be to move backward, which means that you will need to throw a combination of attacks in order to chase him or her down.

Again, good trap fighting requires great preparation, wariness, and consideration of your opponent's favorite tactics. Like the offensive and defensive fighting, there are few hard-and-fast rules—you will have to adapt to changing circumstances.

Sparring Drills

In addition to frequent practice of footwork, which you should include in every sparring session as a warm-up and general drill, you should work on a series of drills specifically designed to help you refine your tactics and techniques. Nothing will help you to gauge and determine your distance better than controlled contact drills. We use three kinds of targets: light kicking pads, body shields, and partners wearing protective gear. In developing drill routines to incorporate into your workouts, be imaginative and practical. Use the suggestions in the sections on tactics to help you develop drills of your own.

Remember that the drills described below reflect only a portion of the drills you might practice. The variety of kicks you can perform on targets is endless, and you should experiment to devise drills and combinations that develop the skills you specifically need to sharpen. Keep some basic rules in mind:

- Many of the drills described under one section ("Kidney Pads," for example), can be performed with the targets described in another section ("Shields or Heavy Bag").
- When devising drills, try to combine techniques that make sense and flow together efficiently.
- Try to make the drills you practice motion-oriented and interactive as opposed to static. In other words, don't just ask your partner to stand still while you take your time setting up and executing the kick; have your partner check and feint and give you different distances. The interactivity of the drill will help your partner too.
- Try to simulate live action, incorporating steps, checks, and feints into your drills. This will improve your ability to respond in actual sparring situations.

Note for pad holders—your job is extremely important both for the effectiveness of the drill and the safety of the kicker. Stay alert at all times, and present the pad properly, quickly, and surely each time your partner kicks.

Move quickly and powerfully. Speed is essential. Remember that the looser and more relaxed you are, the faster you will be. Always keep your body weight moving forward and always recover in a full, agile fighting stance.

Defense drills force you to attack only when the target appears. With practice, you will find yourself straining less to see the perfect moment to strike and beginning to sense the openings. A good fighter's ability to land kicks or punches can seem uncanny—sometimes it just doesn't seem possible to act fast enough to strike during those infinitesimal moments that an opponent's vulnerability is exposed. Yet a good fighter doesn't act by responding solely to a glimpse of an opening. Rather, he or she learns to react to an opponent's overall motion, based on a thorough understanding of how any fighter moves.

Defense marries technique to timing. Concentrate on relaxing, staying light on your feet, and moving only when you need to. Do not anticipate your target; wait for the right moment, and strike hard when it appears.

When drilling trap techniques, it is just as important to work on the check or feint itself as it is to react to the countermotion of the target holder. Make your checks and feints quick, supple, and convincing. Remember that if you are going to check, you need to be mindful of what you are checking for and how you plan to react.

Kidney Pads

Kidney-shaped pads or other focus pads are great tools for developing speed and accuracy. They are particularly useful for developing speedy turning kicks, axe/push kicks, and spinning hook kicks. Back kicks on kidney pads are more difficult, and are better practiced on shields. Try some of the following drills:

SINGLE TECHNIQUES
Warm up by throwing some of your basic sparring kicks (turning kick, axe kick, and spinning hook kick) on these pads held as stationary targets. Then incorporate steps, checks, and feints before the kicks. When practicing these basic kicks, develop a good follow-through, so that you end up in a properly balanced fighting stance as quickly as possible after the kick. For example, when practicing your turning kick, make sure that you rechamber after the kick, quickly scopping your knee up toward your body and forcing the kicking foot down, landing in a good (and not over-rotated) fighting stance, ready to kick again.

COMBINATION TECHNIQUES
After executing single techniques, add to the level of difficulty by kicking in combinations. For example, try the following:

- Double turning kicks: rear leg kicking first and landing in front, followed by turning kick with the other foot
- Rear-leg turning kick, landing in front, followed by front-leg turning kick (either low or high section) with the same foot
- Rear-leg turning kick, landing in front, followed by spinning hook kick with the other foot. For added difficulty, try throwing the spinning

hook kick before your kicking foot lands (essentially a 360-degree spinning hook kick).
- Rear-leg turning kick, landing in front, then switch stance and spinning hook kick with the same foot
- Rear-leg turning kick, landing in front, followed by narabam with the same foot
- Rear-leg turning kick, followed by narabam with the same foot and spinning hook kick with the opposite foot
- Rear-leg bent-leg axe kick, followed by back kick or spinning hook kick
- Skipping-in bent-leg axe kick with the front foot, followed by rear-leg turning kick
- Double, triple, or quadruple turning kick, starting with the back foot; for variety, try kicking off the lead foot or vary the rhythm by executing a double, pausing, then another double

Step-Kick Combinations
These next drills are intended to help you coordinate your steps and kicks, and to make the transition between the step and kick efficient:

- Jeonjin step, followed by rear-leg turning kick
- Ilbo-jeonjin step, followed by rear-leg turning kick
- Ilbo-jeonjin step, then skipping-in front-leg turning kick
- Hoojin step, followed by rear-leg turning kick (launching your kick as soon as your rear foot touches the floor). Practice landing forward after the hoojin step/turning kick and falling back as you kick (i.e., bada-chagi, or underkick)
- Ilbo-hoojin step, then turning kick with the stepping foot (launching your kick as soon as your foot touches the floor). Again, practice both coming forward after the ilbo-hoojin step and bada-chagi.

FLASH DRILLS
In these reaction drills, your aim is to kick the target as quickly as possible when the pad is "flashed" (presented) to you. As you move around in fighting stance, have your partner flash the pad to you. You can either execute a predetermined kick or set of kicks each time, or your partner can call out the name of the kick(s), placing the pad at the appropriate height and distance. For added difficulty, try doing this in rounds of two or three minutes. Pad

holder—note that this is a perfect opportunity for you to practice your checking motions on the kicker.

Shields or Heavy Bag

Here is your chance to practice your techniques with full force. Shields and heavy bags are particularly useful for practicing your turning kick, back kick, and side kick. Heavy bags and shields each have their own advantages. With a heavy bag, a partner is not necessary. Also, because its surface is rounded, the heavy bag is unforgiving of poor targeting. Inaccurate back kicks will slide off. For the most part, the heavy bag is best used for practicing single techniques although a low-hanging bag can be used to practice double and triple kicks. Shields provide the chance to practice with a moving target, allowing you to develop offensive and defensive techniques and techniques in combination with each other as the holder moves back and forth.

These targets are not ideal for all kicks. Generally speaking, spinning hook kicks, cut kicks, and axe kicks are better practiced on kidney pads.

When kicking the shield or bag, make sure you "dig in." Try to penetrate. Don't retract your kick as soon as you hit the surface—in fact, don't worry at all about bringing your foot back, because if you kick the shield hard enough, your foot will often bounce back by itself.

You can practice most of the turning kick and back kick drills listed in the previous pages and below (both kidney pad and hogu drills) with the shield. In addition, try the following:

BACK KICK DRILLS
In these drills, your partner will square off against you, holding the shield straight in front of you.

- Back kick, jeonjin step/back kick or ilbo-jeonjin step/back kick. The shield holder remains stationary. For added difficulty, take a hoojin step back after the back kick (leaving the kicking foot in front), and execute another back kick with the other foot.
- Quick jumping back kick as the shield holder rushes you. For added difficulty, your partner will rush you continually, and you will execute back kick after back kick, alternating your kicking foot. Remember to recover from each kick in fighting stance, rather than leaving your back

facing your partner, and to hoojin step back after each back kick (leaving the kicking foot in front). Note that if you hook your back kick too much, with the knee of the kicking leg rising to the outside, you will miss the shield, so keep your knees close together and your back kick straight.

BADA-CHAGI/BACK KICK COMBINATION DRILL

In this drill, your partner will square off against you, holding the shield sideways to give you a good target for the bada-chagi.

• As your partner takes a jeonjin step forward, meet the advance with a bada-chagi. Let your kicking foot return to its original position, while your partner takes another jeonjin step forward and turns the shield to face you. As soon as you have resumed fighting stance, use the same foot to back kick the shield. Start by pausing after each set of this combination, then build them up to continual sets of bada-chagi, back kick, bada-chagi, back kick, etc.

Partner Hogu Drills

Kicking a person wearing a hogu (and getting kicked while wearing one) are perfect ways to simulate real sparring and to adapt your timing, distance, and power to real body kicks. In the partner drills that follow, one person is a willing and relatively open target for the kicker. A word of caution—you can hurt each other if you are not careful, so make sure you always start off light before building up to full speed and power. Communication between partners is essential in drills of this kind. You may also want to wear two hogus, or even add additional cushioning (such as a kidney pad) between your body and your hogu for the more powerful kicks (like the back kick) or stronger kickers. Here are some of our favorite drills:

ATTACKING DRILLS

Your partner retreats using either a variety of footwork or steps that have been agreed upon in advance. Kick your partner on the hogu with any kick, timing the kicks and adjusting your footwork so that each kick strikes to the front of the body. Note that you can agree in advance upon specific footwork and kicks, or you can improvise as you go.

COUNTERATTACK DRILLS

Closed Stance

- Partner executes a push kick, cut kick, turning kick, or axe kick with the rear leg. As soon as you see your partner is committed to the kick, counter with a bada-chagi.
- Partner executes a back kick or spinning hook kick with the rear leg. Counter with a bada-chagi, kicking low under your partner's kick. (Note for partner—to avoid painful clashes, don't execute a full kick until you get the timing and mechanics down. Start off with just the spinning motion and let yourself get kicked.)
- For added difficulty, have your partner initiate this sequence with a jeonjin step, which you will match with a hoojin step before executing the bada-chagi.

Open Stance

- Partner initiates with an ilbo-jeonjin step, followed by either spinning hook kick or back kick. Match your partner's advance with a hoojin step, then counter with a bada-chagi.
- Partner executes a skipping or sliding push kick, cut kick, turning kick, or axe kick with the front leg. As soon as you see your partner is committed to the kick, counter with a bada-chagi.

TRAP DRILLS

- In closed stance, switch stances. While your partner tries to counter with a bada-chagi, you, in turn, respond with a back kick.
- In closed stance, execute a push kick, cut kick, turning kick, or axe kick with the rear leg. While your partner tries to counter with a bada-chagi, you, in turn, counter with a back kick. (This is an extension of the first counterattack hogu drill.)
- From open stance, execute a skipping or sliding push kick, cut kick, turning kick, or axe kick with the front leg, which your partner tries to counter with a bada-chagi, and which you, in turn, counter with a back kick. (This is an extension of the second counterattack hogu drill.)

Tournament Rules

The basic rules of WTF- and Olympic-style Taekwondo competition are quite simple. Matches are conducted in a series of timed rounds, usually two or three, depending on the particular tournament and the level of competition. For example, the U.S. National Taekwondo Championships are conducted in three rounds, but smaller, local tournaments may use two rounds, with three longer rounds in finals, or they may use two rounds throughout. A break of thirty to sixty seconds between rounds is common. Likewise, the duration of rounds varies from one tournament to another. At the national championships, be prepared to fight at your best for three three-minute rounds.

A tournament ring is square and has defined boundaries. The official-size ring for national and international matches is eight meters square, with an additional two meters per side as an out-of-bounds, or "Alert," area. The eight-meter line is called the Alert Line, and the referee will stop the match whenever a contestant steps over this line, then return the competitors to the contest area, usually just inside the line. The referee will place the contestant driven over the Alert Line just inside the line. That player will have to fight hard to regain a safer position away from the boundary. Intentional crossing of this line will result in a warning from the referee. The outside line is known as the Boundary Line, and crossing this line can result in a full-point deduction by the referee.

Contestants are required to wear padding, although the actual padding required may differ from one tournament to another. All competitors are required to wear a hogu—the chest protector—and men are required to wear cups. All competitors must wear shin protectors, and most tournament rules require instep protectors, forearm pads, a helmet, and a mouthpiece.

All WTF sparring is full contact. All areas below the waist are illegal targets, and punches to the head are illegal. Blows to the spinal region and to the back of the head are also illegal. Only kicks, punches, and blocks are permitted; no knees, elbows, shins, backfists, hammer strikes, grapples, chokes, or throws may be used, and the use of disallowed techniques will result in warnings, full-point deductions, or even disqualification. A clean, powerful shot to a legal target with a legal technique typically scores one point under the current rules. Much of the time, however, judges are reluctant to award points for punches to the body, because their forcefulness is difficult to assess. Usually, a punch must result in a knockdown to be awarded a point, while any clean, strong kick that does not meet with the interference of a block scores.

Except in the case of electronic scoring, the referee collects the judges' score-cards at the end of every round, delivers them to the Head of Court to be tallied, and announces the score for the round. At the end of the match, the referee declares the contestant with the highest cumulative score winner. With electronic scoring, the corner judges press buttons on a handset to award points as they see them. The score is immediately reported on a computer monitor facing the ring, so that contestants and spectators know the score at all times. This innovation has affected sparring strategy, since it is possible to know when one is behind in points and needs to catch up, or when one can safely avoid confrontation without needing to worry about points.

If one opponent is unable to continue after receiving a blow, or if one has received a particularly jarring shot to the body or head, the referee must give a standing eight count to allow time to recover. If, after reaching a full count of ten, the recipient of the blow cannot continue, the referee will declare the winner by knockout, unless the technique used to deliver the blow is illegal enough to receive a full-point deduction. In this case, the downed opponent may be declared winner by disqualification.

Sometimes the score will be tied. In this case, the referee must declare a winner based upon several criteria. The first step is to discount any penalty deductions. The winner will then be declared based on the prepenalty score. If there are no penalties, or if the match is still a tie, the referee will rely upon other criteria. In order, they are: 1) greatest display of initiative and aggressive ring management; 2) greater number of techniques, if the degree of aggression is about equal; 3) greater technical difficulty (for example, more spinning or jumping techniques), including more kicks to the head; 4) best "competition manner."

In general, the rules of superiority encourage a competitor to be aggressive and to attempt to dominate the match both technically and strategically. This implies that offensive tactics are most advantageous, while, all other things being equal, defensive tactics can possibly result in a defeat if the score is tied. This often turns out to be true, except when the defensive fighter displays much greater fighting superiority. It is possible to fight defensively and maintain greater control of the match in this manner, although this calls for a large measure of skill.

Between two perfectly matched competitors who score an equal number of points and who display equal technical ability, the decision will go to the one who has shown a greater knack for ring management. Ring management will, therefore, receive some special discussion in the next section. Note that officials can also be influenced by a fighter's bearing, comportment, and general manner. It is important to display the greatest respect in the tournament setting, and to be a model of Taekwondo values.

The rules governing Taekwondo competition have evolved substantially, even in the past several years. These changes include substantive ones, such as what constitutes a warnable or deductible offense, as well as procedural ones, such as referees' hand signals and the number of corner judges. It is critical for competitors as well as coaches and trainers to keep up to date with respect to these developments.

Ring Management

Simply put, ring management is the ability to stick to the center of the ring without being driven out of bounds and without being forced to move one way or the other at the whim of one's opponent. Maintaining control of the ring means that on a fundamental level you must not only remain in control of your own movement but also influence or control your opponent's motion.

If you find yourself backing up to the Alert Line, you must either draw an attack and counter it effectively, scoring a point even if you are driven over the line, or you must launch an aggressive offense in order to move your opponent back and regain central position. Note that the referee is required to bring out-of-bounds contestants back within the contest area, but not back to the center of the ring. If you have been driven out-of-bounds, a competent referee will reposition you just within the line. It is up to you to fight your way back in.

Always remember that you can use the boundary to your advantage. Once you have initiated an offensive, keep it up. Don't stop until you have driven your opponent out-of-bounds. This can achieve two results. The first is that your aggression will often be rewarded with a point. The second is that if your opponent is consistently driven out-of-bounds, he or she may receive an official warning from the referee, and each set of two warnings will constitute a full-point deduction. Either way, you have benefited.

Conversely, you need to keep in mind that in the ring it can be a real disadvantage to be driven back, unless you have excellent counterattacks and being driven back is part of your scoring strategy. Make full use of your side-steps and your understanding of steps and footwork to make it difficult for your opponent to force you backward. Counterattack at every opportunity. Not only will this reduce your opponent's will to charge aggressively, but it can successfully stop a charge. Also, if the referee sees that you are fighting every step of the way backward, you may avoid receiving official warnings, no matter how often you cross the Alert Line. However, we recommend you not try your luck with a referee's temperament. When you find yourself nearing the line, move sideways.

Coaching

Coaching plays a critical part in the development and success of any Taekwondo competitor. Competition creates needs that differ from those of Taekwondo students who do not compete, and these needs can include emotional and psychological support as well as tournament-specific training and preparation. This is true for competitors at all levels, although it may apply especially to those who have broken through to the elite level of competition—national and international tournaments and team trials, for example—if only because the stakes at these events are so high.

The emotional and psychological support a coach needs to provide has been written about extensively in the literature on sports psychology. An athlete in training needs to remain focused not only on the particular event being trained for, but also on his or her own ability to excel. Maintaining that conviction, that indomitable spirit, can sometimes be difficult, especially when opponents who are believed to be superior are anticipated or when injuries or personal distractions are interfering with training. Throughout all of this, a coach must cajole, nurture, and motivate the athlete to succeed, always working to help the competitor to cope with any obstacles, real or perceived.

Coaches can also perform more tangible duties. It is the coach's responsibility to have all the information pertaining to a given tournament and even to help make travel and lodging arrangements if necessary. More important, it is the coach's responsibility to know something about the other fighters that will be there: how they fight, where they train, what their own competition records are, and, in general, what can be expected of them in the ring. If this information cannot be gathered in advance, the coach should make every effort to scout it out at the tournament itself, watching the matches of potential opponents and rivals. Some of the things the coach should look out for are which stance, left or right leg forward, the fighter favors; whether the fighter habitually throws lead or rear-leg kicks, and what type; and what the fighter's preferred strategy—offense, defense, or trap—might be. The coach then needs to assimilate that information and pass it on in the form of useful strategic advice.

Strategic advice is especially important during the course of the actual match. From the ringside chair, the coach should watch not only his or her fighter but, maybe more important, the opponent. During the break between rounds, the coach should be able to give advice based on those observations. A cool head is often useful at times like this. Few fighters can concentrate well enough to retain a great deal of information during their few seconds of rest, so the advice should be as brief and to the point as possible. In fact, the simplest advice is often the best, because it is easiest to remember in the heat of combat. When the referee declares the winner, the coach deserves credit as well. If Taekwondo is ever a team sport, it is at that moment when a critical piece of information is passed and the winning point is scored.

CHAPTER 10

Poomse

Taegeuk Il Jang • Taegeuk Yi Jang • Taegeuk Sam Jang • Taegeuk Sa Jang •
Taegeuk O Jang • Taegeuk Yuk Jang • Taegeuk Chil Jang • Taegeuk Pal Jang

Poomse makes up the third aspect of Taekwondo. If sparring is the highest test of Taekwondo's sportsmanly values, specially emphasizing the importance of mutual respect and a sense of fairness, then poomse represents the balance of Taekwondo values: focus, concentration, discipline, and a sense of aesthetics. To execute poomse is to demonstrate mental and physical refinement, to achieve the highest form of conduct.

A number of different sets of poomse have been devised for Taekwondo practitioners, such as the Taegeuk, the Palgwe, the Hyung, and the Kicho, to name a few. In this book we will cover the fundamental poomse recognized everywhere by World Taekwondo Federation dojangs, the Taegeuk.

"Taegeuk" is the Korean name for the familiar symbol depicting the yin/yang relationship. It denotes the universal immortal principle from which life springs and the manner in which we, as humans, experience the universe. The final form of the symbol, complete with the eight sets of triple bars surrounding it—the Kwae—was completed by the philosopher Kim Il-bu after passing through a lengthy procession of scholars, beginning with Sinsi Bonki around 35 B.C.E. It is said that Heaven commanded Sinsi Bonki to glimpse the universal truths, allowing him to observe the rituals of Heaven. From this experience he received the eight Kwae. The circle symbolizes infinity, the extent and mystery of the cosmos. The two parts within the circle symbolize "yin" ("um" in Korean), the negative, and "yang," the positive. Um and yang exist in equal balance within the infinite cosmos, and move constantly in rotation about each other. The Kwae, the sets of three bars appearing eight times around the perimeter of the Taegeuk, symbolize the trinity of Taegeuk, infinity, and um/

yang. The various configurations of the Kwae represent the constant shifting of balance between the members of the trinity. Finally, "Taegeuk" signifies the union of the infinite with the positive and negative aspects of existence, along with all the combinations of experience and knowledge found therein.

At the most elementary level, poomse calls for a sense of composure and confidence. Performing poomse with excellence calls for perfect technique, great balance, power, and a sense of rhythm. There is another ineffable quality that distinguishes great poomse from the technically competent. It might be described as a sense of presence, or as a projection of power. When you watch someone with that quality execute poomse, you can practically feel the force in every blow and every block.

It has been said that the first stage in understanding poomse, and therefore of doing them well, is knowledge of technique, the ability to focus on every motion, and the imbuement of every move with power. At the second stage, you see an opponent at every turn; you strike and block with real conviction. You breathe life into the form. At the third stage, you perform the poomse with such conviction that you actually make the audience see the opponent. You fill the room with your presence. Every movement is palpable. Every movement *is* real. Onlookers cannot look away as you do your form.

The various stages of achievement in poomse require great practice. The first thing you need to work on, of course, is the perfection of your technique, so that every move looks effortless and bursts with power. And every time you practice a form, visualize not just your technique but especially your target. Make it real to yourself. The more real it becomes, the more interesting you will find every motion, and the more meaning the form will acquire.

Common Principles

To develop excellent poomse, you must keep in mind the basic principles behind Taekwondo technique. In poomse, these principles become especially emphasized, so we will reiterate them here.

Stance

Nothing is more important to good form than your basic stances. As we mention in Chapter 4, "Stances," your stance is the foundation of your strength and your power. The earth under your feet gives you power and solidity; it grounds you, and your stance allows you to transmit that power and solidity into your techniques.

Take special care to maintain a front stance that is long and wide, a walking stance that is natural and relaxed, and a back stance that sits easily on the rear leg, with both knees bent. When you turn, be sure to place the moving foot—as opposed to the pivoting foot—exactly where it should be to result in a stable stance upon completion of the turn. Many Taekwondoists, especially beginners, find themselves off balance after turning to face a new direction. Avoid this by learning to plant the ball of the moving foot carefully.

Finally, avoid stomping. In the first eight Taegeuk forms, your energy and power should thrust forward or backward, not down into the floor.

Explosiveness

Execute every kick, strike, or block with maximum power and speed. Do not rush between moves; your transitions should be smooth, but your actions should be forceful and passionate. Think of your blocks as blows against an attacker's limbs, and visualize devastating attacks

Use your motion, whether forward, backward, or rotational, to add power to every move. Keep your shoulders loose and your body relaxed.

Chamber Position

The importance of your basic chamber positions is magnified during poomse. Make sure that the chamber for every technique is perfect; that way, you will never look rushed during the form, and you will have time to bring out the full potential of every strike or block. Solid chambering also enhances your appearance of certainty and conviction.

When you have to turn before executing a technique, make sure you reach your chamber position before you complete the turn, and execute the technique itself the moment you complete your turn or your step.

Keep Your Eyes on Your Target

Before you turn in any direction, look first. It is critical to see where you are going. Looking first will improve your balance, the accuracy of your blows, power, and the appearance of certainty. It will also heighten your ability to visualize an opponent.

Relaxation and Tension

Make sure your breath is regular. Exhale with the performance of every technique. Stay loose and relaxed until the moment a block, strike, or kick is complete; then lock in before rechambering.

Basic Technique

All of the techniques displayed in the poomse have appeared previously in this book in their appropriate chapters. For your convenience, we have cross-referenced techniques in this chapter with the pages where they appear throughout the book. If you have any questions that are not adequately answered by the "Notes on Individual Moves" following the pattern chart for each form, you can easily refer to the appropriate cross-reference. Where the poomse requires a variation from the standard performance of a given technique, those differences are explained in the notes.

Starting Position and Directions

Each of the eight Taegeuk forms begins in standard joon bi position. For the sake of clarity, we designate all motion forward from this position as north; similarly, we will refer to other directions by the points of the compass. For example, a turn to the left from this position is a turn toward the west, a turn to the right would face east, and so on. Joon bi itself always faces north. We also include references to right and left for clarity.

For movements headed north and south, we have provided profile views in addition to the front or back view. These profile views are indicated by the ➡ *symbol.*

Generally, a hand technique corresponding to the lead leg (for example, a left-arm down block in left walking stance) will be designated by the simple name of technique, while a hand technique performed with the opposite leg forward will be designated as a reverse technique. Thus, a left-hand down block with your left leg forward will be referred to as a down block, while a down block with the right hand and the left leg forward will be referred to as a reverse down block, and so forth.

Learning Poomse

The first step in learning a new form is to make sure you know each technique appearing in that form. For example, you can hardly hope to do Taegeuk Sam Jang well if you cannot stand in Back Stance or do not understand the inside knife-hand strike. Practice every one of the techniques that appear in a form until you are comfortable with all of them.

Once you have a basic understanding of all the techniques in any given form, including the stances, you can begin to learn the pattern. By "pattern" we mean the basic steps, stances, and techniques that make up the form itself. All eight of the lower poomse have the same basic shape, modeled after the Kwae. Each of them has a trunk with three branches growing from each side. All of these forms, except for the eighth, begin with a turn to the left, and the first technique in all eight of the forms is some kind of block, emphasizing the principle that Taekwondo is used solely for self-defense.

After you learn a form's pattern, you can begin to study the best way to deliver power with every technique, and how to adjust your timing of the techniques so that your movements look natural. Even though the patterns of the poomse are standard, everyone does forms differently according to their own sense of style, their specific abilities, and their limitations. Make each form your own by applying your sense of style to it.

For a one-page summary of each of the poomse, see the "Poomse Summary" section following this chapter.

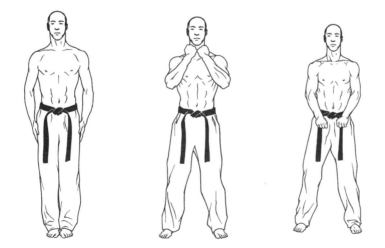

Taegeuk Il Jang

Taegeuk Il Jang represents *keon,* the yang: positive energy, the beginning of Creation, and Heaven. To see a one-page illustrated summary of this form, see p. 259.

Pattern Chart

Movement Number	Finishing Direction	Movement	Finishing Stance	Technique Combination
1.	West	Pivot on right foot and turn 90° left to face west	Left Walking Stance	Down block
2.	West	Step forward	Right Walking Stance	Front middle punch
3.	East	Pivot right 180° on left foot to face east	Right Walking Stance	Down block
4.	East	Step forward	Left Walking Stance	Front middle punch
5.	North	Pivot left 90° on right foot to face north	Left Front Stance	Down block, followed by reverse middle punch
6.	East	Pivot right 90° on left foot to face east, drawing the right foot forward	Right Walking Stance	Reverse inside block
7.	East	Step forward	Left Walking Stance	Reverse middle punch
8.	West	Pivot left 180° on right foot to face west	Left Walking Stance	Reverse inside block
9.	West	Step forward	Right Walking Stance	Reverse middle punch
10.	North	Pivot right 90° on left foot to face north	Right Front Stance	Down block, followed by reverse middle punch
11.	West	Pivot left 90° on right foot to face west, drawing the left foot forward	Left Walking Stance	High block
12.	West	Step forward	Right Walking Stance	Right-leg front snap kick landing in Right Walking Stance; followed by front middle punch

Movement Number	Finishing Direction	Movement	Finishing Stance	Technique Combination
13.	East	Pivot right 180° on left foot to face east	Right Walking Stance	High block
14.	East	Step forward	Left Walking Stance	Left-leg front snap kick landing in Left Walking Stance, followed by front middle punch
15.	South	Pivot right 90° on right foot to face south	Left Front Stance	Down block
16.	South	Step forward	Right Front Stance	Front middle punch and kihap
17.	North	Pivot left 180° on right foot, drawing left foot parallel	Ba ro	

Notes on Individual Moves

1. When you pivot out of joon bi position, make sure you move the left foot as well as pivot on the right, so that you end up in a stable walking stance rather than looking as if you are walking a tightrope.

3. Sweep your right foot *across* your line of travel so that your stance is wide enough once you complete the turn.

6 & 11. Notice that the *rear* foot in these front stances is the foot that moves, not the front foot. In movement #6, for instance, turn your head to look to the right. At the same time, pull your right foot forward until it is in position for Right Walking Stance. Note that the hand technique here is a reverse block, using the hand opposite the lead leg.

12 & 14. Hold the high block in position while you kick. As you rechamber your kick, and before you set the foot down, assume the chamber position for the punch. Then, as your foot comes down in walking stance, punch.

15. Although you are turning to the right out of a Left Walking Stance, it is still the left foot that moves. You will be in a left stance before the turn and a left stance after the turn.

Taegeuk Il Jang

1. From joon bi, pivot to your left (west) into Left Walking Stance (p. 60) and down block (p. 88) with the left arm. When you pivot out of joon bi position, make sure you move the left foot slightly to the left as you pivot the right foot, so that you end up in a stable walking stance rather than standing as if you were walking a tightrope.	
2. Step forward into Right Walking Stance and front middle punch (p. 102) with the right arm.	
3. Turn all the way around to your right (east) into Right Walking Stance and down block with the right arm. As in step #1, you need to finish in a stable stance. When you turn around to face the opposite direction, sweep your right foot not only behind yourself in order to come about-face but also *across* your line of travel so that your stance is secure once you complete the turn. This principle of movement applies to all forms and basic techniques.	
4. Step forward into Left Walking Stance and middle punch with the left arm.	

5. Turn to the left (north) and step forward with the left foot into Left Front Stance (p. 61). Immediately throw left down block (**a**), followed by reverse punch with the right hand (**b**). Each of these hand techniques should be sharp and powerful. Make each one distinct, rather than blur them together.

6. Turn to the right (east) by drawing your right leg—your rear leg in the Left Front Stance— forward as you turn into Right Walking Stance. At the same time, reverse inside block with the left hand (p. 88). Give the block extra power by using the motion of your rightward rotation.

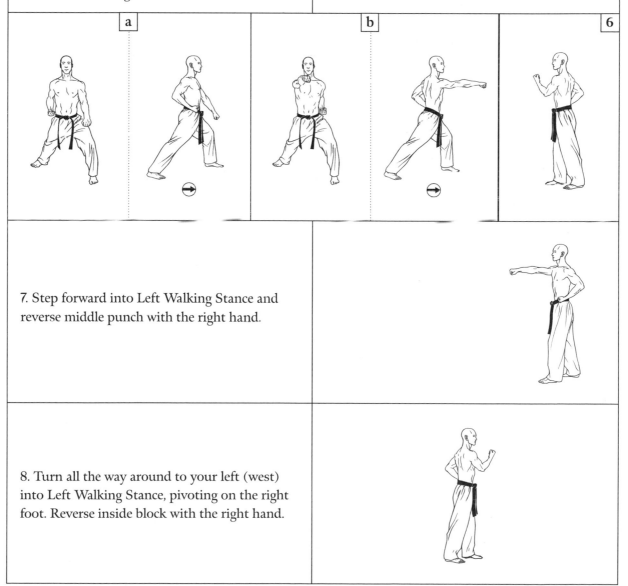

7. Step forward into Left Walking Stance and reverse middle punch with the right hand.

8. Turn all the way around to your left (west) into Left Walking Stance, pivoting on the right foot. Reverse inside block with the right hand.

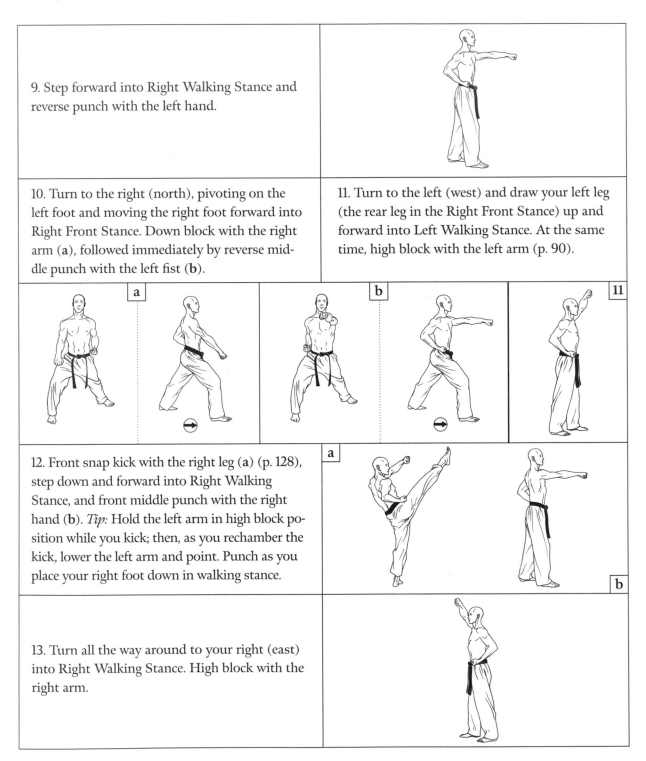

9. Step forward into Right Walking Stance and reverse punch with the left hand.

10. Turn to the right (north), pivoting on the left foot and moving the right foot forward into Right Front Stance. Down block with the right arm (**a**), followed immediately by reverse middle punch with the left fist (**b**).

11. Turn to the left (west) and draw your left leg (the rear leg in the Right Front Stance) up and forward into Left Walking Stance. At the same time, high block with the left arm (p. 90).

12. Front snap kick with the right leg (**a**) (p. 128), step down and forward into Right Walking Stance, and front middle punch with the right hand (**b**). *Tip:* Hold the left arm in high block position while you kick; then, as you rechamber the kick, lower the left arm and point. Punch as you place your right foot down in walking stance.

13. Turn all the way around to your right (east) into Right Walking Stance. High block with the right arm.

14. The opposite of #12. Front snap kick with the left leg, holding the right arm in the high block position (**a**). As you rechamber the kick, point the right arm toward the middle target. Then throw the left front middle punch as you step down and forward into Left Walking Stance (**b**).

15. Turn to the right (south) and step forward with the left leg—not the right—into Left Front Stance. Down block with the left arm.

16. Step forward into Right Front Stance, front middle punch with the right arm, and kihap!

17. Pivoting on the right foot and moving the left foot, turn all the way around to the left to face north again, finishing in ba ro position.

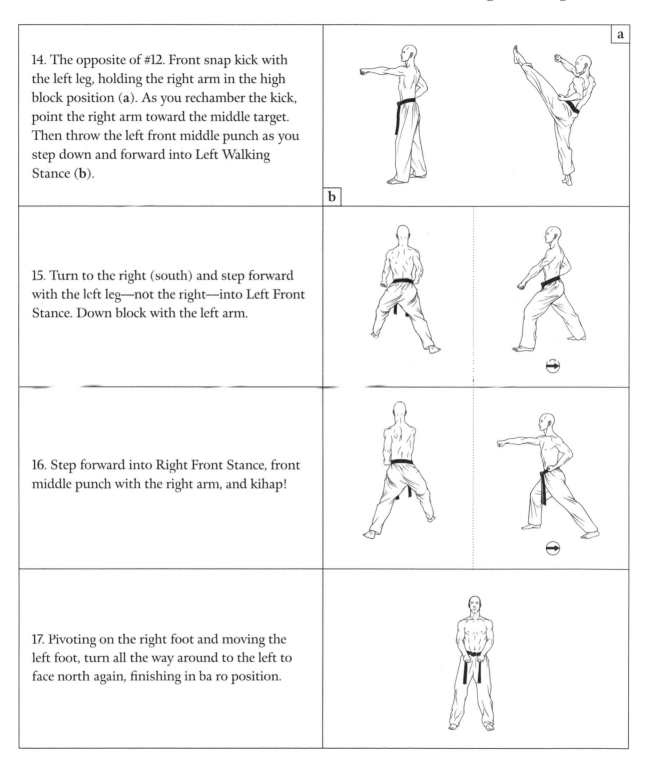

Taegeuk Yi Jang

Taegeuk Yi Jang represents *tae*. *Tae* signifies internal firmness and external softness. The familiar maxim that one should speak softly but carry a big stick would be a familiar example of the idea inherent in *tae*. Other illustrative images come to mind: the iron fist in a velvet glove, or peacefulness, tact, and diplomacy supported by inner strength and will. Indomitable spirit, not forcefulness, lies within each of us. To see a one-page illustrated summary of this form, see p. 260.

Pattern Chart

Movement Number	Finishing Direction	Movement	Finishing Stance	Technique Combination
1.	West	Pivot left 90° on right foot to face west	Left Walking Stance	Down block
2.	West	Step forward	Right Front Stance	Front middle punch
3.	East	Pivot right 180° on left foot to face east	Right Walking Stance	Down block
4.	East	Step forward	Left Front Stance	Front middle punch
5.	North	Pivot left 90° on right foot to face north	Left Walking Stance	Reverse inside block
6.	North	Step forward	Right Walking Stance	Reverse inside block
7.	West	Pivot left 90° on right foot to face west	Left Walking Stance	Down block
8.	West	Step forward	Right Front Stance	Right-leg front snap kick, landing in right front stance, followed by front high punch
9.	East	Pivot right 180° on left foot to face east	Right Walking Stance	Down block
10.	East	Step forward	Left Front Stance	Left-leg front snap kick, landing in front stance, followed by front high punch
11.	North	Pivot left 90° on right foot to face north	Left Walking Stance	High block

Movement Number	Finishing Direction	Movement	Finishing Stance	Technique Combination
12.	North	Step forward	Right Walking Stance	High block
13.	East	Pivot left 270° on right foot to face east	Left Walking Stance	Reverse inside block
14.	West	Pivot right 180° on left foot to face west	Right Walking Stance	Reverse inside block
15.	South	Pivot left 90° on right foot to face south	Left Walking Stance	Down block
16.	South	Step forward	Right Walking Stance	Right-leg front snap kick, followed by front middle punch
17.	South	Step forward	Left Walking Stance	Left-leg front snap kick, followed by front middle punch
18.	South	Step forward	Right Walking Stance	Right-leg front snap kick, followed by front middle punch and kihap
19.	North	Pivot left 180° on right foot, drawing left foot alongside	Ba ro	

Notes on Individual Moves

1. See the note on move #1 for Taegeuk Il Jang.

8 & 10. See the note on moves #12 and 14 in Taegeuk Il Jang. Although the specific techniques are different, the principle is the same. Chamber the punch at the same time that you rechamber after the kick.

13. The principle that applies to this 270-degree turn applies to all 270-degree turns. In this case, you are turning to the left. Because it is always advisable to look in the direction you intend to turn, yet impossible to turn your head so far around in one direction, first look over your right shoulder rather than your left. Then, as you begin the pivot, turn your head the other way so that you can spot your finishing position. As you turn, extend the left fist to point and chamber the right hand for the reverse inside block.

16–18. Punch at the exact moment that you step down after each kick, chambering each punch as you rechamber the kick. The timing of the chamber and the step will help ensure a powerful punch.

Taegeuk Yi Jang

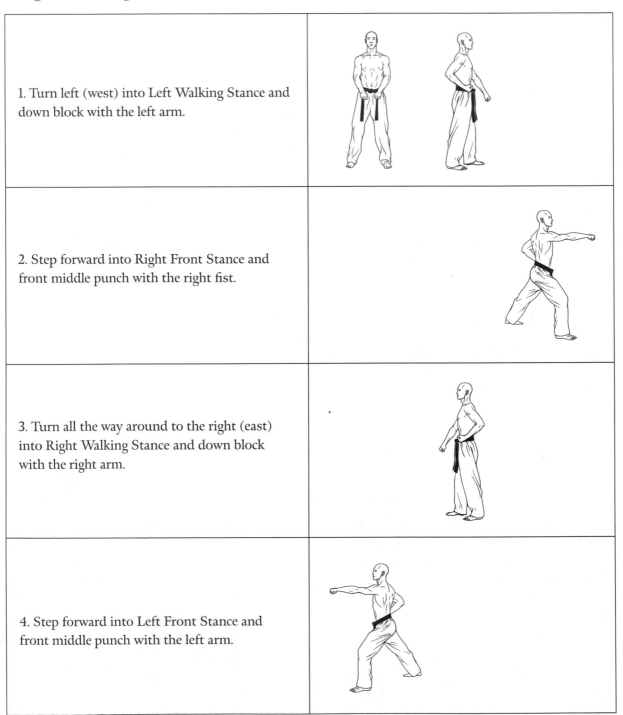

1. Turn left (west) into Left Walking Stance and down block with the left arm.	
2. Step forward into Right Front Stance and front middle punch with the right fist.	
3. Turn all the way around to the right (east) into Right Walking Stance and down block with the right arm.	
4. Step forward into Left Front Stance and front middle punch with the left arm.	

5. Pivot left (north), pulling the left foot in and placing it in front of you to assume Left Walking Stance. At the same time, throw a reverse inside block with the right arm.

6. Step forward into Right Walking Stance and reverse inside block with the left arm.

7. Pivot left (west), moving the left foot into Left Walking Stance, and down block with the left arm.

8. Front snap kick with the right leg (**a**). Land forward in Right Front Stance and front high punch with the right hand (**b**). The timing of the chamber for the high punch is the same here as for steps 12 and 14 in Taegeuk Il Jang.

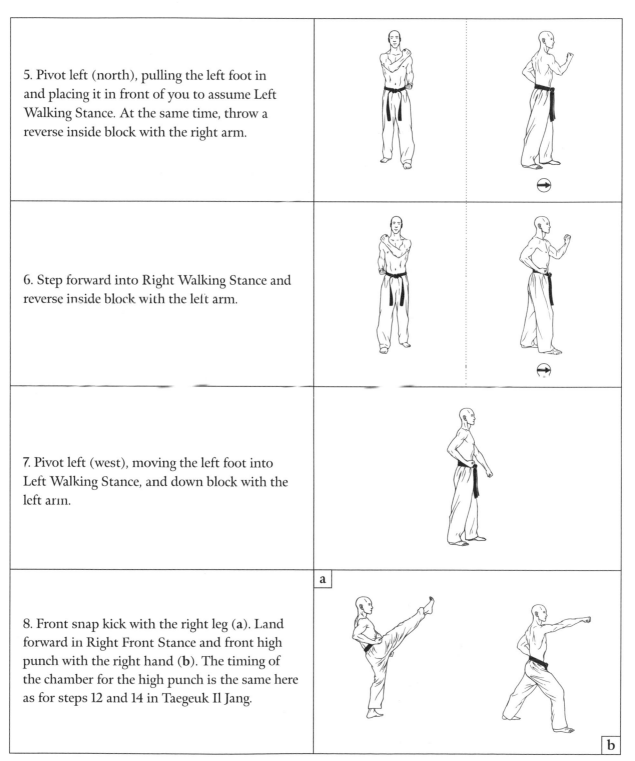

9. Moving the right foot, pivot all the way around to the right (east) into Right Walking Stance and down block with the right hand.

10. Front snap kick with the left leg (**a**) and land forward in Left Front Stance. Front high punch with the left hand (**b**).

a

b

11. Turn to the left (north), moving the left foot into Left Walking Stance, and high block with the left arm.

12. Step forward into Right Walking Stance and high block with the right arm.

13. Pivoting on your right foot, turn 270 degrees (east), sweeping your left foot around to finish in Left Walking Stance. Reverse inside block with the right arm as you complete the turn. Since it is impossible to turn your head far enough around to see where you are going before you begin the turn, first look over your right shoulder rather than your left. Then, as you begin the pivot, turn your head the other way so that you can spot your finishing position. As you turn, extend the left fist to point and chamber the right hand for the reverse inside block.

14. Turn around to your right (west), sweeping your right foot across behind you to finish in Right Walking Stance. Reverse inside block with the left arm as you come into position.

15. Pivot left (south), moving the left foot into Left Walking Stance with a left-arm down block.

16. Right-leg front snap kick (**a**), stepping forward into Right Walking Stance with right-arm front middle punch (**b**). Chamber for the punch as you rechamber the front kick, and punch at the precise moment that you step down from the kick.

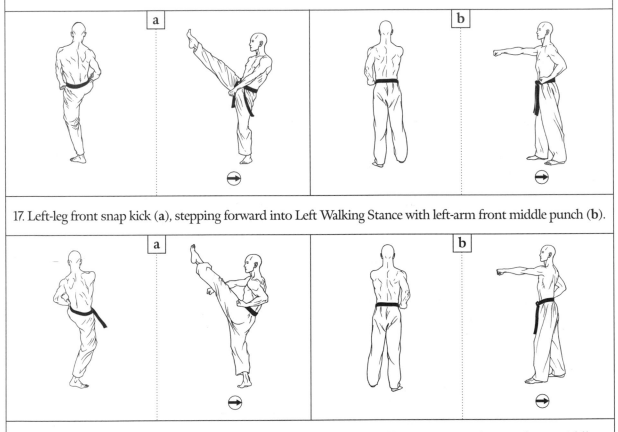

17. Left-leg front snap kick (**a**), stepping forward into Left Walking Stance with left-arm front middle punch (**b**).

18. Right-leg front snap kick (**a**), stepping forward into Right Walking Stance, right-arm front middle punch (**b**), and kihap!

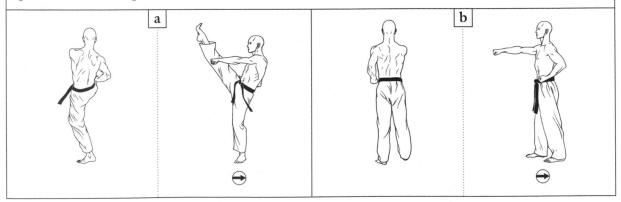

19. Moving the left foot, pivot all the way around to the left (north) to come back to ba ro.	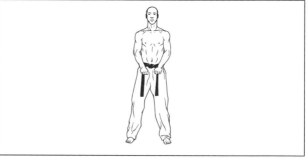

Taegeuk Sam Jang

Taegeuk Sam Jang represents *Ra,* fire. The heat and brilliance of *Ra* encourages the Taekwondoist to pursue training with both passion and intensity.

As you practice Taegeuk Sam Jang, notice the emphasis on counterattacks. Many of the steps in this form involve blocks immediately followed by counter-attacks. To see a one-page illustrated summary of this form, see p. 261.

Pattern Chart

Movement Number	Finishing Direction	Movement	Finishing Stance	Technique Combination
1.	West	Pivot left 90° on right foot to face west	Left Walking Stance	Down block
2.	West	Step forward	Right Front Stance	Right-leg front snap kick, landing in Right Front Stance, followed by double middle punch, right hand first
3.	East	Pivot right 180° on left foot to face east	Right Walking Stance	Down block
4.	East	Step forward	Left Front Stance	Left-leg front snap kick, landing in Left Front Stance, followed by double middle punch, left hand first
5.	North	Pivot right 90° on right foot to face north	Left Walking Stance	Reverse inside knife-hand strike
6.	North	Step forward	Right Walking Stance	Reverse inside knife-hand strike

Movement Number	Finishing Direction	Movement	Finishing Stance	Technique Combination
7.	West	Pivot left 90° on right foot to face west	a) Left Back Stance b) Left Front Stance	a) Single knife-hand middle block, b) Reverse middle punch
8.	East	Pivot right 180° on left foot to face east	a) Right Back Stance b) Right Front Stance	a) Single knife-hand middle block, b) Reverse middle punch
9.	North	Pivot left 90° on right foot to face north	Left Walking Stance	Reverse inside block
10.	North	Step forward	Right Walking Stance	Reverse inside block
11.	East	Pivot left 270° on right foot to face east	Left Walking Stance	Down block
12.	East	Step forward	Right Front Stance	Right-leg front snap kick, landing in Right Front Stance, followed by double punch, right hand first
13.	West	Pivot 180° on left foot to face west	Right Walking Stance	Down block
14.	West	Step forward	Left Front Stance	Left-leg front snap kick, landing in Left Front Stance, followed by double punch, left hand first
15.	South	Pivot left 90° on right foot to face south	Left Walking Stance	Down block followed by reverse middle punch
16.	South	Step forward	Right Walking Stance	Down block followed by reverse middle punch
17.	South	Step forward	Left Walking Stance	Left-leg front snap kick, landing forward in Left Walking Stance, followed by down block and reverse middle punch
18.	South	Step forward	Right Walking Stance	Right-leg front snap kick, landing forward in Right Walking Stance, followed by down block and reverse middle punch with kihap
19.	North	Pivot left 180° on right foot to face north	Ba ro	

Notes on Individual Moves

2 & 4. As in Taegeuk Il Jang and Taegeuk Yi Jang, hold the block position while you kick; then, as you rechamber the kick, chamber for the punch. Punch as you step down into your stance.

5 & 6. These knife-hand strikes are aimed at your imaginary opponent's neck. They must be delivered with power—take the time to develop the strength of these useful hand techniques.

7 & 8. Don't rush through these single knife-hand blocks. Make sure the block is solid, with a true, balanced back stance, before opening up to the front stance reverse middle punch.

11. Sec the note on movement #13 in Taegeuk Yi Jang.

15–18. Make sure your down blocks are crisp; don't meld them into the punches. In steps 17 and 18, chamber the block as you rechamber the front snap kick.

Taegeuk Sam Jang

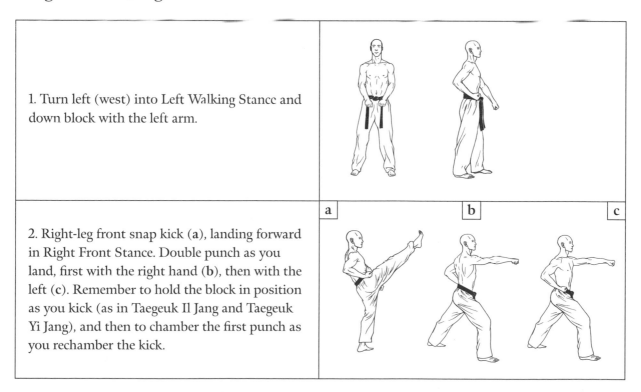

1. Turn left (west) into Left Walking Stance and down block with the left arm.	
2. Right-leg front snap kick (**a**), landing forward in Right Front Stance. Double punch as you land, first with the right hand (**b**), then with the left (**c**). Remember to hold the block in position as you kick (as in Taegeuk Il Jang and Taegeuk Yi Jang), and then to chamber the first punch as you rechamber the kick.	**a** **b** **c**

3. Turn all the way around to the right (east) into Right Walking Stance with right down block.

4. Left-leg front snap kick (**a**), landing forward in Left Front Stance. Double punch as you land, punching first with the left hand (**b**), then with the right (**c**).

c **b** **a**

5. Turn to the left (north), moving the left foot into Left Walking Stance, and reverse inside knife-hand strike to the neck with the right hand (p. 118). Bring your elbow up high for the reverse inside knife-hand strike and draw your hand back behind your ear. When you turn to your left into the first walking stance with reverse inside knife hand strike, use the power available to you as you turn to make that strike strong. When you step forward for the next strike, use your shoulders to make the strike even more powerful.

6. Step forward into Right Walking Stance, and reverse inside knife-hand strike with the left hand.

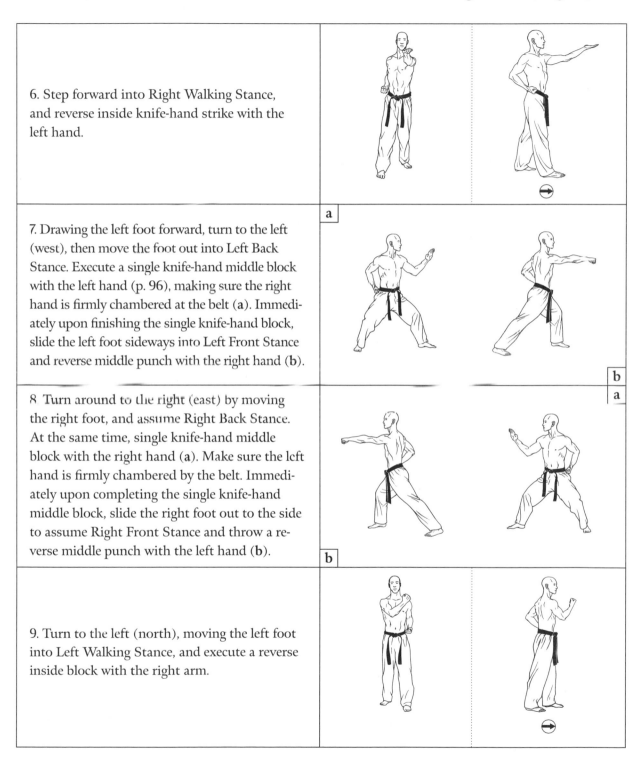

7. Drawing the left foot forward, turn to the left (west), then move the foot out into Left Back Stance. Execute a single knife-hand middle block with the left hand (p. 96), making sure the right hand is firmly chambered at the belt (**a**). Immediately upon finishing the single knife-hand block, slide the left foot sideways into Left Front Stance and reverse middle punch with the right hand (**b**).

8. Turn around to the right (east) by moving the right foot, and assume Right Back Stance. At the same time, single knife-hand middle block with the right hand (**a**). Make sure the left hand is firmly chambered by the belt. Immediately upon completing the single knife-hand middle block, slide the right foot out to the side to assume Right Front Stance and throw a reverse middle punch with the left hand (**b**).

9. Turn to the left (north), moving the left foot into Left Walking Stance, and execute a reverse inside block with the right arm.

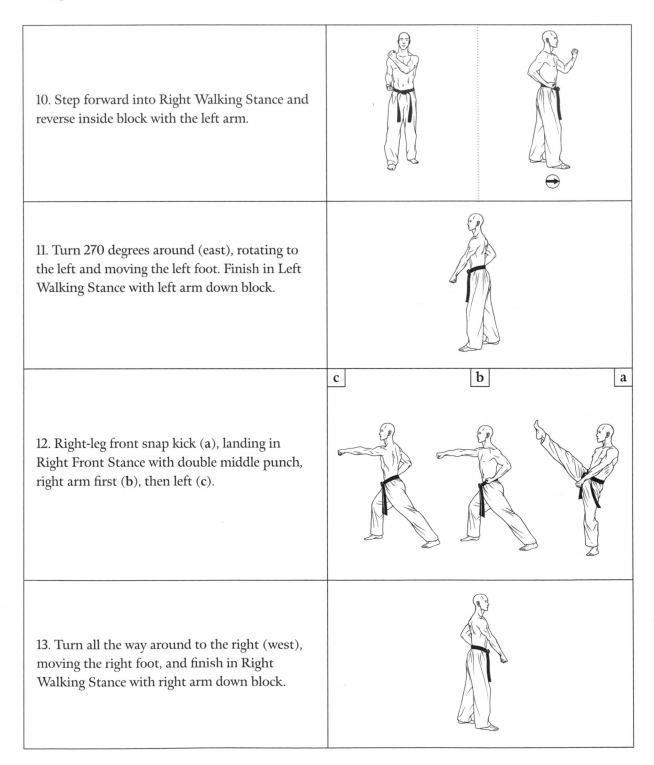

10. Step forward into Right Walking Stance and reverse inside block with the left arm.

11. Turn 270 degrees around (east), rotating to the left and moving the left foot. Finish in Left Walking Stance with left arm down block.

12. Right-leg front snap kick (a), landing in Right Front Stance with double middle punch, right arm first (b), then left (c).

c   b   a

13. Turn all the way around to the right (west), moving the right foot, and finish in Right Walking Stance with right arm down block.

14. Left-leg front snap kick (**a**), landing in Left Front Stance with double punch, left arm first (**b**), then right (**c**).

15. Turn to the left (south) into Left Walking Stance. Down block with the left arm (**a**), immediately followed by reverse middle punch with the right fist (**b**).

16. Step forward into Right Walking Stance. Down block with the right arm (**a**), immediately followed by reverse middle punch with the left fist (**b**).

17. Left-leg front snap kick, landing in Left Walking Stance (**a**). Down block with the left arm (**b**), immediately followed by reverse punch with the right fist (**c**).

18. Right-leg front snap kick, landing in Right Walking Stance (**a**). Down block with the right arm (**b**), immediately followed by reverse punch with the left fist (**c**), and kihap!

19. Turning all the way around to the left (north), moving the left foot, return to ba ro.

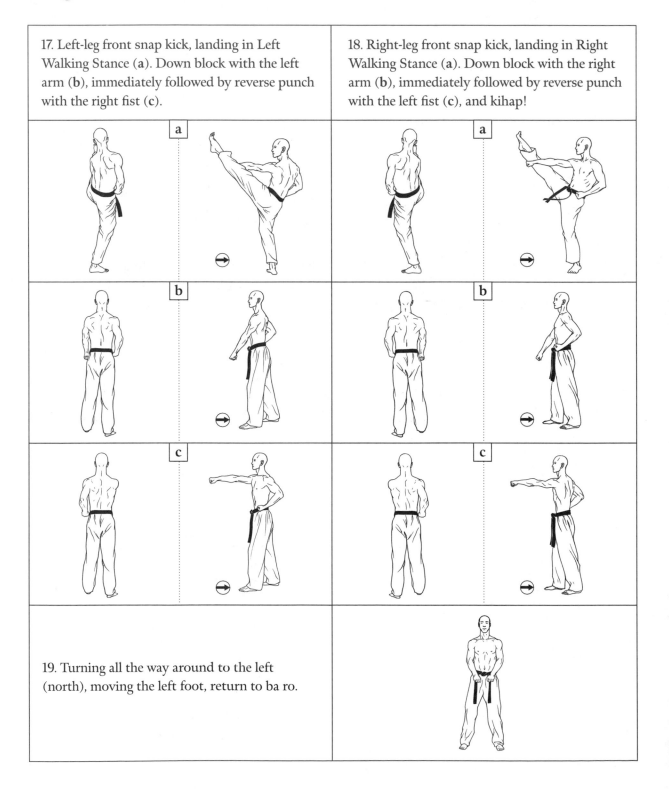

Taegeuk Sa Jang

Taegeuk Sa Jang represents *Jin* in the Taegeuk: thunder, which in turn signifies power and courage. Concentrate especially hard on cultivating grace and power. This poomse is the first of the lower forms to demand great perseverance from you in order to display these qualities. To see a one-page illustrated summary of this form, see p. 262.

Pattern Chart

Movement Number	Finishing Direction	Movement	Finishing Stance	Technique Combination
1.	West	Pivot left 90° on right foot to face west	Left Back Stance	Double knife-hand middle block
2.	West	Step forward	Right Front Stance	Reverse pressing-down block followed by right spear hand
3.	East	Pivot right 180° on left foot to face east	Right Back Stance	Double knife-hand middle block
4.	East	Step forward	Left Front Stance	Reverse pressing-down block followed by left spear hand
5.	North	Pivot left 90° on right foot to face north	Left Front Stance	Simultaneous open-hand high block with reverse inside knife-hand strike
6.	North	Step forward	Right Front Stance	Right-leg front snap kick, landing in Right Front Stance, followed by reverse middle punch
7.	North	Step forward twice	a) Left Walking Stance b) Right Back Stance	a) Left-leg side kick, landing in Left Walking Stance, fists in guard position b) Right-leg side kick, landing in Right Back Stance with double middle knife-hand block
8.	East	Pivot left 270° on right foot to face east	Left Back Stance	Outside forearm block
9.	East	None	Left Back Stance	Right-leg front snap kick, stepping back into Left Back Stance; reverse inside block as stance is reassumed

Movement Number	Finishing Direction	Movement	Finishing Stance	Technique Combination
10.	West	Pivot right 180° on left foot to face west	Right Back Stance	Outside forearm block
11.	West	None	Right Back Stance	Left-leg front snap kick, stepping back into Right Back Stance; reverse inside block as stance is reassumed
12.	South	Pivot left 90° on right foot to face south	Left Front Stance	Simultaneous open-hand high block with reverse inside knife-hand strike
13.	South	Step forward	Right Front Stance	Right-leg front snap kick, landing in Right Front Stance, with backfist strike to the nose
14.	East	Pivot left 90° on right foot to face east	Left Walking Stance	Inside block followed by reverse middle punch
15.	West	Pivot right 180° on left foot (standard about-face) to face west	Right Walking Stance	Inside block followed by reverse middle punch
16.	South	Pivot left 90° on right foot to face south	Left Front Stance	Inside block followed by double middle punch, right hand first
17.	South	Step forward	Right Front Stance	Inside block followed by double middle punch, left hand first, and kihap
18.	North	Pivot left 180° on right foot, drawing left foot back to face north	Ba ro	

Notes on Individual Moves

2 & 4. Execute the pressing-down block directly out of the double knife-hand block. Keep the blocking hand in position as you thrust forward with the spear hand so that the elbow of your striking arm is supported by the back of the blocking hand.

5. The blocking hand should be to the right of center—your blocking surface is actually the wrist, not the hand itself. Strike powerfully with the reverse inside knife hand.

8. See the note on movement #13 in Taegeuk Yi Jang on page 197. Chamber the outside forearm block as you turn.

9 & 11. When you rechamber your kick, chamber the reverse inside block. Throw the block as you step back into the Back Stance, turning your body slightly inward to give the block more power. You can achieve this with more grace, ease, and power if you chamber your arm for the block at the same time that you rechamber the front kick. Then, as you bring your leg back to its former position in back stance, turn your shoulders in slightly and throw the reverse inside block.

14 & 15. Apply the principle of action/reaction to this inside block. Although you are turning opposite the direction of your arm's motion as you block, you can use those opposite motions to make the block snappier and the turn sharper.

Taegeuk Sa Jang

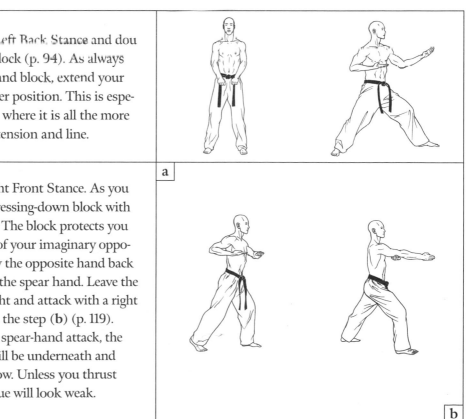

1. Turn left (west) into Left Back Stance and double knife-hand middle block (p. 94). As always with the double knife-hand block, extend your arms fully in the chamber position. This is especially critical in poomse, where it is all the more important to display extension and line.	**a**
2. Step forward into Right Front Stance. As you step, execute a reverse pressing-down block with the left hand (**a**) (p. 98). The block protects you from the reverse punch of your imaginary opponent. As you block, draw the opposite hand back to chamber position for the spear hand. Leave the block at midsection height and attack with a right spear hand as you finish the step (**b**) (p. 119). When you complete the spear-hand attack, the left hand, palm down, will be underneath and supporting the right elbow. Unless you thrust with power, this technique will look weak.	**b**

3. Turn all the way to the right (east) into Right Back Stance and double knife-hand middle block.

4. Step forward into Left Front Stance. As you step, execute a reverse pressing-down block with the right hand (**a**). Leave the block at midsection height and attack with a left spear hand as you finish the step (**b**). When you complete the spear-hand attack, the right hand, palm down, will be underneath and supporting the left elbow.

5. Turn left (north), moving the left foot into Left Front Stance, and throw a simultaneous open-hand high block with the left hand and a reverse inside knife-hand strike with the right hand. Chamber this double-hand technique with both hands drawn back behind the right shoulder, palms apart and facing each other as if holding a ball. Turn the shoulders back slightly. When you step forward into the Left Front Stance, snap your shoulders into place, simultaneously bringing your hands into position.

6. Right-leg front snap kick (**a**), landing forward in Right Front Stance. Reverse punch with the left hand as you land in the front stance (**b**).

a

b

7. This step consists of three separate moves: the first is a left-leg side kick (p. 138) with hands raised in guard position, stepping forward into Left Walking Stance (**a**). Immediately throw right-leg side kick, hands kept in guard position (**b**). Land forward in Right Back Stance with double knife-hand middle block (**c**).

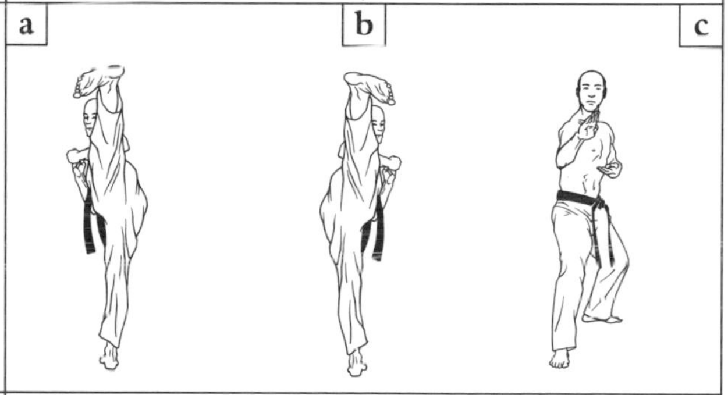

a

b

c

8. Turn 270 degrees to the left (east), pushing the left foot out into Left Back Stance, with a left-arm outside forearm block as you complete the step (p. 91). Remember to turn your head first to the right before you begin the turn.

9. Right-leg front snap kick from the back stance (**a**). Do not step forward. Return to the Left Back Stance, chambering the right arm for the reverse inside block as you rechamber the kick, and execute the reverse inside block (**b**). Turn your rear shoulder forward as you block. *Tip:* When you throw the front snap kick, keep your weight forward, rather than anticipating your return to back stance and leaning back while you kick.

a

b

10. Turn all the way around to the right (west), moving the right foot and finishing in Right Back Stance with right arm outside forearm block.

11. As in step #9, left-leg front snap kick (**a**), returning to Right Back Stance with reverse inside block (**b**).

12. Turn to the left (south), moving the left foot into Left Front Stance, and, as in step #5, open-hand high block with a simultaneous reverse inside knife-hand strike using the right hand.

13. Right-leg front snap kick, landing in Right Front Stance (**a**), with a right-hand backfist to the nose (**b**) (p. 112).

14. Moving the left leg, turn to the left (east) into Left Walking Stance. As you come into position, block with a left-arm inside block (**a**) and follow up immediately with a right-fist reverse middle punch (**b**).

15. Moving the right leg, turn completely around to the right (west) into Right Walking Stance. Block with right-arm inside block (**a**) and immediately follow with a left-fist reverse middle punch (**b**).

16. Moving the left foot, turn to the left (south) into Left Front Stance. Inside block with the left arm (**a**) and double middle punch, punching first with the right fist (**b**), then the left (**c**).

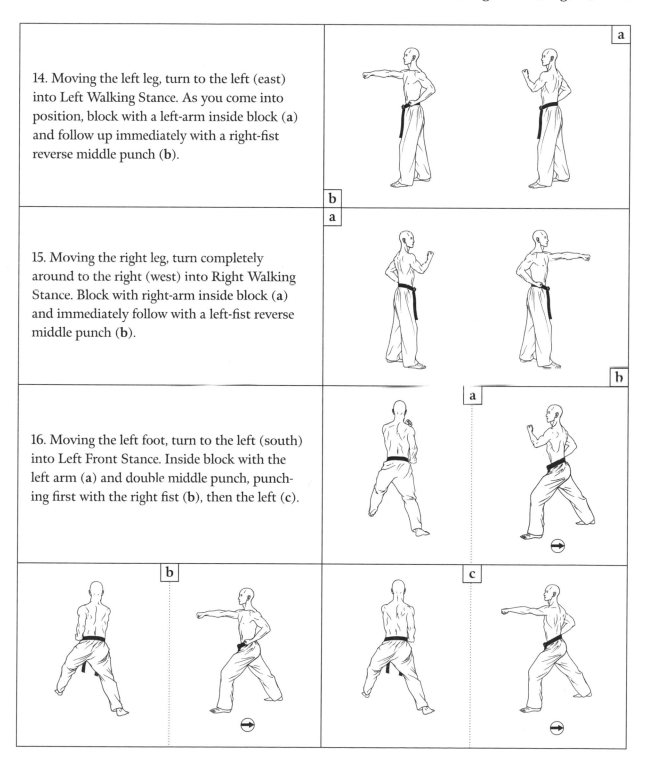

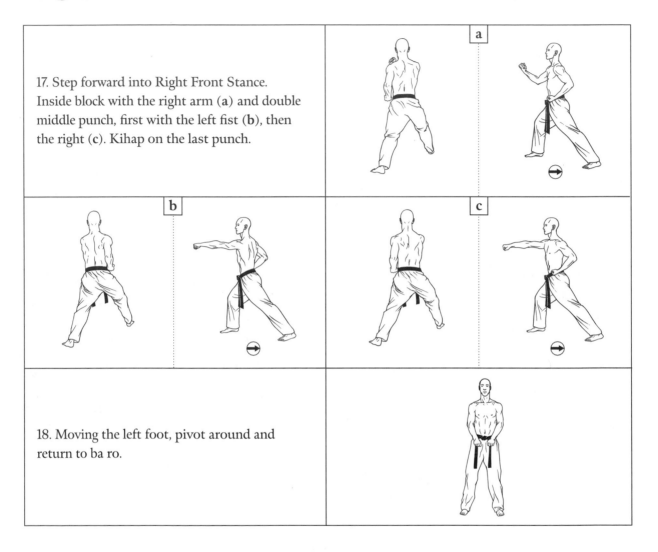

17. Step forward into Right Front Stance. Inside block with the right arm (**a**) and double middle punch, first with the left fist (**b**), then the right (**c**). Kihap on the last punch.

18. Moving the left foot, pivot around and return to ba ro.

Taegeuk O Jang

Taegeuk O Jang represents *Seon,* the paradox of air: the might of a powerful wind and the weakness of still air, reflecting the strength and weakness within all things. Each of us contains this paradox, and through our practice of martial arts we expand our capacity in both directions. By developing the means to generate great power, we increase our potential ability. Yet by understanding that power, we also acquire calmness. One is not complete without the other. To see a one-page illustrated summary of this form, see p. 263.

Pattern Chart

Movement Number	Finishing Direction	Movement	Finishing Stance	Technique Combination
1.	West	Pivot left 90° on right foot	Left Front Stance	Down block
2.	West	None	Withdraw left foot into Natural Stance (feet in joon bi position), body facing north, head turned to face west	Escape, drawing the left hand low across the front of the body and circling into a downward hammer strike
3.	East	Pivot right 90° on left foot	Right Front Stance	Down block
4.	East	East	Withdraw right foot into Natural Stance (feet in joon bi position), body facing north, head turned to face east	Escape, drawing the right hand low across the front of the body and circling into a downward hammer strike
5.	North	Step forward	Left Front Stance	Inside block followed by reverse inside block
6.	North	Step forward	Right Front Stance	a) Right-leg front snap kick b) Right-hand backfist to nose c) Reverse inside block
7.	North	Step forward	Left Front Stance	a) Left-leg front snap kick b) Left-hand backfist to nose c) Reverse inside block
8.	North	Step forward	Right Front Stance	Right backfist to nose
9.	East	Pivot left 270° on right foot to face east	Left Back Stance	Single knife-hand middle block
10.	East	Step forward	Right Front Stance	a) Clasp right fist in left hand b) Inside elbow strike as you step forward
11.	West	Pivot right 180° on left foot to face west	Right Back Stance	Single knife-hand middle block

Movement Number	Finishing Direction	Movement	Finishing Stance	Technique Combination
12.	West	Step forward	Left Front Stance	a) Clasp left fist in right hand b) Inside elbow strike as you step forward
13.	South	Pivot left 90° on right foot to face south	Left Front Stance	Down block followed by reverse inside block
14.	South	Step forward	Right Front Stance	Right-leg front snap kick, landing in Right Front Stance; down block followed by reverse inside block
15.	East	Pivot left 90° on right foot to face east	Left Front Stance	High block
16.	East	Step forward	Right Front Stance	a) Right-leg side kick, simultaneously extending right fist in outside hammer strike b) Landing in Right Front Stance, reverse inside elbow strike into open hand
17.	West	Pivot right 180° on left foot to face west	Right Front Stance	High block
18.	West	Step forward	Left Front Stance	a) Left-leg side kick, simultaneously extending left fist in outside hammer strike b) Landing in Left Front Stance, reverse inside elbow strike into open hand
19.	South	Pivot left 90° on right foot to face south	Left Front Stance	Down block followed by reverse inside block
20.	South	Hop forward	Right Twist Stance	a) Right-leg front snap kick b) Hop forward off of left leg, landing in Right Twist Stance c) Right-hand backfist to nose and kihap
21.	North	Pivot left out of Twist Stance 180° to face north	Ba ro	

Notes on Individual Moves

2 & 4. This is a standard escape from a same-side wrist grab. After the escape, bring the fist up high in a circle as you draw your lead foot in from the front stance and assume natural stance. Then strike sharply downward with your hammer fist, finishing with your arm parallel to the floor.

5, 6 & 7. Take care to perform each technique well, without blending them into one another. Be precise.

16 & 18. Strike with your hammer fist as you throw the side kick. As you rechamber the kick prior to stepping down into front stance, open your fist as if grabbing the head of your opponent. Then, with your open hand holding the opponent's head in place, reverse elbow strike into the open hand.

Taegeuk O Jang

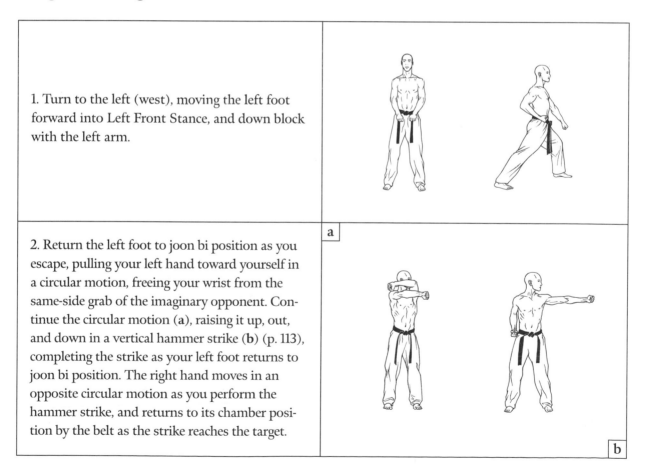

1. Turn to the left (west), moving the left foot forward into Left Front Stance, and down block with the left arm.

a

2. Return the left foot to joon bi position as you escape, pulling your left hand toward yourself in a circular motion, freeing your wrist from the same-side grab of the imaginary opponent. Continue the circular motion (**a**), raising it up, out, and down in a vertical hammer strike (**b**) (p. 113), completing the strike as your left foot returns to joon bi position. The right hand moves in an opposite circular motion as you perform the hammer strike, and returns to its chamber position by the belt as the strike reaches the target.

b

3. Turn to the right (east), moving the right foot forward into Right Front Stance, and down block with the right arm.

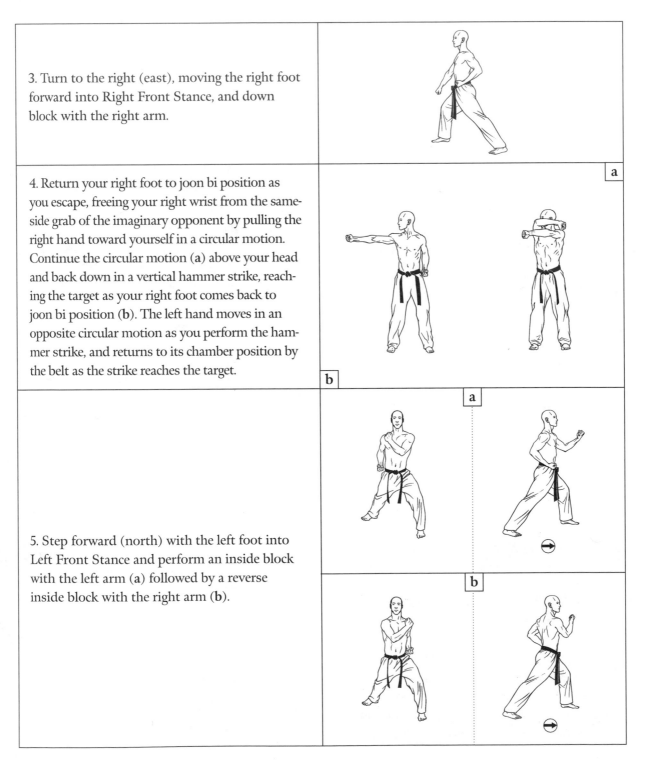

4. Return your right foot to joon bi position as you escape, freeing your right wrist from the same-side grab of the imaginary opponent by pulling the right hand toward yourself in a circular motion. Continue the circular motion (**a**) above your head and back down in a vertical hammer strike, reaching the target as your right foot comes back to joon bi position (**b**). The left hand moves in an opposite circular motion as you perform the hammer strike, and returns to its chamber position by the belt as the strike reaches the target.

5. Step forward (north) with the left foot into Left Front Stance and perform an inside block with the left arm (**a**) followed by a reverse inside block with the right arm (**b**).

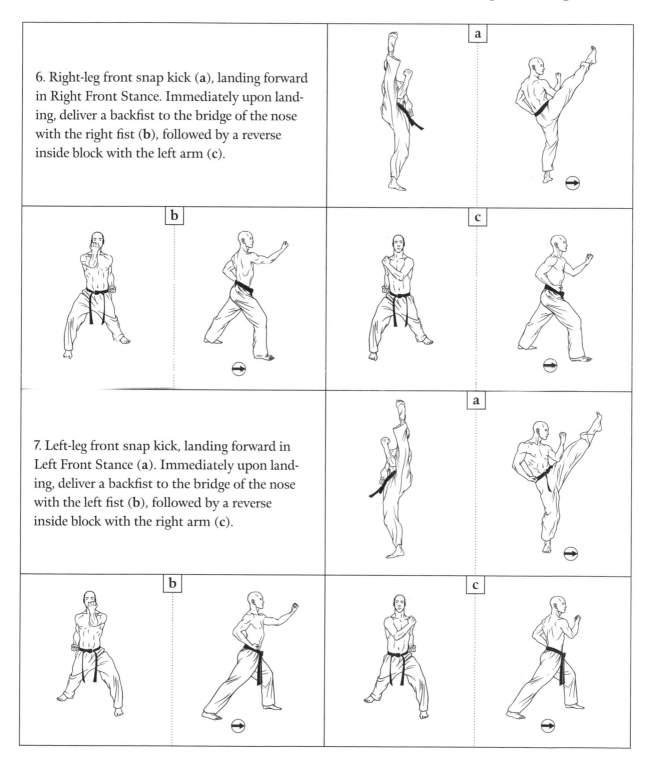

6. Right-leg front snap kick (**a**), landing forward in Right Front Stance. Immediately upon landing, deliver a backfist to the bridge of the nose with the right fist (**b**), followed by a reverse inside block with the left arm (**c**).

7. Left-leg front snap kick, landing forward in Left Front Stance (**a**). Immediately upon landing, deliver a backfist to the bridge of the nose with the left fist (**b**), followed by a reverse inside block with the right arm (**c**).

8. Step forward into Right Front Stance and backfist to the bridge of the nose with the right fist.

9. Moving the left foot, turn 270 degrees around to the left (east) into Left Back Stance, and single knife-hand middle block with the left arm.

10. Raise the chambered right fist in front of the chest and draw the left hand in to clasp it lightly. Step forward with the right foot into Right Front Stance and elbow strike to the head with the right elbow (p. 114).

11. Moving the right foot, turn all the way around to the right into Right Back Stance and single knife-hand middle block with the right arm.

12. Raise the chambered left fist in front of the chest and draw the right hand in to clasp it lightly. Step forward with the left foot into Left Front Stance and elbow strike to the head with the left elbow.

13. Moving the left foot, turn left (south) and step forward into Left Front Stance. Down block with the left arm (**a**), immediately followed by reverse inside block with the right arm (**b**).

14. Right-leg front snap kick, landing forward in Right Front Stance (**a**). Follow the kick with right-arm down block (**b**) and left-arm reverse inside block (**c**).

15. Moving the left foot, turn to the left (east) into Left Front Stance and high block with the left arm.

16. Right-leg side kick, extending the right fist simultaneously in an outside hammer strike, fist held horizontally (**a**). The right arm and the right leg should be parallel. As you rechamber the kick, open the right fist to hold the head of the imaginary opponent, then step down into Right Front Stance, and, using the left elbow, reverse elbow strike into the opened right hand (**b**) (p. 114).

17. Moving the right foot, turn all the way to the right (west) into Right Front Stance and high block with the right arm.

18. Left-leg side kick, extending the left fist simultaneously in an outside hammer strike, fist held horizontally (**a**). The left arm and the left leg should be parallel. As you rechamber the kick, open the left fist to hold the head of the imaginary opponent, then step down into Left Front Stance and, using the right elbow, reverse elbow strike into the opened left hand (**b**).

19. Moving the left foot, turn to the left (south) into Left Front Stance. Immediately down block with the left arm (**a**), followed by reverse inside block with the right arm (**b**).

20. Right-leg front snap kick (**a**) and hop forward as you rechamber, landing on the right foot in Twist Stance (p. 65). Right-hand backfist to the bridge of the nose (**b**) and kihap! As always, don't stint on this hand technique. Use the momentum from your jump forward to charge this backfist with power. Note that the chamber position for this technique differs from the standard chamber for a backfist to the nose. Chamber under the opposite shoulder, rather than above it. Don't stiff-leg the landing—the Twist Stance is a light, springy, dynamic position. Keep the knees slightly bent and relaxed after landing.

21. Untwist from the Twist Stance to face north and ba ro.

Taegeuk Yuk Jang

Taegeuk Yuk Jang represents *Kam*, water, and water's incessant flow and softness. While the flow of water may not be irresistible at all times, it nonetheless persists until it carves channels and canyons and valleys, reducing stone to grit. *Kam* may be seen as a reflection of one of Taekwondo's core values: indomitable spirit. Like flowing water, never give up. To see a one-page illustrated summary of this form, see p. 264.

Pattern Chart

Movement Number	Finishing Direction	Movement	Finishing Stance	Technique Combination
1.	West	Pivot left 90° on right foot to face west	Left Front Stance	Down block
2.	West	None	Left Back Stance	a) Right-leg front snap kick, stepping back into Left Back Stance b) Outside forearm block
3.	East	Pivot right 180° on left foot to face east	Right Front Stance	Down block
4.	East	None	Right Back Stance	a) Left-leg front snap kick, stepping back into Right Back Stance b) Outside forearm block
5.	North	Pivot left 90° on right foot to face north	Left Front Stance	Reverse open-hand high block
6.	West	After turning kick (see "Technique Combination" column), pivot left 90° on right foot to face west	Left Front Stance	a) Facing north, throw right-leg turning kick, holding open-hand high block in place b) Land the kick next to the left foot and face left (west) c) Step to the left (west) with left leg into Left Front Stance d) High outside forearm block, followed by reverse middle punch

Movement Number	Finishing Direction	Movement	Finishing Stance	Technique Combination
7.	West	Step forward	Right Front Stance	Right-leg front snap kick, landing in Right Front Stance; reverse middle punch
8.	East	Pivot right 180° on left foot to face east	Right Front Stance	High outside forearm block followed by reverse middle punch
9.	East	Step forward	Left Front Stance	Left-leg front snap kick, landing in Left Front Stance; reverse middle punch
10.	North	Pivot left 90° on right foot to face north	Natural Stance (feet in joon bi position)	Slow double down block to the sides, beginning with fists crossed in front of face
11.	North	Step forward	Right Front Stance	Reverse open-hand high block
12.	West	After turning kick (see Technique column), pivot right 270° on left foot to face west	Right Front Stance	a) Facing north, throw left-leg turning kick, holding open-hand high block in place and kihap b) Land the kick next to the right foot and pivot right 270° to face west c) Step forward with right leg into Right Front Stance d) Down block
13.	West	None	Right Back Stance	a) Left-leg front snap kick, stepping back into Right Back Stance b) Outside forearm block
14.	East	Pivot left 180° on right foot to face east	Left Front Stance	Down block
15.	East	None	Left Back Stance	a) Right-leg front snap kick, stepping back into Left Back Stance b) Outside forearm block
16.	North	Pivot left 90° on left foot to face north	Left Back Stance	Double knife-hand middle block

Movement Number	Finishing Direction	Movement	Finishing Stance	Technique Combination
17.	North	Step backward	Right Back Stance	Double knife-hand middle block
18.	North	Step backward	Left Front Stance	a) Crossing palm block b) Reverse middle punch
19.	North	Step backward	Right Front Stance	a) Crossing palm block b) Reverse middle punch
20.	North	Left foot steps forward	Ba ro	

Notes on Individual Moves

2 & 4. See the note for Taegeuk Sa Jang, moves 10 and 12.

6. Use the open-hand high block to grab the imaginary opponent's wrist after blocking the punch; holding the wrist, deliver your turning kick. This move requires great control of the kick and the rechamber. Keep your balance as you rechamber the kick and set the right foot down next to the left foot. Then step out with the left foot into the Left Front Stance (facing west) and execute the hand combination.

10. This is two slow down blocks, executed simultaneously, protecting you from attacks coming from your sides. Finish with your fists to the sides, not in front of you.

12. This move is substantially the same as movement #6, with the addition of the 270-degree turn. According to the standard method of the turning kick, your supporting foot should rotate 180 degrees until the heel is pointing directly toward your imaginary opponent. Leave the supporting foot in that position as you rechamber and step down from the kick; that way, your left foot will neatly line up next to your right foot when you step down, and you should be able to complete a smooth 270-degree turn into the Right Front Stance facing west.

18 & 19. Put a lot of snap into these crossing palm blocks—make them strong.

Taegeuk Yuk Jang

1. Turn left (west) into Left Front Stance, moving the left leg, and down block with the left arm.	
2. Right-leg front snap kick (**a**), stepping back into Left Back Stance, and left-arm outside forearm block (**b**). Don't anticipate stepping back while you are throwing the front snap kick, or it will look weak.	
3. Turn completely around to the right (east), moving the right leg into Right Front Stance, and down block with the right arm.	
4. Left-leg front snap kick (**a**), returning to Right Back Stance and outside forearm block with the right arm (**b**).	

5. Turn to the left (north), moving the left foot into Left Front Stance, and reverse open-hand high block with the right hand. Chamber the block above the opposite shoulder.

a

6. Right-leg turning kick (**a**) (p. 134), holding the open-hand block in place (the application is that the block becomes a wrist grab). This technique is most impressive if thrown high, but it requires great control. Place the kicking foot down just ahead of the left foot and turn to the left (west), moving the left foot forward into Left Front Stance. Once in the front stance, high outside forearm block with the left arm (**b**) followed by reverse punch with the right fist (**c**).

b

c

7. Right-leg front snap kick (**a**), landing forward in Right Front Stance, and reverse middle punch with the left fist (**b**).

a

b

8. Turn completely around to the right (east), moving the right foot into Right Front Stance, and high outside forearm block with the right arm (**a**) followed by reverse middle punch with the left fist (**b**).

9. Left-leg front snap kick (**a**), landing forward in Left Front Stance, and reverse middle punch with the right fist (**b**).

10. Moving the left foot, turn to the left (north) with the feet in joon bi position. Slowly execute a double down block, crossing the arms in front of the face and finishing with the arms blocking to either side of the body. The slow movement of this step is meditative, demonstrating focus and intensity.

11. Step forward with the right foot into Right Front Stance and reverse open-hand high block with the left arm.

12. Left-leg turning kick, holding the open-hand block in place (**a**), and kihap! As you kick, the supporting foot will turn 180 degrees. Place the kicking foot down next to the supporting foot and step out to the right (west) with the right foot—this will complete a 270-degree turn to the right—into Right Front Stance and right-arm down block (**b**).

13. Left-leg front snap kick (**a**), stepping back into Right Back Stance and outside forearm block with the right arm (**b**).

14. Moving the left leg, turn completely around to the left (east) into Left Front Stance and down block with the left arm.

15. Right-leg front snap kick (**a**), stepping back into Left Back Stance and outside forearm block with the left arm (**b**).

16. Moving the right leg, turn to the left (north) into Left Back Stance and double knife-hand middle block.

17. Step backward into Right Back Stance and double knife-hand middle block.

18. Step backward into Left Front Stance and crossing palm block with the left hand (**a**) (p. 97). Follow with reverse middle punch with the right fist (**b**).

a

b

19. Step backward into Right Front Stance and crossing palm block with the right hand (**a**). Follow with reverse middle punch with the left fist (**b**).

20. Draw the left foot up alongside the right foot and ba ro.

Taegeuk Chil Jang

Taegeuk Chil Jang represents *Kan,* a mountain: solid, ponderous, firm, majestic, wise. Develop these qualities even in the graceful but narrow cat stance, and maximize them in the front stances and back stances. Concentrate on stability. Make the twin uppercut punches explosive and the lower X blocks invulnerable, with a very long and low Front Stance. It requires special effort to display the combination of grace and power called for in Taegeuk Chil Jang, particularly because the cat stances do not provide the same kind of firm grounding available in front stances. To see a one-page illustrated summary of this form, see p. 265.

Pattern Chart

Movement Number	Finishing Direction	Movement	Finishing Stance	Technique Combination
1.	West	Pivot left 90° on right foot to face west	Left Cat Stance	Reverse crossing palm block
2.	West	None	Left Cat Stance	a) Right-leg front snap kick, returning to Left Cat Stance b) Inside block
3.	East	Pivot right 180° on left foot to face east	Right Cat Stance	Reverse crossing palm block
4.	East	None	Right Cat Stance	a) Left-leg front snap kick, returning to Right Cat Stance b) Inside block
5.	North	Pivot left 90° on right foot to face north	Left Back Stance	Double knife-hand lower block
6.	North	Step forward	Right Back Stance	Double knife-hand lower block
7.	West	Pivot left 90° on right foot to face west	Right Cat Stance	a) Reverse crossing palm block, with the left fist, palm down, supporting the right elbow b) Reverse backfist to nose as left fist continues to support the right elbow

Movement Number	Finishing Direction	Movement	Finishing Stance	Technique Combination
8.	East	Pivot right 180° on left foot to face east	Left Cat Stance	a) Reverse crossing palm block, with the right fist, palm down, supporting the left elbow b) Reverse backfist to nose as right fist continues to support the left elbow
9.	North	Pivot left 90° on right foot to face north	Feet side by side	With both hands at waist, clasp right fist in left hand and slowly raise and push hands out in front of chest while exhaling
10.	North	Step forward	Left Front Stance	Double scissor block: a) Simultaneous outside block/reverse down block, followed by b) Simultaneous down block/reverse outside block
11.	North	Step forward	Right Front Stance	Double scissor block: a) Simultaneous outside block/reverse down block, followed by b) Simultaneous down block/reverse outside block
12.	East	Pivot left 270° on right foot to face east	Left Front Stance	Double outside forearm block
13.	East	None	a–b) Left Front Stance c) Right Twist Stance d) Right Front Stance	a) Head grab b) Right knee strike, slapping both hands down to knee c) Hop forward slightly, landing in a crouching Right Twist Stance with twin uppercut punch d) Extend left leg back, ending in Right Front Stance with low X block
14.	West	Pivot right 180° on left foot to face west	Right Front Stance	Double outside forearm block

Movement Number	Finishing Direction	Movement	Finishing Stance	Technique Combination
15.	West	None	a–b) Right Front Stance c) Left Twist Stance d) Left Front Stance	a) Head grab b) Left-knee strike, slapping both hands down to knee c) Hop forward slightly, landing in a crouching Left Twist Stance with twin uppercut punch d) Extend right leg back, ending in Left Front Stance with low X block
16.	South	Pivot left 90° on right foot to face south	Left Walking Stance	Backfist to temple
17.	South	Step forward	Right Horse Stance	Open the backfist as target and a) Right-leg inside crescent kick to open hand, stepping down into Horse Stance, right foot toward the south; b) Right elbow strike to extended left hand
18.	South	None	Right Walking Stance	Draw left foot up to a Right Walking Stance and backfist to temple
19.	South	Step forward	Left Horse Stance	Open the backfist as target and a) Left-leg inside crescent kick to open hand, stepping down into Horse Stance, left foot toward the south b) Left-elbow strike to extended right hand
20.	South	None	Left Back Stance	Change to Left Back Stance and single knife-hand middle block
21.	South	Step forward	Right Horse Stance	Side punch and kihap
22.	North	Pivot left 90° on right foot to face north	Ba ro	

Notes on Individual Moves

1. Cat Stance is a graceful, fluid position. Nevertheless, you need to be sure that your hand techniques in Cat Stance are strong.

7 & 8. Again, power can be difficult to come by here. Keep your legs loose and use the movement of your hips and shoulders to create the power you need.

10 & 11. The scissor block is one of the most interesting techniques in all the Taegeuk poomse. Many students maintain a stiff upper body while performing them. While it is certainly easier at first to throw these double blocks with a rigid, mechanical motion, try instead to allow your shoulders some free motion and use that to add grace and power to this showcase technique.

12 & 14. Chamber the double outside forearm block with your arms crossed in front of your chest, with the left arm on the outside when stepping into Left Front Stance and the right arm outside when stepping into Right Front Stance.

13 & 15. A step-by-step description of this complex series:

- First, reach out and up to grab the head of your imaginary opponent by the sides. Pull your hands in and down while drawing the knee of the rear leg up sharply. Slap your hands against the knee to emphasize the force of the blow.
- Hop forward slightly before you land on the foot of the striking leg, and as you land, draw the opposite leg up, crossing its foot behind the lead foot. Both knees should be bent; your stance at this point is a crouching Twist Stance, feet crossed.
- As you lower yourself into the crouch, chamber the twin uppercut with your fists palm down at your sides and throw the punches simultaneously, attacking your opponent's midsection with two punches at the same time. Finish the twin uppercut with the elbows bent and the fists snapped over, palms up.
- Finally, extend the rear leg straight out behind yourself, assuming Front Stance, and execute the low X block. The hand on top corresponds to the lead leg.

16 & 18. Make sure this backfist has power. Again, loose shoulders are the key.

17 & 19. Do your best to slap first your foot and then your elbow into the

target hand accurately. A loud slap is especially impressive, and requires accuracy. Keep in mind that the target hand should also be strong, and not held out limply. It is first holding the head of the imaginary opponent, and then seizing the opponent's shoulder.

21. Finish strong with a solid Horse Stance and a punch thrown with all your weight behind it.

Taegeuk Chil Jang

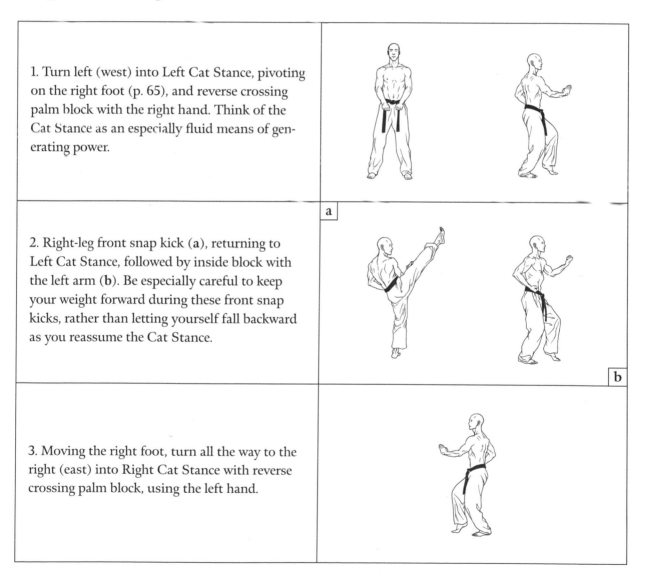

1. Turn left (west) into Left Cat Stance, pivoting on the right foot (p. 65), and reverse crossing palm block with the right hand. Think of the Cat Stance as an especially fluid means of generating power.	a
2. Right-leg front snap kick (**a**), returning to Left Cat Stance, followed by inside block with the left arm (**b**). Be especially careful to keep your weight forward during these front snap kicks, rather than letting yourself fall backward as you reassume the Cat Stance.	b
3. Moving the right foot, turn all the way to the right (east) into Right Cat Stance with reverse crossing palm block, using the left hand.	

4. Left-leg front snap kick (**a**), returning to Right Cat Stance, followed by inside block with the right arm (**b**).

5. Turn to the left (north), moving the left foot forward into Left Back Stance and double knife-hand lower block (p. 94).

6. Step forward into Right Back Stance and double knife-hand lower block.

7. Turn left (west), drawing the left foot forward into Left Cat Stance. Reverse crossing palm block with the right hand (**a**), followed by reverse backfist to the nose, also with the right hand (**b**). Throughout both hand techniques, the left fist is held palm down underneath the right elbow, supporting it. Use your hips and shoulders to generate power for these techniques.

8. Turn all the way to the right (east) into Right Cat Stance, pivoting on the left foot. Reverse crossing palm block with the left hand (**a**), followed by reverse backfist to the nose, also with the left hand (**b**). Throughout both hand techniques, the right fist is held palm down underneath the left elbow, supporting it.

9. Moving the left foot, turn left (north) and place the left foot next to the right. Inhale and bring both hands to chamber position at the waist, palms up, right hand balled into a fist. As you exhale, clasp the right fist in the left hand in front of the navel and then extend the arms slowly in front of the chest. This is a standing meditation.

10. Step forward with the left foot into Left Front Stance and double scissor block: the left arm performs an outside block while the right simultaneously performs a down block (**a**); then the left arm down blocks while the right arm outside blocks (**b**). Note that the arm performing the outside block remains on the outside. For both this and the following step, it is important to keep the shoulders relaxed and mobile. It is easy to make this complex block look mechanical, when it should look more fluid.

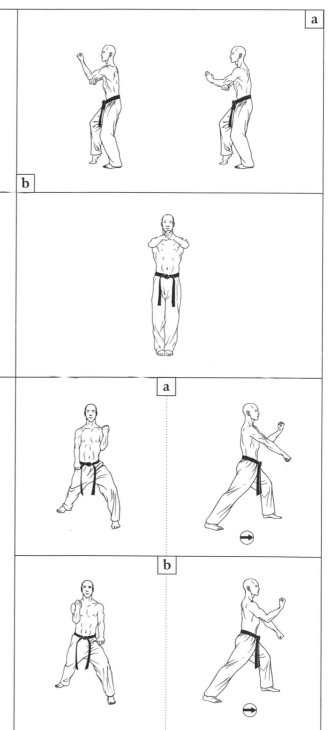

11. Step forward with the right foot into Right Front Stance and repeat the double scissor block: the right arm performs an outside block while the left arm performs a down block (**a**); then the right arm down blocks while the left arm outside blocks (**b**).

12. Moving the left foot, turn 270 degrees to the left (east) into Left Front Stance and simultaneous double outside forearm block. This technique is in fact a strike dislodging an assailant's hands from your collar. Chamber with the left arm on top.

13. Remaining in the front stance, reach up with both hands to grab your assailant by the sides of the head (**a**). Second, draw the hands down and bring your right knee up sharply, slapping your hands against the knee (**b–c**). This is a knee strike to the face, with the hands pulling the opponent's head down. Third, hop forward slightly after delivering the knee strike, landing on the right foot with the left crossed behind. This is a crouching Right Twist Stance, with the weight on the right foot and the left foot resting lightly on its ball. Chamber your fists, palms down, on either side of your rib cage, and immediately upon landing in Twist Stance throw simultaneous double uppercut punches, palms up, into your opponent's midsection (**d**). Last, extend the left foot back to finish in Right Front Stance, and low X block (p. 93), right wrist on top (**e**).

14. Moving the right foot, turn all the way around to the right (west), finishing in Right Front Stance and double outside forearm block, chambering the right arm on top.

15. This move mirrors step #13. First, remaining in the front stance, reach up with both hands to grab your assailant by the sides of the head (**a**). Second, draw the hands down and bring your left knee up sharply, slapping your hands against the knee as it rises (**b–c**). This is a knee strike to the face, with the hands pulling the opponent's head down. Third, hop forward slightly after delivering the knee strike, landing on the left foot with the right foot crossed behind. This is a crouching Left Twist Stance, with the weight on the left foot and the right foot resting lightly on its ball. Chamber your fists, palms down, on either side of your rib cage and immediately upon landing throw simultaneous double uppercut punches, palms up, into your opponent's midsection (**d**). Last, extend the right foot back to finish in Left Front Stance, and low X block, left wrist on top (**e**).

16. Turn to the left (south), moving the left foot and assuming Left Walking Stance with left backfist to temple, chambering the backfist above the right shoulder.

17. Open the left hand, palm facing in, and right leg inside crescent kick (p. 133), slapping the palm of the left hand with the sole of the foot (**a**). Keep the hand in position with the forearm parallel to the floor and land in Right Horse Stance (p. 58). As you land, right elbow strike into the open palm of the left hand (**b**).

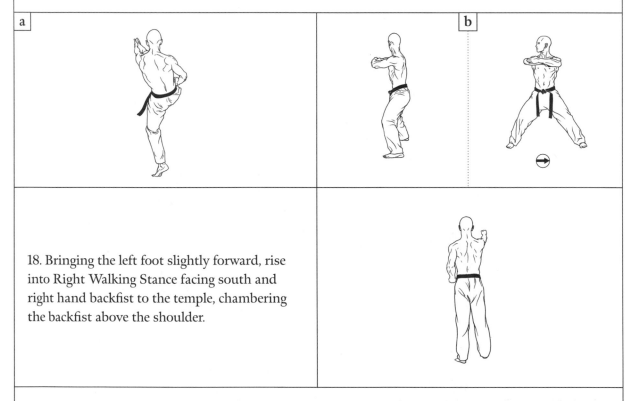

18. Bringing the left foot slightly forward, rise into Right Walking Stance facing south and right hand backfist to the temple, chambering the backfist above the shoulder.

19. Open the right hand, palm facing in, and left-leg inside crescent kick, slapping the palm of the right hand with the sole of the left foot (**a**). Keep the hand in position with the forearm parallel to the floor and land in Left Horse Stance. As you land, left elbow strike into the open palm of the right hand (**b**).

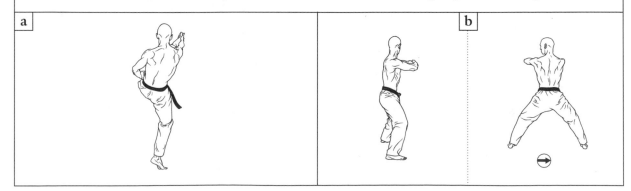

20. Pivot the left foot into Left Back Stance and, with the left hand, single knife-hand middle block.

21. Step forward into Right Horse Stance, side punch with the right fist, and kihap!

22. Moving the left foot, turn left (north) into ba ro.

Taegeuk Pal Jang

Taegeuk Pal Jang is a magnificent form that admirably fills its role as the highest of the Taegeuk forms. Taegeuk Pal Jang represents *Kon* in the Taegeuk: um and earth. As yang is positive energy and the representation of heaven and the origin of all things, so um, negative energy, represents earth, the opposite of heaven, and the end of all things. Considering the cycle of mortal life, earthly energy is also a beginning, a fruition. Students who have advanced to the study of Taegeuk Pal Jang are eligible for promotion to black belt, with a black belt's richer understanding of Taekwondo and dedication to a new beginning.

When you perform Taegeuk Pal Jang, strive to show everything you've learned about power and presentation. Make your movements grand and dramatic. To see a one-page illustrated summary of this form, see p. 266.

Pattern Chart

Movement Number	Finishing Direction	Movement	Finishing Stance	Technique Combination
1.	North	Step forward with left foot	Left Back Stance	Double-fist middle block
2.	North	None	Left Front Stance	Open up to Front Stance and reverse middle punch
3.	North	Hop forward	Left Front Stance	a) Left-leg scissor front kick, landing in Left Front Stance b) Inside block c) Double punch, right hand first
4.	North	Step forward	Right Front Stance	Middle front punch and kihap
5.	East	Pivot left 270° on right foot to face east	Reverse Right Front Stance	Slowly execute a simultaneous down block over the straight leg and a high outside block over the bent leg
6.	East	None	Pivot from Reverse Right Front Stance to Left Front Stance	Slowly execute a reverse uppercut punch while drawing the left fist in across the face
7.	West	Step backward, left foot passing in front of the right	Reverse Left Front Stance	Slowly execute a simultaneous down block over the straight leg and a high outside block over the bent leg

Movement Number	Finishing Direction	Movement	Finishing Stance	Technique Combination
8.	West	None	Pivot from Reverse Left Front Stance into Right Front Stance	Slowly execute a reverse upper-cut punch while drawing the right fist in across the face
9.	North	Pivot left 270° on left foot to face north	Left Back Stance	Double knife-hand middle block
10.	North	None	Left Front Stance	Open to Front Stance and reverse middle punch
11.	North	Step back	Right Cat Stance	a) Right-leg front snap kick b) Place right foot down behind the left foot and slide left foot back, ending in Right Cat Stance with crossing palm block
12.	West	Pivot left 90° on right foot to face west	Left Cat Stance	Double knife-hand middle block
13.	West	None	a) Left Cat Stance b) Left Front Stance c) Left Cat Stance	a) Left-leg front kick, landing in Left Front Stance b) Reverse middle punch c) Draw left foot backward to reassume Left Cat Stance with crossing palm block
14.	East	Pivot right 180° on left foot to face east	Right Cat Stance	Double knife-hand middle block
15.	East	None	a) Right Cat Stance b) Right Front Stance c) Right Cat Stance	a) Right-leg front kick, landing in Right Front Stance b) Reverse middle punch c) Draw right foot backward to reassume Right Cat Stance with crossing palm block
16.	South	Pivot right 90° on left foot to face south	Right Back Stance	Double-fist lower block
17.	South	Hop forward	Right Front Stance	a–b) Double front scissor kick, kicking first with left leg, then with right and kihap, landing in Right Front Stance c–e) Inside block followed by double punch

Movement Number	Finishing Direction	Movement	Finishing Stance	Technique Combination
18.	West	Pivot left 270° on right foot to face west	Left Back Stance	Single knife-hand middle block
19.	West	None	Left Front Stance	Open to Front Stance and a) Reverse elbow strike to face b) Reverse backfist to nose c) Front punch
20.	East	Pivot right 180° to face east	Right Back Stance	Single knife-hand middle block
21.	East	None	Right Front Stance	Open to Front Stance and a) Reverse elbow strike to face b) Reverse backfist to nose c) Front punch
22.	North	Pivot left 90° on right foot	Ba ro	

Notes on Individual Moves

1. Emphasize the chamber position here. Advance the left foot into a deep, solid Back Stance, and throw the block as strongly as possible.

3. Don't rush this motion. Hold the right knee up for a moment before jumping up and forward into the left scissor front kick. Make sure you fully rechamber the kick before you come down in the Left Front Stance.

5. This position is essentially a backward Front Stance. The right knee is deeply bent, the left leg is straight, and you are looking back over your left shoulder. There are two hand techniques performed simultaneously: a high outside block with the right hand, and a reverse down block with the left hand.

6. Pivot around from the reverse Right Front Stance to Left Front Stance. Raise the left hand from the down block position. Slowly pull the left fist in toward the opposite side of your face, palm facing in. At the same time, slowly throw a reverse uppercut with the right hand, beginning with the palm facing down and ending with the palm facing inward, the punch heading directly up into the opponent's jaw. This combination is performed slowly, taking 3–5 seconds to complete, with a sudden snap at the end.

7. To move from the last position into the new one, look over your right

shoulder and step backward, crossing the left foot in front of the right foot before moving the right foot backward into the reverse Left Front Stance. Otherwise, execute the move in the same way as move #6.

8. See notes for move #7, adjusting for the different right/left direction.

Taegeuk Pal Jang

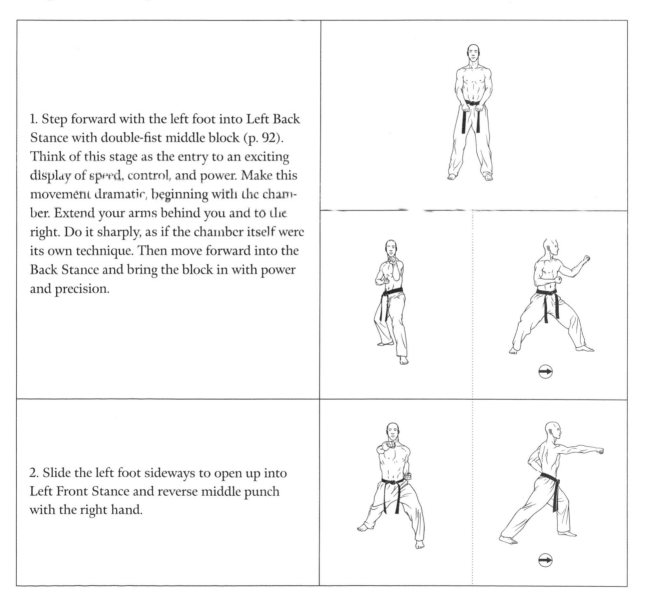

1. Step forward with the left foot into Left Back Stance with double-fist middle block (p. 92). Think of this stage as the entry to an exciting display of speed, control, and power. Make this movement dramatic, beginning with the chamber. Extend your arms behind you and to the right. Do it sharply, as if the chamber itself were its own technique. Then move forward into the Back Stance and bring the block in with power and precision.

2. Slide the left foot sideways to open up into Left Front Stance and reverse middle punch with the right hand.

3. Left-leg front scissor kick: draw the right knee up, hold for a moment, then front snap kick with the left leg (**a**), hopping forward and landing in Left Front Stance. Don't rush. Inside block with the left arm (**b**) immediately followed by a double punch, right arm first (**c–d**).

4. Step forward into Right Front Stance. Front middle punch with the right hand and kihap!

5. Moving the left foot, pivot 270 degrees to the left (east), finishing in a Reverse Right Front Stance. You will be in a Right Front Stance oriented toward west, but you will be looking back over your left shoulder (east) rather than straight ahead. As you come into position, chamber the left hand as you normally would a down block, with the palm of the fist facing you and the hand up across your face. Chamber the right hand for the outside block a bit lower than the normal chamber for this technique, reaching down across your body. Your elbows should nearly meet. Slowly execute a simultaneous down block over your left leg with your left arm and a high outside block with your right arm, as if you were protecting yourself from two attackers coming at you from opposite sides. It should take 3–5 seconds to complete the double block. However, make sure that at the very end of the technique, you snap your hands into place.

6. Pivot your feet to switch into Left Front Stance while continuing to face the same direction. You will need to open the left foot slightly. At the same time, reach forward with the left hand as if to grab an opponent's collar; slowly draw the left hand in toward you, finishing with the left hand near the right side of your face. At the same time, execute a slow uppercut punch with the right hand, chambered palm down and finishing at chin height (p. 110). Snap the wrist over at the end of the technique.

7. Step backward to the west by crossing your left foot in front of the right, finishing in Reverse Left Front Stance, looking back over your right shoulder. Slowly execute a simultaneous down block with the right arm over the right leg with the left arm rising into a high outside block. Snap the hands into position at the end of the technique.

8. Pivot your feet to switch into Right Front Stance while continuing to face the same direction. At the same time, reach forward with the right hand as if to grab an opponent by the collar; slowly draw the right hand in toward you, finishing with the right hand near the left side of your face. At the same time, execute a slow uppercut punch with the left hand, finishing at chin height. Snap the punch at the moment of completion.

9. Moving the right foot, turn 270 degrees to the left (north), finishing in Left Back Stance with double knife-hand middle block. Again, don't stint on this chamber.

10. Slide the left foot sideways to open into Left Front Stance and reverse middle punch with the right hand.

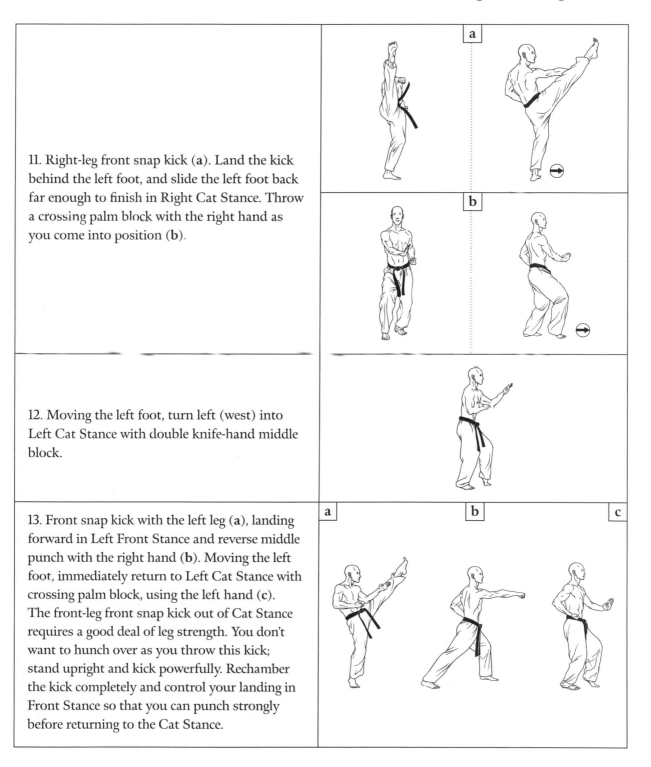

11. Right-leg front snap kick (**a**). Land the kick behind the left foot, and slide the left foot back far enough to finish in Right Cat Stance. Throw a crossing palm block with the right hand as you come into position (**b**).

12. Moving the left foot, turn left (west) into Left Cat Stance with double knife-hand middle block.

13. Front snap kick with the left leg (**a**), landing forward in Left Front Stance and reverse middle punch with the right hand (**b**). Moving the left foot, immediately return to Left Cat Stance with crossing palm block, using the left hand (**c**). The front-leg front snap kick out of Cat Stance requires a good deal of leg strength. You don't want to hunch over as you throw this kick; stand upright and kick powerfully. Rechamber the kick completely and control your landing in Front Stance so that you can punch strongly before returning to the Cat Stance.

14. Turn around to the right (east), moving the right foot into Right Cat Stance, and double knife-hand middle block.

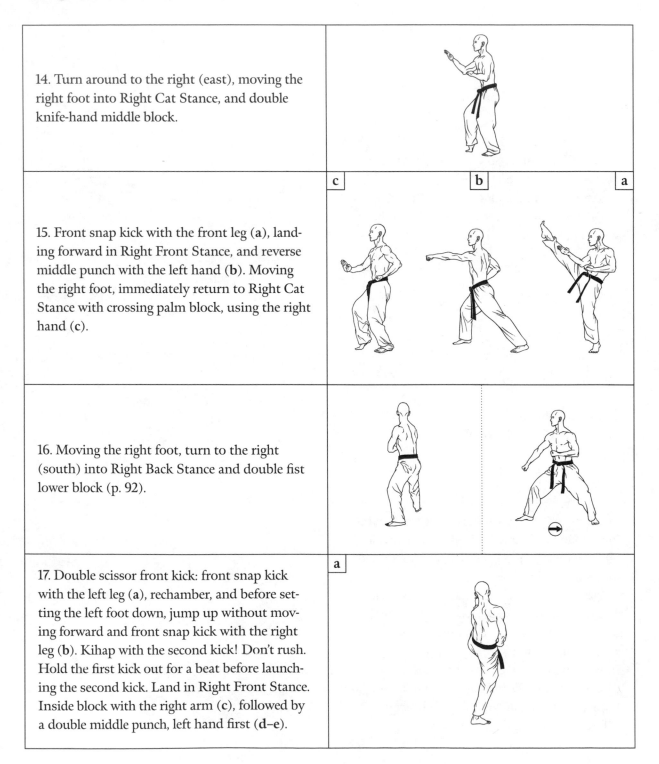

c   b   a

15. Front snap kick with the front leg (**a**), landing forward in Right Front Stance, and reverse middle punch with the left hand (**b**). Moving the right foot, immediately return to Right Cat Stance with crossing palm block, using the right hand (**c**).

16. Moving the right foot, turn to the right (south) into Right Back Stance and double fist lower block (p. 92).

17. Double scissor front kick: front snap kick with the left leg (**a**), rechamber, and before setting the left foot down, jump up without moving forward and front snap kick with the right leg (**b**). Kihap with the second kick! Don't rush. Hold the first kick out for a beat before launching the second kick. Land in Right Front Stance. Inside block with the right arm (**c**), followed by a double middle punch, left hand first (**d–e**).

a

18. Moving the left foot, turn 270 degrees to the left (west) into Left Back Stance and single knife-hand middle block.

	a	b	c

19. Slide the left foot sideways into Left Front Stance and perform three hand techniques in sequence: (**a**) reverse elbow strike with the right arm; (**b**) reverse backfist to the nose with the right fist (the fist is already chambered for this technique from the finishing position of the elbow strike); (**c**) front middle punch with the left fist. Make each technique crisp. Don't blur them together.

20. Moving the right foot, turn around to the right (east), finishing in Right Back Stance, and single knife-hand middle block.

	c	b	a

21. Slide the right foot sideways into Right Front Stance and perform three hand techniques in sequence: (**a**) reverse elbow strike with the left arm; (**b**) reverse backfist to the nose with the left fist (the fist is already chambered for this technique from the finishing position of the elbow strike); (**c**) front middle punch with the right fist.

22. Moving the left foot, turn left (north) and ba ro.

Taegeuk Il Jang

Taegeuk Yi Jang

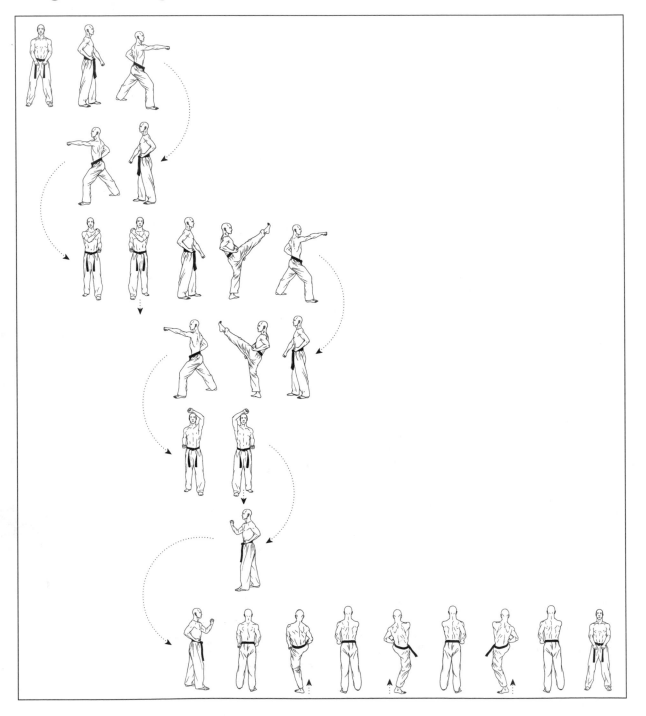

Taegeuk Sam Jang

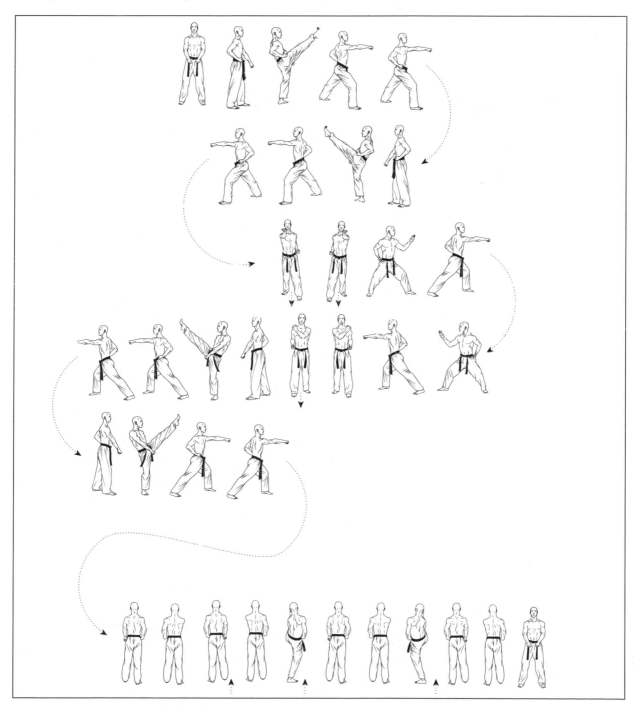

Taegeuk Sa Jang

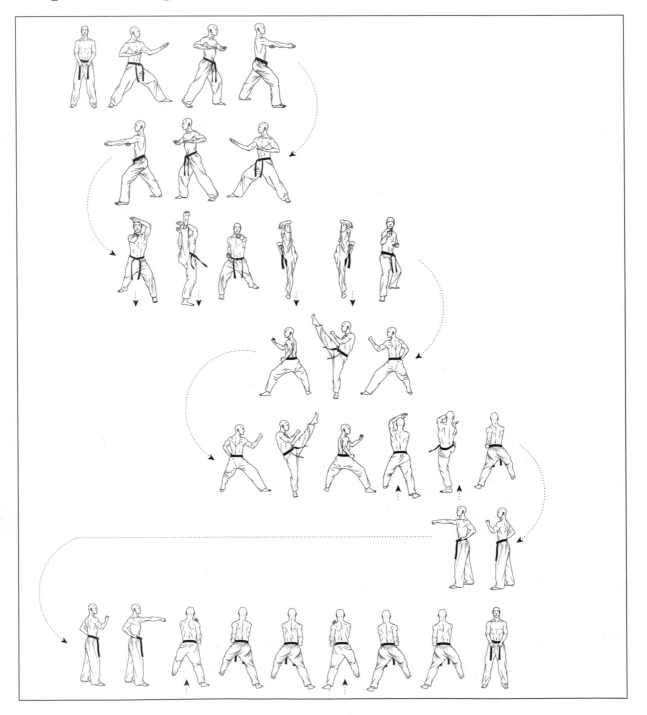

Taegeuk O Jang

Taegeuk Yuk Jang

Taegeuk Chil Jang

Taegeuk Pal Jang

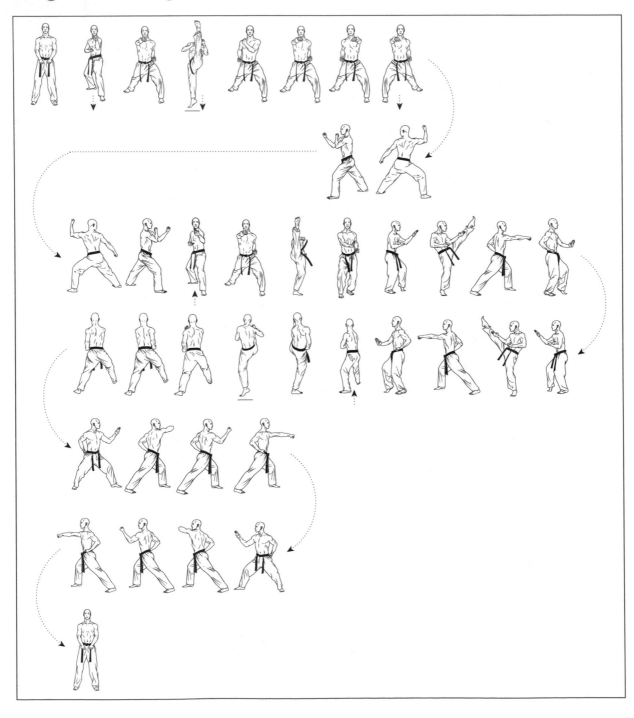

GLOSSARY

AEROBIC: Exercise—such as running, cycling, and a range of Taekwondo activities—that stresses increased respiratory levels and the use of oxygen in large quantity.

AGILITY: Best described as a fighter's ability to explode off the mat into an attack, agility refers to the speed and precision with which one can move one's body.

ANAEROBIC: Exercise that stresses the use of energy without heightened respiratory levels. Examples include sprints, weight lifting, and phases of Taekwondo sparring or speed drills.

BLOCK: A defense, usually by redirection, against a striking or kicking attack. Blocks most often use the arms or hands, but in some systems they can use the knees or shins as well.

CARDIOVASCULAR: Of or pertaining to the heart and the circulatory system.

CHAMBER: The position at which blocking or striking hand is held prior to execution of the technique, or the position at which the foot and leg are held prior to execution of a kick.

COUNTERPUNCH: Also reverse punch, this is a punch thrown with the hand corresponding to the rear leg.

COUNTING: The numbers, from one to ten, are: *hana, dul, set, net, dasot, yasot, ilgup, yodol, ahop, yeol.*

FRONT (*ap*): In regard to hand techniques, front refers to the hand corresponding to the lead leg. In regard to kicks, front designates a kick that attacks a frontal target without turning the body.

GLUTEUS: Any of three large muscles of the buttocks, instrumental in side kicks and back kicks.

HAMMER FIST/HAMMER STRIKE: Hammer fist refers to the outer edge of the clenched fist; hammer strike is the downward or sideways motion used to deliver a blow with this portion of the fist.

ISOMETRIC: Tension upon a muscle without shortening or lengthening it.

JAB: A quick punch with the lead hand, one of the basic tools of self defense or hand-to-hand combat.

KICK: An attack with the foot.

KNIFE HAND: The outer edge of the open hand, which, when rigid, can deliver a powerful blow.

PHALANGES: The bones of the fingers (distal, middle, proximal from the tip of the finger to the hand).

POWER: In physics, power is equal to work divided by time. The implication for Taekwondo is that the more quickly a blow can be delivered (reducing time as much as possible), the more power will result.

PUNCH: An attack using the front two knuckles of the clenched fist.

QUADRICEP: The large four-part frontal muscle of the thigh.

RESPIRATION: The process of breathing.

REVERSE: Usually refers to the hand corresponding to the rear leg, but can also refer to a step where the rear foot passes by the heel side, rather than the toe side, of the front foot, or where the front foot passes by the toe side, rather than the heel side, of the rear foot.

SOLAR PLEXUS: The network of nerves found immediately below the sternum and behind the stomach. A blow to the solar plexus can cause acute pain and partial respiratory paralysis.

SPEAR HAND: An attack using the tips of the extended fingers.

STANCE: How one stands, especially when performing an action.

SWITCH KICK: A defensive turning kick, where the lead foot is pulled back as the kick is thrown with the rear foot.

THANK YOU: *Kamsa hamnae da.*

YOU'RE WELCOME: *Chunmunayo.*

KOREAN TERMS

A note about Korean pronunciation: *A* sounds like the "a" in "father," not the "a" in "back." *D* is a soft sound, slightly aspirated, almost like a "t." *I* sounds like a long "e," as in "see." *J* is more like the "ch" in "church." *R* is a light sound, with the tongue tapping the roof of the mouth. *U* sounds more like a double "o," as in "flu."

AP: Front, as in front kick.

CHAGI: Kick.

CHARYUT: Attention.

CHIRUGI: Strike or punch.

CHUNMUNAYO: You're welcome.

COUNTING: The numbers, from one to ten, are: *hana, dul, set, net, dasot, yasot, ilgup, yodol, ahop, yeol.*

DOBOK: The Taekwondo uniform.

DOJANG: A Taekwondo school or gymnasium.

DOLLYO: Turning, as in "turning kick."

DWI: Back, as in "back kick" or "back stance."

DWIRO DORA: Turn around.

GYOROOGI: Sparring.

HOGU: A padded chest protector used in sparring.

HOOJIN: Backward motion, as in a backward sliding step.

ILBO-HOOJIN: Backward motion, with change, as in a full step backward.

ILBO-JEONJIN: Forward motion, with change, as in a full step forward.

JEONJIN: Forward motion, as in a forward sliding step.

JOON BI: Literally "ready," joon bi also refers to a stance in which the feet are one shoulder width apart and the fists are held slightly away from the body in front of the belt.

KAESOK: Command meaning continue.

KALYO: Command meaning break, or stop action.

KAMSA HAMNAE DA: Thank you.

KIHAP: A powerful yell from the diaphragm, the kihap increases power, eliminates fear and pain, and may frighten opponents.

KUMAN: Command meaning stop.

KWANJANGNIM: Grandmaster; one who has attained higher than fifth dan.

KYOBUNIM: Instructor.

KYUNGNET: Bow.

MAKKI: Block.

MOMTONG: Inner or inside.

OLGUL: Face or head.

POOMSE: The prearranged sequences of moves that all Taekwondo students must learn. Poomse provides one means of learning the basic stances and techniques of Taekwondo.

SABOMNIM: A master instructor of fourth or fifth dan.

SEOGI: Stance.

SHIJAK: Command meaning start.

UM: *Yin,* negative energy, and the earth.

YEOP: Side, as in side step or side kick.

SELECTED RESOURCES

In recent years, a number of Taekwondo books have begun to grace the shelves of American bookstores. Two of these have proven to be valuable to us as references. The third, while not widely available, is worth seeking out as the last word on orthodox Kukkiwon Taekwondo. Ki-Back Yi's *A New History of Korea* is fascinating and enlightening—recommended reading for anyone interested in the general history of the Korean peninsula.

Chun, Richard. *Tae Kwon Do: The Korean Martial Art*. New York: HarperCollins, 1976.

Gerrard, Jon, Yeon Hee Park, and Yeon Hwan Park. *Tae Kwon Do: The Ultimate Reference Guide to the World's Most Popular Martial Art*. New York: Facts on File, Inc., 1989.

Yi, Ki-Baek. *A New History of Korea*. Cambridge: Harvard University Press, 1984.

Taekwondo Textbook. Kukkiwon edition. Seoul, South Korea: Oh Sung Publishing Co., 1995 (English ed.).

A huge number of Taekwondo-related sites have appeared on the World Wide Web as well, far too many for us to include a comprehensive list here. Below are the addresses of a select few. The addresses for the USTU and for the Taekwondo program at George Washington University both include extensive links to other sites. Of particular interest are the listings of collegiate Taekwondo programs, which often have fairly extensive cross-referencing to other sites of interest to martial arts enthusiasts.

United States Taekwondo Union: www.ustu.com
World Taekwondo Federation: www.worldsport.com/sports/taekwondo
George Washington University Taekwondo: www.gwu.edu/~gwtkd/

INDEX

Double outside forearm block, 240, 244, 245

Double punch *(doo bon-chirugi)*, 104

Double scissor block, 243, 244

Double scissor front kick, 256

Double turning kick, 154

Down block *(arae-makki)*, 88

Drilling trap techniques, 175

Drills, types of, 165–67

E

Ego (idea of self), 26–27

Elbow strikes, 114–17, 221, 224, 226, 246, 258

Exercise, value of, 23

Exhale, through mouth, 102

Explosiveness, importance of, 187

Eyes on target, 187–88

F

Fake step, 77–78

Fast cut kick, 161

Fast kick. *See* Front-leg turning kick.

Feint, with jeonjin step, 71, 72

Fidelity. *See Sa Chin Yi Hyo.*

Fighting stance *(gyoroogi-seogi)*, 43, 65–66

Final hamstring/groin stretch, 55

Fist, 101–3, 217

    attacks, 112–14

Fist blocks, 92–93

Flash drills, for sparring, 176–77

Flying back kick *(twio on mom dollyo dwi-chagi)*, 148

Flying kicks, 147–48

Flying side kick *(twio bakkuwo yeop-chagi)*, 147–48

Foot, pivoting, 125

Football, 32

Foot positions, and kicking surfaces, 127–28

Footwork, 67–83, 172

    drills for, 82–83

    principles of, 68–69

Forearm. *See* Outside forearm block.

Forward hammer strike *(maejoomok nae ryo-chigi)*, 113

Forward motion, 70–74

Four abilities, for sparring, 152–68

Front kicks, 128–30

Front-leg axe kick, 159, 161–62

Front-leg front snap kick, 255

Front-leg kicks, 160, 255

Front-leg side kick *(apbal yeop-chagi)*, 139–40

Front-leg turning kick, 160

Front middle punch, 235, 258

Front push kick *(meereo chagi)*, 129–30, 159, 161

Front snap kick *(ap-chagi)*, 128–29, 194, 195, 256

Front splits, 51–52

Front stance *(apkeubi)*, 48, 61–63, 255

Front stretch, 50–51

G

Games. *See* Sports.

Gluteus/hamstring stretch, 54

Gluteus stretch, 54

Groin, hamstring, and hip stretch/straddle split, 50–51

Groin stretch, 49. *See also* Final hamstring/groin stretch.

    standing, 47–48

ABOUT THE AUTHORS

Twin brothers MASTERS SUNG CHUL WHANG and JUN CHUL WHANG have studied Taekwondo since they were six years old. At eighteen, they founded their first Taekwondo program at Dartmouth University. They now own and operate New York City's West Side Taekwondo, the largest Taekwondo school in New York City. Masters Whang are also attorneys in private practice with New York City law firms and serve on various committees of the United States Taekwondo Union, including the National Tournament Committee. They live in New York City.

MASTER DAE SUNG LEE, a nine-time U.S. national sparring champion and a ten-time U.S. team member, holds the world record for most consecutive times representing his country on a national sports team. Master Lee serves various leadership functions within the United States Taekwondo Union and is a frequent guest instructor around the U.S. and abroad. He owns and operates U.S. Taekwondo Center in Honolulu, Hawaii.

BRANDON SALTZ has studied Taekwondo for fourteen years and is a national poomse champion. He is an instructor at West Side Taekwondo and runs several after-school Taekwondo programs. He is also a writer and makes his home in Brooklyn.